What Would Jesus Sing?

Experimentation and Tradition in Church Music

What Would Jesus Sing?

Experimentation and Tradition in Church Music

Marilyn L. Haskel, Editor

CHURCH PUBLISHING
an imprint of
Church Publishing Incorporated, New York

Unless otherwise noted, the Scripture quotations contained herein are from the New Revised Standard Version Bible, copyright © 1989 by the Division of Christian Education of the National Council of Churches of Christ in the U.S.A. Used by permission. All rights reserved.

Library of Congress Cataloging-in-Publication Data

What would Jesus sing? : experimentation and tradition in church music / Marilyn L. Haskel, editor.
  p. cm.
 ISBN 978-0-89869-563-2 (pbk.)
 1. Church music—21st century. I. Haskel, Marilyn L. II. Title.

ML3001.W54 2007
264'.2—dc22

2007020995

Church Publishing Incorporated
445 Fifth Avenue
New York, NY 10016
www.churchpublishing.org

5 4 3 2 1

Contents

Introduction
John L. Bell. 1

What About Jazz?
Richard Birk. 5

What About Synthesizers?
J. Owen Burdick. 15

What About Handbells?
Judith C. Dodge. 35

What About Electronic Music?
Isaac Everett. 45

What About Contemporary Ensembles?
Mark Glaeser. 57

What About Instrumentalists?

Young and Amateur Musicians
Cynthia Holden. 71

Using Professionals in Worship
John Marsh. 87

What About Guitars?
Robert C. Laird 97

What About Cantors?
Joel Martinson 105

What About Choirs and Organs?
Robert P. Ridgell 129

What About Unaccompanied Congregational Song?
Donald Schell. 143

What About Additional Services?

First Friday
at Christ Church Cathedral, Nashville, Tennessee
    Sheldon Curry 155

Taizé
at All Saints' Episcopal Parish, Beverly Hills, California
    Thomas Foster 163

Before the Ending of the Day: Compline
at Christ Church, New Haven, Connecticut
    Robert W. Lehman 169

The HipHopEMass
at Trinity Episcopal Church of Morrisania, Bronx, New York
    Lucas Smith 181

Introduction

Years ago I attended a conference for church musicians organized by the Royal School of Church Music. There were seminars on choral tone, the playing of Bach fugues, repertoire from current British composers, and my sectional, which was about congregational song.

The final session was a plenary in which the audience members were invited to ask any question they wished of the presenters. All went well until one very unassuming lady asked if anyone on the panel could advise her as to what to do with the "Emerald Gems."

We all imagined this was a query better directed to an antique jeweler. Then she explained that the title referred to a trio of ladies who were the remnants of a choir that had once been vibrant but had long since passed its peak. We—the presenters—were stumped. Here was a woman making an enquiry that could have been replicated in any gathering of church musicians in the Western hemisphere. But, sadly, none of our areas of expertise bordered on it.

I somehow feel that any of the contributors to this volume would have made a better response, because irrespective of their expertise, they speak as practitioners whose authority comes not from a narrow specialism, but from a broad experience of church music.

For some, this will be a primer, enabling them to discover in-roads into a style of music-making they have not hitherto investigated. For others it will be a resource book of proven practices and recommended texts which will help to develop their current interests. For others yet, it will be a travel guide through the variety of musical phenomena that in different places and at different times enable the worship of the church.

It is neither my role nor intention to comment on individual chapters. This is an introduction, not a précis. But what I would like to do is to identify some common chords which are worth our collective pondering.

1. Horses for Courses

The world of church music today is very different from a century ago, when denominational correctness and the presumption of cathedrals or large city churches to model good practice both held sway. As regards repertoire, we are increasingly eclectic, freely transgressing both denominational and national boundaries to discover music suited to our congregation. And because few rural or suburban Episcopal, Methodist, or Lutheran churches would claim to be cathedrals in miniature, that which works in the city-center historic space is now less likely to be emulated on the periphery.

The potential of the congregation, its musicians, its physical worship space, its socio-economic and racial mix all contrive to demand of church music and musicians that which will be an honest reflection of the congregation's soul and sensitivity, rather than a damaged carbon copy of what other people in other places do well.

2. Performance and Participation

Liturgy is a performance, irrespective of how high or low church the congregation may be. But at odds with much in contemporary culture, it is not a performance by a few in order to satisfy or delight the many. It is a performance by all the people gathered for the benefit of Almighty God who gave each their voice and their creative potential.

It is in that context and only that context that musicians play preludes and choirs sing anthems—not as the gifted exhibiting their skills for the musically challenged, but as those with special gifts making a rehearsed offering to God on behalf and with the consent of the whole congregation.

Thus there are no active and passive partners in worship. All are involved. When some give of their singing, then others give of their listening, and thus the Body of Christ is built up in faith and makes a corporate offering to God.

3. Planning and Preparation

Being both a preacher and an occasional church musician, I see from both sides the need for the diet of worship to be a matter of concern to the ministers of word and music together. Too often musicians find a list of seemingly random numbers on the music stand indicating what the priest or minister wishes sung on Sunday coming, while just as often preachers discover that the anthem has been chosen in accordance with the choir's abilities rather than the season of the year or the lectionary being followed.

It is in no small way regrettable that church musicians and pastors in most countries share no common training, the more so when they are jointly responsible for the sound, sense, and silence in corporate worship. For good relations among the leadership team, it is essential that people know each other as more than functionaries with individual responsibilities. Worship needs to be planned on the big canvas well in advance, with the fine tuning coming nearer the time of the liturgy. Advent and Lent particularly are deserving of involved discussion as these seasons prepare people for the two major feasts in the Christian year.

But pastors and musicians should also be talking abut the conduct and content of weddings and funerals in order to prevent banality or insipid repetitiveness to replace appropriateness and imagination.

Important as this is for the building of a dynamic and trusting relationship among leaders, it is even more important for ensuring that the offering of worship to God is worthy, has integrity, represents and speaks to the congregation, and exploits the potential of all involved.

Coda D'Amore

Apart from their romantic predilections, there are three loves without which no pastor or church musician can survive or fulfill his or her calling.

There has to be a love of God, without which leading worship is a grueling business. And that love cannot necessarily be cultured in the time when the leaders are fulfilling their professional calling. It has to be nurtured when far away from the music stand or pulpit, the ministers of word and music celebrate their value as loved children of God not for what they can do or how well, but simply because of who they are.

The second love is a love of language. For some that is spoken words, for others it is musical notation. Both languages can fill those who hear with a sense of desire for God or a feeling of disgust with the random way in which the offering of worship has been made. The language of music, as the language of speech, is the means by which conversion, commitment, grace, forgiveness, and reconciliation can move from concept to reality. They are the tools which will only deliver the best when they are cherished.

And thirdly there has to be a love of people. For in the church we are not called to be a separate caste by dint of our professional engagement. We are expected to be members of a joined-up body. And the best musicians in churches are not those who ferret around for compliments on their improvised saxophone descant or hymn-tune prelude, but those who befriend the congregation for no other reason than that they too are partners in the praise of God.

I commend this broad book to a wide readership and pray that it will provide good nourishment and enable best practice.

John L. Bell
Glasgow, Scotland
May 2007

John L. Bell is an ordained minister of the Church of Scotland and a member of the Iona Community. After a period in the Netherlands and two posts in church youth work, he became employed full time in the areas of music and worship with the Wild Goose Resource Group. He is a past convener of the Church of Scotland's Panel on Worship and presently convenes the committee revising the Church Hymnary.

In 1999 he was honored by the Presbyterian Church of Canada and the Royal School of Church Music, which bestowed a fellowship on him; and in 2002 he was awarded an honorary doctorate by the University of Glasgow.

John has produced (some in collaboration with Graham Maule) many collections of original hymns and songs and two collections of songs of the World Church. These are published by the Iona Community in Scotland and by G.I.A. Publications (Chicago) in North America. He is an occasional broadcaster, lectures in theological colleges in Britain and the United States, but is primarily concerned with the renewal of congregational worship at the grassroots level.

What About Jazz?

RICHARD BIRK

> Every man prays in his own language. There is no language God does not understand.
>
> *Duke Ellington*

Leave it to Duke to cut right to the heart of the matter and eloquently and succinctly state the essence of this article! Anyway, here it goes. . . .

Jazz is the musical language with which I have chosen to praise God. So what is jazz? Louis Armstrong once answered, "Man, if you have to ask what it (jazz) is, you'll never know." The *Encarta Dictionary*, however, is a little more helpful:

> Jazz (noun): popular music that originated among black people in New Orleans in the late 19th century and is characterized by syncopated rhythms and improvisation. It has since developed various styles.

The things that leap out at me in this definition (so brief, yet implying so much more—kind of like Christ and some of his teachings) are:

1. Jazz is American.
2. Jazz is about rhythm.
3. Jazz is about improvisation.
4. Jazz is a huge umbrella that covers a number of different sustyles.

In reverse order, jazz is tremendously *diverse* and encompasses dixieland, big band, bebop, cool, free, fusion, and smooth to name just a few *substyles*. This diversity always reminds me of the fable of the blind men and the elephant. The first man touches the elephant's side and says the elephant is like a wall. The second man encounters the elephant's leg and says the elephant is like a tree. The third man feels the elephant's trunk and says the elephant is like a snake, while the fourth man concludes the elephant is like a fan after touching the elephant's ear. While they're all partially correct, none can "see" the big picture. I think this analogy can be applied not only to how we view jazz but even in fact how we view various religions and denominations. Maybe we're all "correct" from our narrow point of view, but we must realize that the face of God is so much bigger than what we can see individually, socially, or culturally.

Improvisation is a key element of jazz, and Mark Gridley in his book *Jazz Styles: History and Analysis* says "to improvise is to compose and perform at the same time."[1] Since the psalms exhort us to "Sing to the Lord a new song," then improvisation is one avenue to achieve this scriptural mandate. Improvisation is also the ultimate "living in the moment" experience for musicians. Divine inspiration during an improvised solo is a powerful and moving experience for both the listener and the performer.

One of the earliest and most recognizable characteristics of jazz is its *swing rhythm*. Deriving from the syncopation of ragtime, swing has evolved to become one of the signature features of jazz. Since its inception, jazz has continued to develop rhythmically and now includes Latin rhythms, rock rhythms, and world rhythms to name just a few. Rhythm is a unifying force not just in music, but in our daily lives. It can bridge social and cultural gaps, helping us to dance as brothers and sisters in Christ.

Jazz is a distinctly *American music* (which Congress in 1987 designated as a "rare and valuable national American treasure") that grew out of African and European traditions. It could only have happened in this great melting pot where different cultural identities were blended together to create a new art form that has influenced and transformed music throughout the world.

Historical Overview

The roots of jazz are ragtime and blues. Ragtime music was written for solo piano originally and contained infectious syncopated rhythms while using traditional European harmonies and form. Blues grew out of the slaves' experience and was their deeply expressive vocal music that contained moans, shouts, and growls. These musical traditions merged in New Orleans in the early 1900s when instrumentalists would recreate the vocal effects of the blues while taking liberties with ("jazzing up") traditional ragtime melodies.

Born in 1901, trumpeter/singer Louis Armstrong grew up in New Orleans and was the first great (and some say greatest) jazz musician. Louis influenced the whole course of jazz with his brilliant, virtuosic improvisations and his refined sense of swing. The advent of recordings near the same time as Louis' rise allowed his spontaneous performances to be captured and preserved for musicians far and wide to hear. As Louis moved first to Chicago and later New York, his music and influence spread even farther.

Jazz evolved from dixieland in its infancy to big band/swing in the 1930s, bop in the '40s, cool in the '50s, free/avant garde in the '60s, fusion in the '70s, and smooth in the '80s. Along the way, countless jazz pianists like Fats Waller,

Art Tatum, and Thelonious Monk got some of their initial musical experience as church musicians. Several significant jazz compositions such as "The Preacher" by Horace Silver and "Come Sunday" by Duke Ellington incorporate church music elements (gospel in particular).

This link between church and jazz has been solidified through the years through such things as Duke Ellington's Sacred Concerts, Dave Brubeck's *Mass: To Hope! A Celebration*, and Louis Armstrong's album *Louis and the Good Book*. Father John Garcia Gensel established a Ministry to the Jazz Community at New York's St. Peter's Church in 1965. This ministry was a direct outreach to jazz musicians and also included a weekly jazz vespers where jazz musicians could share their art in the context of a worship service.

My Personal Journey

I am the son of a Lutheran pastor and have been a professional jazz musician and taught jazz at the community college level for over twenty years. I was raised in the church with the rich Lutheran musical heritage of Bach and his counterparts. Additionally, my father was a campus minister so I was also exposed to the "contemporary" church music of the '60s and '70s. As a jazz musician and educator, I have lived and breathed the music of the jazz giants like Louis Armstrong, Duke Ellington, Count Basie, Charlie Parker, Dizzy Gillespie, Miles Davis, Dave Brubeck, John Coltrane, Herbie Hancock, Chick Corea, and Pat Metheny.

Yet despite my church and jazz upbringing or perhaps because I grew up in Texas (neither a Lutheran nor jazz "hotbed"), the thought of jazz *in* church never really crossed my mind until 1990. My pastors at that time, David Henske and Jennie Jones of Christ Lutheran Church in Lake Jackson, Texas, repeatedly approached me about leading a jazz worship. I repeatedly turned them down. Having never seen nor heard of one, I had no concept of "jazz worship." Additionally, most of my Lutheran worship experience was traditional and *conservative*. Finally with great reluctance and trepidation on my part, Pastor David and Pastor Jennie convinced me to give it a go. Fully expecting jazz in church to go over about the same as a stripper doing liturgical dance, I was pleasantly surprised—no, shocked!—to find a very warm and receptive response. Annual invitations to lead a jazz worship service at Christ Lutheran followed and inspired me to form the Christian jazz sextet, Jazz Sunday. We gradually became more adventuresome with the depth of our jazz, recorded our first compact disc, and began branching out to lead jazz worship services at other churches. As of this point in time, Jazz Sunday has led Baptist, Catholic, Episcopal, Lutheran, Methodist, and Presbyterian worship services and recorded three compact discs.

So What Have I Learned?

First and foremost, I have learned that this is a *dual ministry* for Jazz Sunday. While our music (hopefully) has enriched worship services and helped shed a new light on the musical face of God, we as musicians and worshipers have been perhaps even more richly blessed by encountering these different faith communities. We have had the opportunity to hear and witness the word of God in countless manifestations. I know that my faith and understanding have been broadened and strengthened thanks to the Christian brothers and sisters that I have met while on my Jazz Sunday journey.

Being a jazz musician can be a thankless undertaking at times. Years of practice, typically small and/or inattentive crowds, dingy club environments, and late hours are just a few of the obstacles that tend to drag down jazz musicians. Playing jazz in church *honors our musical gifts*. Church is a positive environment. People listen. The hours are good. (OK, sometimes Sunday morning does come a little early after those late Saturday night gigs.) People say thank you. We can really feel that our music touches people.

There really is something to this "body of Christ" that the Apostle Paul writes about in 1 Corinthians. Just as the parts of the body, every instrument has its role. In fact Rev. Dr. James Reiter perhaps said it best in his RSV—Revised Satchmo Version—of Paul's epistle:

> For just as the band is one and has many players, and all the players of the band though many are one band, so it is with Christ . . .
>
> Indeed, the band does not consist of one instrument but of many. If the drummer should say, "Because I am not a clarinet, I do not belong to the band," that would not make it any less a part of the band. And if the trombone should say, "because I am not a bass, I do not belong to the body," that would not make it any less a part of the band.
>
> If the whole band were a drum, where would the melody be? If the whole band were a clarinet, where would the rhythm be?
>
> But as it is, God has arranged and orchestrated the parts of the band, each of them as he chose. If all were a single instrument, where would the band be? As it is there are many instrumentalists, yet one band. The drummer cannot say to the clarinetist, "I have no need of you" nor again the pianist to the bass, "I have no need of you."
>
> But God has arranged and conducts the band in such a way that there is no disharmony within the band, [rather] the players harmonize. If one sings the blues, all sing the blues together; if one has cause to ragtime, all ragtime with it.
>
> Now you are the band of Christ and individually instrumentalists within it.[2]

Finally, I've learned that there is a *depth to jazz* that parallels scripture. Jazz is a music that is harmonically rich. Jazz melodies are intricate and take unexpected twists and turns. Jazz rhythms are vibrant and complex. Jazz honors diversity. Jazz requires a lifelong pursuit of understanding—there is always more to learn/discover. Yet there is something in jazz that touches and speaks to people.

So You Want to Try Jazz Worship?

I believe that having a jazz worship boils down to two primary things—musicians and material.

Musicians—If you want "real" jazz, you need "real" jazz musicians. Otherwise it's like expecting Chinese food from Taco Bell.

"It's hard enough finding an organist/pianist/choir director, where am I going to find jazz musicians?" Well if you're fortunate enough to have "home-grown" organists/pianists/choir directors in your congregation, perhaps there are some jazz musicians in your congregation that you aren't aware of because you haven't asked. Many students have played in their school jazz ensembles and have received wonderful training. Maybe they just need an invitation to apply their expertise in your worship.

If there are no jazz musicians in your church, there are other places to look for them. (No, not the unemployment office. . . .) Jazz education is increasingly strong in our schools. Check with your local music teacher(s) and see if they can provide you with some leads. Go to local jazz concerts or clubs. Check with professional organizations like the American Federation of Musicians or the International Association for Jazz Education. (See the list of resources at the conclusion of this article for specific contact info.)

"But what if they've never played in a church before?" You will need to provide some education/training on how to "play church." Let them know how the service is structured and what is appropriate attire/conduct etc. Invite them to attend some "regular" services beforehand. Mostly though, trust that God is working with you and that you don't have to do it all yourself. The Holy Spirit and his Word can provide wonderful guidance if we'll only take the time to listen.

Materials—Many jazz musicians learn best by ear. Consequently recordings sometimes can be more helpful than sheet music. With more and more resources becoming available for download from the Internet on a daily basis, be sure to do regular Web searches.

Published sacred/religious jazz sheet music is gradually becoming more prevalent; however, it's important to remember two things: (1) the ability level of the musician and (2) improvisation. There is a mentality among some musicians that "you have to play what's on the page." This is not the case with jazz. Jazz sheet music is usually only a "guide." Notes can be added and notes can be deleted. Rhythms can be changed. In this way, the music can be adapted to the ability level (and personality) of the musician.

Instrumentation—There is no "standard" instrumentation for a jazz worship ensemble so there is tremendous flexibility. The following are common "jazz" instruments along with their typical roles and necessary skills:

- **Piano**—The piano in jazz can carry both melody and harmony. Much of the sheet music for jazz piano may have chord symbols instead of a fully notated part. A knowledge of jazz chords and appropriate jazz voicings is critical. The ability to improvise and the ability to comp (play chords to accompany other improvised solos) are important skills as well.
- **Bass**—The bass (acoustic or electric) provides the harmonic and rhythmic foundation in jazz. Walking bass is common in jazz songs with swing rhythm. This is where the bass plays a note from the corresponding scale/chord on every beat. Much of the sheet music for jazz bass may have chord symbols instead of a fully notated part. A knowledge of harmony and how to construct walking bass lines is critical. Equally important (if not more so) is a strong rhythmic sense and ability to play at a steady tempo.
- **Drums**—Drums help provide the "time" and establish the rhythmic style in jazz. (In swing, however, it is actually the bass with its walking lines that has the primary role of "timekeeper.") Drum parts in jazz are rarely fully notated and often only have very vague instructions, i.e., "2-beat swing," etc. A knowledge of various styles/beats (swing, Latin, funk, rock), an ability to play at a steady tempo, and a sensitivity to volume are critical skills.
- **Horns (saxophone, trumpet, trombone, etc.)**—Horn parts in jazz typically carry the melodic lines. Appropriate stylistic nuances and jazz inflections help make the melodic lines authentic. While horn parts are usually well-notated, the ability to improvise is a decided plus. For maximum flexibility in utilizing parts written for other instruments, the ability to transpose is also a helpful skill.
- **Guitar**—Jazz guitar is highly specialized and requires significantly more training than "contemporary" or "folk" guitar styles. A talented jazz guitarist can fill many roles including the comping (piano), melody (horns), and rhythm (drums). Most jazz guitarists are able to improvise and have a thorough knowledge of jazz harmony.

A Few Other Things

A truly effective jazz worship involves more than just the music. You can't just plug "jazz" into the musical slots in the service and expect it to always work. I believe that the best jazz is collaborative—a spontaneous dialogue between all the instruments. Consequently, I also believe that the "best" jazz worship services occur when all the worship leaders collaborate. This doesn't mean that everything within the service occurs spontaneously. Quite the contrary, since most of the jazz services that I've been involved with are special, one-time events, they require *more* advance planning. The dialogue between me, the pastor(s), and/or the music director includes the overall structure, mood, and flow of the service, the musical repertoire of the congregation, and how to balance listening and participation.

Yet within this advance planning and structuring of the service, there is a flexibility that allows for the Holy Spirit to be present and provide guidance during the actual service. We sometimes improvise interludes between congregational hymn verses just as do some church organists. We also must be able to extend the music if the offering or communion runs longer than expected. A particularly memorable spontaneous event was the first time our sax player "walked the aisle" during an improvised solo. (This refers to the tradition of saxophone players "walking the bar" where they climb onto the bar and improvise while walking back and forth.) We were playing "Reverend Ron," a bluesy original composition of mine that features saxophone throughout, at the early service with a small, mostly elderly crowd. Johnny, our fearless and very spontaneous sax player, suddenly left the band and began walking up and down the center aisle of the church. He "got in people's faces" as he played and definitely connected with them. It was a very powerful moment for us and for the congregation.

Most people in a congregation are familiar with jazz sounds. It's the context of hearing those sounds in church that tends to challenge them. There is a lot of musical material that is somewhere between jazz and traditional worship music that could serve as a bridge to prepare a congregation for jazz in worship. While preparation and communication about an upcoming jazz worship is always helpful, I believe in the end that the best approach is to plunge into jazz worship headfirst—the "immersion principle." One of the reasons Jazz Sunday typically gets a warm reception when we lead a jazz worship for the first time in a church is that we "jazz up" *familiar* hymns or spirituals. By using 90 percent familiar songs, we find congregations more receptive to the 10 percent of original material that we do.

In Conclusion

Jazz is a significant musical style with a lengthy historical link to the church. By including jazz in worship you can create a powerful experience for both congregations and musicians. While jazz is usually associated with spontaneity, an effective jazz worship experience requires careful planning. The key ingredients for a jazz worship are suitable musicians and materials. There is no "standard" instrumentation or model for jazz worship, so be bold and be flexible. With sufficient prayer and planning, you can make the energy and beauty of jazz a part of your worship experience. May God richly bless your worship services and don't forget what Duke said: "Every man prays in his own language. There is no language God does not understand."

Notes

1. Mark Gridley, *Jazz Styles: History and Analysis*, 9th ed. (Upper Saddle River, NJ: Prentice Hall, 2006).

2. Used with permission of Dr. James Reiter.

Resources

Christian Jazz Artists Network
http://www.songsofdavid.com/christian_jazz_artists.html
Christian Jazz Artists
PO Box 87
Elm Springs, AR 72728

The Jazz Ministry at Saint Peter's
http://www.saintpeters.org/jazz/
St. Peter's Church
619 Lexington Avenue at 54th Street
New York, NY 10022

Jim Martinez & Jazz Praise.com
www.jimmartinez.com
Invisible Touch Music
PO Box 1836
Rocklin, CA 95677

International Association for Jazz Education
http://iaje.org/
International Association for Jazz Education
PO Box 724
Manhattan, KS 66505

Jamey Aebersold Jazz, Inc.
www.jazzbooks.com
Jamey Aebersold Jazz®, Inc.
PO Box 1244
New Albany, IN 47151-1244

American Federation of Musicians
www.afm.org
American Federation of Musicians
1501 Broadway
Suite 600
New York, NY 10036

Jazz Sunday
www.st-john.org/jazzsunday
St. John Lutheran Church
2227 North Downing Road
Angleton, TX 77515-3709

Richard Birk is leader/founder of the Christian jazz sextet, *Jazz Sunday*, which has led jazz worship services since its inception in 1990. They have also performed concerts in Texas and throughout the country including the 2006 Episcopal General Convention in Columbus, Ohio. Birk is also associate professor and coordinator of music at Brazosport College in Lake Jackson, Texas, being twice recognized as Brazosport College's Piper Professor Nominee and Teacher of Excellence. He has been conductor of the Community College All-Star Jazz Ensemble at the International Association for Jazz Education (IAJE) conference in New York and is currently president of IAJE-Texas.

Richard serves as the director of contemporary worship for St. John Lutheran in Angleton, Texas, and has been involved with the 2000 Youth Gathering Jazz Ensemble in St. Louis and the Evangelical Lutheran Worship Introductory Team for the Texas-Louisiana Gulf Coast Synod. Greatly in demand as a clinician, composer/arranger, and professional freelance trombonist in Houston, he has performed with such noted jazz artists as John Pizzarelli, Phil Woods, Bob Mintzer, Bobby Shew, Denis DiBlasio, and Frank Mantooth. He is the son of a Lutheran pastor.

What About Synthesizers?

Electronic Music in the Church:

Lions, and Tigers, and Bears! Oh My!
or
Let Not Your Hearts Be Troubled!

J. OWEN BURDICK

The master of ceremonies waved his arm . . . the bishop was waiting. After months of preparation, my colleague, Bruce Blair, and I were to begin the play-over of the first hymn. The congregation of over 1,600—crammed into two adjoining Anaheim Hilton ballrooms—was on its feet . . . waiting. And waiting . . . Nothing. No sound. Nada, rien, zippo—not even speaker hiss. Our executions seemed imminent.

This was, after all, our big chance—our coup. Ever since the demolition of St. Paul's Cathedral years ago due to its unearthquakeproof construction, the Diocese of Los Angeles had often, of necessity, held its annual convocation in a convention center ballroom. This always necessitated the importing of church furnishings, which resulted in the installation of either a small pipe, or electronic, organ—believed to be required at such events.

As members of the Diocesan Commission on Liturgy and Music, Bruce and I had been asked by our fellow members if we believed Synthurgy—our production company and the liturgical electronic music we'd produced in previous years—was suitable for such a "ballroom liturgy." We responded with an emphatic "yes!" and were assigned the responsibilities.

Our equipment was mistakenly delivered to the Disneyland Hotel, two miles away. The delay in retrieving it meant that the night—I should say rather, the wee hours of the morning—before the principal Eucharist, witnessed the frenetic laying down of what seemed miles of loudspeaker cable. Attaching it to the carpet so people wouldn't trip over it was a tedious, hands-and-knees job. One hour before the service, I was finishing the cabling, and inadvertently walked into a stack of electronic equipment, sending a rented $10,000 reverb unit crashing to the floor.

With only twenty minutes to go, we powered-up our "nuclear power plant" in the middle of the convention floor, and nothing! Nothing? How was this possible? We had checked and rechecked the stacks of synthesizers, samplers, amplifiers, and speakers that were wired together.

In the corner of the ballroom sat an old, (barely) upright piano. Would it come to this—pounding an entire service onto a Hamilton spinet in front of 1,600 people in a 60,000-square-foot carpeted ballroom, with all this TECHNOLOGY sitting here? Lord, take me now! The humiliation was unfathomable—members of AAM (Association of Anglican Musicians) would find out! Somehow (there *is* a Holy Spirit!), Bruce checked the reverb unit, which appeared to be working perfectly. He opened the back of the blamed thing, noticed that a printed circuit board had been dislodged in the tumble, and clicked it back into place. Lights illumined! Dials delineated! We were ready—Thanks be to God!

I realized the moral of the story: keep things simple.

There was no reason why we couldn't have made do with one-tenth all that hardware we lugged into the convention center—or even none of it at all. If the city of Anaheim hadn't paid its electric bill, and we were stranded in the dark, that old piano would've worked just fine—wouldn't it?

That night, after everyone had gone home, Bruce and I sat around that piano. We played Duke Ellington, Cole Porter, and extolled the virtues of an instrument you don't have to plug into the wall. We also gave thanks for the fact that when everything finally worked, the ability of this technology to facilitate musical community was overwhelmingly affirmed.

Electronic Instruments Aren't Inherently Evil

The premise of this article is that electronic music *does* have a place in the worship of God. It is hoped that those who disagree with this assertion will read these pages and be otherwise convinced, and will be encouraged to get their feet wet.

Musicians with little or no experience in the field of electronic music will find a basic explanation of the various types of synthesis, how synthesizers work, and where their use is appropriate in worship. Those already acquainted with the subject will find a discussion of some currently available equipment and resources for further investigation and expansion of their programs.

The electronic keyboard (including all synthesizers and organs—analog or digital) has been with us since the early part of the last century and, given recent advances in digital technology, shows no sign of waning in popularity.

Admittedly, there are challenges and limitations inherent in the design of all digital instruments—whether their sounds are sampled or synthesized—which have hindered them from sounding completely "real." Advances in technology, however, are constantly narrowing this gap. Furthermore, unlike a handcrafted instrument, there is no "suchness" to digital instruments—they have, after all, the same intrinsic value as a computer, because they are computers.

It could be argued that a Stradivarius violin when put away in its case at the end of the day is still a work of art even when silent. A computer when idle is a dormant box of printed circuits. I suggest that a Stradivarius is to digital organs as still photography is to motion pictures. Yes, a Stradivarius is inherently a work of art when dormant, as are Ansel Adams's stunning prints of Yosemite when the lights of the museum are turned off for the night and no one is viewing the prints.

Take a group of individual images and rush them through a projector at 24 frames per second and the photographic images appear to meld seamlessly together to create motion. This, of course, is entirely an illusion—the "art" of the motion picture only comes to life with its activation. Otherwise, a movie in storage is just a canister of 35-millimeter celluloid. And yet who, now, would argue that film isn't a legitimate art form?

The same can be said for the medium of the digital organ. Its beauty isn't apparent until it is activated. As with the motion picture, when this activation occurs, an entirely new medium is created.

Undeniable advances in technology allow us instantly to perceive the difference between a silent film of a hundred years ago and the latest Hollywood special effects. The very same advances are occurring in the realm of computer-based electronic music.

The question ultimately with any medium must be, "Is it beautiful?" "Is it capable of communication?"—and the answer with the digital organ is ever increasingly: "Yes."

I will posit that, even today, there are occasions when the installation of a digital instrument might not only be appropriate, but actually preferable, over a traditional acoustic instrument.

A case in point that I shall describe is Trinity Church's recent acquisition of a prototypical computer instrument by Marshall & Ogletree of Boston, Massachusetts. Given Trinity's proximity to Ground Zero just 600 feet away, the disastrous effects of 9/11 have necessitated the removal and eventual restoration—or complete rebuilding—of the main organs. It was agreed that an electronic interim instrument would be musically far superior, and allow for greater continuity within the extensive music program, than "making do" with a small pipe instrument.

I believe that these digital instruments present a much-needed wake-up call to the pipe organ industry: mediocre instruments will no longer be tolerated when such an attractive, relatively low-cost, and increasingly musically satisfying alternative exists.

History: The Path to the Present State of the Synthesizer Is the Same As That of the Development of the Pipe Organ

I had lunch recently with an old friend, who considers himself a gourmet. When I explained what recommendations I was considering with regard to the Trinity Church and St. Paul's Chapel organs, he suggested an analogy that could both enlighten and guide those who are trying to understand the situation.

He suggested I consider myself the *chef de musique* of Trinity Church and St. Paul's Chapel. He described my job as selecting the menus of the music to be served to the Trinity community, finding the right recipes, gathering the necessary ingredients, making sure to have the right equipment, and directing those responsible for the preparation so that people gathering to partake of our offerings—whether on our premises or by way of our Webcasts—would be completely satisfied.

He suggested that the gourmet concept of "substitution" might interest me, and so he sent to me a quote from the introductory "Memo to the Cook" from what he considers to be the classic American guide to cooking: Volume I of *The Gourmet Cookbook* (Gourmet Distributing Corporation © 1957). I found it illuminating.

> Substitutions arise from three motives, economy, expediency, preference. We never suggest using ersatz ingredients. If you feel you must, for false economy's sake, we will find it in our hearts to forgive but not to condone. Expedience is another matter. Many a culinary masterpiece was invented because one bottle was empty and another full. Substitutions for preference are the secret of infinite variety.

Let's see how the concept of substitution in cooking applies to the problems we tried to solve, and have solved, at Trinity Church, Wall Street.

Our first motive, as we faced the dilemma of having no organ at Trinity Church after the pipe organ was ruined on September 11, 2001, was expediency. Any organist knows that the quickest organ one can buy is a digital organ. It is also the most economical answer to replacing a pipe organ, although I believe— as do most professionals—that the standard, production line digital organs are ersatz. They can do in a pinch, but they can't do for long.

Still, the prospect of waiting until we could collect insurance to replace our pipe organ meant that we could make no decisions for at least two years, which was the time we estimated it would take to collect the insurance award. Only at that time could we have been able to contemplate purchasing a pipe organ. The investigation could easily take a year or more to determine which of several builders we should choose. Then, having determined a builder, we would have faced two to three more years while a pipe organ was being built, shipped, installed, and voiced for our acoustics. Even at that point, no one could accurately predict or guarantee a success. There was no question that we'd have to wait five to seven years for a decent replacement pipe organ, during which time I felt that we'd be starving for good organ sound.

An organ salesman from Boston alerted me to some groundbreaking research that had recently been made in reproducing pipe organ sound using innovative digital technology. As a musician trained in electronic music, I understood the approach immediately, and asked to hear what they had to offer.

To make a long story short—Trinity Church signed a contract with the firm of Marshall & Ogletree; and by September 11, 2003, we inaugurated an impressive interim substitute for our lost instrument. Since it was the first such instrument of its kind, it was—and is—the company's "prototype organ." In the four years since it was installed, it has played efficiently and well, and has gone through many changes and improvements as its creator has developed its technology—both for our sake and for others', because Marshall & Ogletree now actively sells and builds new instruments for churches and concert halls around the world.

The *New York Times* has called their instrument "the Virtual Pipe Organ," and I've come to realize that it is the organ for which organists have waited: a twenty-first-century, virtually maintenance- and tuning-free organ of unprecedented quality.

Nevertheless, the question is still very much in the air about rebuilding the old Aeolian-Skinner organ, or at least replacing the Marshall & Ogletree instrument with a traditional pipe organ. The Aeolian-Skinner of 1970 vintage is currently in storage. We have been told that it would cost about $3 million to rebuild. An adequate newly built organ to meet Trinity's needs musically, acoustically, and spatially would cost a similar amount or more. On July 3, 2007, Trinity Church announced that the Marshall & Ogeltree instrument would be the permanent organ and that one would also be commissioned for St. Paul's Chapel.

Trinity Church can be proud of its role in developing the "virtual pipe organ," which could only exist in this new century because of the continuing geometric growth of computer speed and memory. Without Trinity Church having taken advantage of its historic opportunity and daring to consider such an interim instrument, the music world would not now have its first major new musical instrument of the twenty-first century.

Synthesizer: This device is capable of both the production and modification of sounds.

If this is true, then the human voice is arguably the ultimate example. The voice is capable of an extensive range of dynamics, pitch fluctuation, timbral change (harmonic content), portamento, and can sustain a pitch as long as there is breath to sing. The voice has the additional benefit of being able to communicate language and music simultaneously. The next, most versatile, acoustic "synthesizer" candidates would undoubtedly be the bowed string instruments, followed closely by the organ. Whereas the strings and organ are both capable of sustained tone, a violin has the ability to make gradual and continuous changes in pitch (portamento, vibrato,) and the organ has a greater timbral and dynamic range (from dolcan celestes to state trumpets).

From its beginnings, the organ, if not a direct attempt to duplicate the human voice, was surely an attempt to create an instrument with which many different pitch levels or registers, each with its own harmonic content, could be combined to produce "orchestral" effects. The organ, throughout history, has witnessed an expansion of these various registers and the effects produced by their combination. Indeed, the individual timbres of the stops themselves have given rise to numerous schools and styles of registration. Whether in imitation of an existing musical instrument or not, the process of building complex harmonic spectra through the coalition of diverse stops is central to the concept of the organ's tonal design and evolution. Those who argue against the use of electronic music in worship fail to recognize what is, after all, the logical extension and expansion of a very historic goal.

In the last ten years, astonishing technological developments have been made in the field of electronic music; synthesizers manufactured fifteen years ago are today considered primitive antiques. In fact, 2008 will mark the forty-fifth anniversary of the advent of voltage-controlled synthesis, whose initial offerings sounded to many like audible wall current. Today, however, the technology of the processors that affect this current before it reaches our ears has been greatly refined—as have the sonic results. Impressions of early electronic compositions were often characterized as "raw" and "mechanical," as often by limitation as by choice. Many of the earliest synthesizers were so cumbersome and unstable as to be useless in a "live" performance situation. With the advent of modular analog synthesizers—and such publicly accepted realizations as "Switched on Bach"—it was obvious that the electronic synthesizer was here to stay.

The development of computer technology has directly affected the development of electronic music more than any other single factor. Forty years ago, synthesizers were computer-less monophonic devices. In a live performance, the formation of dense textures required as many instruments as notes in a desired chord. In the studio, however, "multi-track" tape recorders enabled chordal textures to be assembled (using a single synthesizer) through the technique of "overdubbing." Today, synthesizers *are* digital computers. These polyphonic, multitimbral instruments may be combined and controlled simultaneously by a single player. Multitrack capability still exists—but it too is digital, obviating the use of recording tape.

I believe the exclusive use of prerecorded material in any form is anathema to worship, which must surely be a *present* expression of faith and praise; today's electronic instruments are designed to be used in live performance. Furthermore, they may be very successfully used in connection with the ubiquitous pipe organ, as well as other less commonly employed acoustic instruments. This is not to say that electronic music is appropriate in all locations and liturgical settings.

Synthesizers have been referred to as the organist's "fourth manual." Indeed, in a reverberant room, it is often difficult to tell when organ and synthesizer overlap. A stentorian melody can be effectively soloed against full organ and, with the rapidity of the finest combination action, instantly transformed to a hushed, accompanimental, stringlike quality. Whether accompanying gospel choirs or English cathedral choirs; whether augmenting the sound of handbells, accompanying *Kol Nidrei*, or underscoring the eucharistic drama, the potential for the ecumenical use of electronic music is vast and challenging. If the climate is right—and borrowing or renting equipment is the most practical and least expensive way to find out—then we can begin to establish a place, if only occasionally, for electronic music in our worship.

Although the technique of using prerecorded electronic music in conjunction with live performers is still available, with the advent of today's computerized, fully automated mixing consoles, it is now possible to "sculpt" a prerecorded sound-scape to the individual requirements of a particular building or performance. Difficult signal-processing effects and timbral changes may be "sequenced," or preprogrammed, for use in live performance.

I mustn't fail to mention that not all synthesizers and samplers must be con-trolled by a keyboard! A number of different companies manufacture guitar and wind instrument controllers. "Wind controllers" are available in either the Boehm system for reed players, or a three-valve arrangement familiar to brass players. All external controllers operate on the same principle: they produce analog voltages that are converted into digital information for use in controlling a particular synthesizer. Guitar and wind controllers, however, naturally lend the indigenous flavors of their acoustic counterparts to the sound of whichever synthesizer they are connected to, and offer a level of expression unavailable from a keyboard.

For this reason, music that requires one or more obbligato instruments may be realized in numerous ways. For instance, the obbligato flute part to a Lenten anthem could be played by a wind player controlling a synthesizer, producing a hauntingly beautiful solo line over chorus and organ.

Types of Synthesis: Two words bandied about, but often misunderstood, are *analog* and *digital*. We know, somehow, that a watch with dials and hands is *ana-log*, and those that beep during concerts and display the exact time to the second (1:40:23) are *digital*. The best way to understand these terms is to visualize the following description: analog is to a slope or ramp what digital is to a staircase. Thus, analog equations can describe gradual and/or continuous gradations, fluc-tuations, or variations in a parameter or event; digital equations represent the same data in numerically discrete, binary units (on-off, 0-1, yes-no, up-down, etc.). Thus, a circle could be described as a fundamental analog form, while a square could easily be described as digital. As we increase the number of sides in a polygon from four, say, to eight or twelve, the square begins to take on a "rounded" appearance. As we approach an infinite number of sides, we can no longer describe them as individual, discrete events. At infinity, the sides blur into a single, continuous event: step "becomes" slope; digital "becomes" analog.

Analog synthesizers use analog oscillators to produce the basic continuous waveforms which are then given attack and release characteristics, timbrally modified or filtered, and finally amplified. It is primarily in the filtering pro-cess that analog synthesizers take on their characteristic "sound," which, as one might expect, has been described as "warm" and "fat." Indeed, although antique by today's standards, many beautiful compositions are still being realized using these technological "dinosaurs." Analog oscillators are inherently difficult to sta-bilize, however, and can "drift" in pitch. Furthermore, many modular analog syn-thesizers require that interconnections be made with patch chords that are not very efficient or "user friendly" in a performance situation. Modern examples are most often polyphonic, but most early analog synthesizers were monophonic. The omnipresent monophonic "Mini-Moog" (no longer manufactured but easily obtainable, secondhand, through the Internet) is still used for solo lines and bass figures by countless rock bands, and often found tucked away in the corner of many commercial studios.

Digital synthesis has been available for many years. Like its analog counterpart, digital synthesis uses oscillators, envelope generators, filters, and amplifiers to produce sounds. In these digitally operated components, however, every action taking place is described as a series of numbers, which are then mathematically manipulated to form a desired numerical model. It is ironic, perhaps, that digital information must be reconverted into sound by a device that has remained basically unchanged since it was developed in the 1920s—the loudspeaker. Not until we can bypass the speaker entirely, going directly from computer to brain, will we have a completely digital system!

The easiest way to understand the digital process in the recording of music is to examine the way a motion picture works. As mentioned earlier, still photographs, each capturing a frozen, visual slice of time, pass in front of the eye 24 times per second. This frequency is sufficiently rapid that the brain can no longer separate the individual "digital" images. They blur into an "analog" continuum. While the eye is easily fooled by such a slow frame rate, the ear is quite a bit more discerning. Until the 1980s, computers weren't fast enough to produce enough "sonic images" (or samples) so that the ear did not also perceive the spaces between them as "noise." Nowadays, computers capable of recording and/or reproducing as many as 200,000 samples per second are commonly available. Compact disc players use a standardized rate of 44,100 samples per second to reproduce an acceptably wide bandwidth of high and low frequencies within an extended dynamic range.

An exciting recent development is Physical Modeling Synthesis which is accomplished by simulating the physical properties of a real or imagined musical instrument mathematically by defining "exciters" and "resonators." Exciters trigger the mathematical model to begin generating sound. The initial buzz of an oboe reed, the pluck of a harpsichord quill, the chiff of an organ pipe are acoustic examples. Depressing a key on a keyboard and the speed or velocity of the press is translated into the parameters for imitating the physical properties of an instrument's input—the vibration of a string, or column of air. Resonators imitate the instrument's response to the exciter, which usually defines how the instrument's physical elements vibrate. Requiring an enormous amount of computational power, this type of synthesis has only recently been made available to consumers.

Sampling: In this recording technique a single acoustic event (cymbal crash, cello pizzicato, door slam, etc.) is digitally recorded and then processed so that other pitches are "cloned" from the original, and made available throughout the compass of the sampler's keyboard or control surface.

One property unique to sampling is that any sound that can be recorded can be played back by the sampling device. You can have an entire symphony orchestra at your fingertips, or play the sitar, or manipulate the sounds of a Japanese shaku-hachi, or Javanese gamelan!

This technique is not synthesis at all, but really just a manual triggering of the playback of a digital recording and is, in fact, how most modern digital organs produce sound: the recording of a single organ pipe, say, middle "C" from an 8-foot principal stop, is then looped so as to sound continuously, and then trans-posed to create the adjacent pitches.

An inherent problem is that as one gets farther and farther above or below the original recorded event, distortion is introduced into the sound. For this rea-son, many samplers offer "cross-fading" capabilities. If samples of the chalumeau, middle, and clarion registers of a clarinet are gradually blended, or cross-faded, into one another, the resulting composite can be very realistic.

This transposition and looping conserves computer memory; for a typical sixty-one-note rank of pipes, as few as ten samples may be employed. The play-back of these individual digital recordings—which can be done polyphonically, with many recordings or samples being played back simultaneously—creates the various combinations of notes and stops required.

Since the tone of most acoustic instruments changes greatly with increased velocity and/or force on the part of the player, many samplers allow multiple recordings of the same pitch—at different volume levels—to be cross-faded through the option of "key-pressure sensitivity." These refinements effect some very expressive and convincing extensions of the original event. They can also produce some disappointments. Sampling Itzhak Perlman playing middle "C" on his violin will not allow us to sound like the maestro by simply playing up and down our sampler's keyboard!

Sampling raises other moral issues: recording a sample from a commercially released CD, however unrecognizable when used in a different context, is none-theless a copyright infringement. Although sampling is technically not a method of sound synthesis, these techniques form the basis of most electronic music production.

Synthesizers are, I believe, more useful in liturgical settings than samplers. True, samplers allow you to play digital recordings of orchestral instruments (or any other recordable sound for that matter) up and down the keyboard—but is this really the most effective use of electronic music in the church? I'm not advo-cating the denial of employment to my fellow acoustical musicians! If worship is not a present expression of praise using whatever the available resources, then let's be done with it and simply listen to tape-recorded sermons of Desmond Tutu, play CDs of King's College Choir, and replace the organist with a disc jockey. No, the real advantage of electronic music is that musicians can produce beautiful, indigenous, otherworldly, and nonimitative sounds that add a stunning dimen-sion to corporate worship. The musician from a small A-frame church may not be able to imitate the sonic opulence of a Gothic cathedral, but can nonetheless provide an organic, genuine, and ethereal musical experience—which perfectly matches the space.

Samplers and synthesizers are not necessarily as easy to play and program as the salesperson in the music store would have you believe. In fact, many notation and sequencing programs have fairly steep learning curves. Most electronic keyboards are designed so you can "plug 'em in and play" but the stock factory preset sounds are not always useful; how many of us have a use for "heavy metal" guitar sounds during Sunday worship? Those factory presets that *are* useful can grow tiresome, and many musicians eventually wind up "customizing" the sounds to their liking or even taking the time to learn how to program the instrument from scratch. I'm no longer as convinced as I once was, however, that in order to be a real synthesist, one must program sounds from scratch. This would, after all, be like saying you're not a *real* organist if you can't design, build, and voice the stops on a pipe organ. Third-party programmers have flooded the market with excellent (and not so excellent!) sound libraries for most of the popular synth models. For a modest sum you can purchase these libraries on a CD, pop them into an instrument or computer, and give yourself a whole new pallet of sounds to work with—a far less expensive solution than buying a second or third keyboard.

Technical Information: What You Need to Know

MIDI (Musical Instrument Digital Interface): This standardized international protocol is employed in musical instruments containing microprocessors for the purpose of communicating data with other similarly controlled instruments. MIDI is notable for its success, both in its widespread adoption throughout the industry, and in remaining essentially unchanged in the face of technological developments since its introduction in 1983. A player may simultaneously control numerous synthesizers and signal processors with a single keyboard and data format. Moreover, the player doesn't need to understand this protocol: his/her actions are automatically translated and understood by the interconnected devices.

A composer (and most players) of electronic music will undoubtedly want, and need, a computer. Every major computer company produces models that will support a myriad of music software packages. The various configurations of IBM PCs, and Apple Macintoshes, have all been used extensively in the production of electronic music. Of course, these same computers support many nonmusical applications as well: library cataloguing, budget and data management, word processing, etc. The ability to control the parameters of the compositional process—as well as the actual realization of the score—using a personal computer, is invaluable.

Graphically oriented users will want to select a computer whose operating system interacts with the user through the use of "icons" (e.g., Apple's Macintosh). These graphic mnemonics permit the implementation of rapid program changes with the single click of a button. Although IBM-compatible PCs are becoming more commonplace in musical applications, the Macintosh, with its graphically interactive software is, at present, more widely employed.

In order for a synthesizer to be able to connect with an external computer, a synthesizer's MIDI data must first be "translated" before it can be "understood" and processed by that computer. This translation task is sometimes performed by the host computer itself, but often necessitates the purchase of a separate MIDI interface. Many of these relatively inexpensive, yet indispensable, devices are designed to fit alongside or under the "footprint" of a desktop computer. Digidesign, Mark of the Unicorn, Edirol—these, and other manufacturers, produce MIDI interfaces as well as the synchronizers used in video production. *Nota bene*: a company's interfaces are often designed to support its other software products (e.g., sequencers); check compatibility before you purchase any sequencer/MIDI interface combination.

Interconnecting the various electronic components has been greatly simplified in recent years through the use of the Universal Serial Bus. USB was devised to help retire all serial and parallel ports on personal computers since these were not standardized and required a multitude of device drivers to be developed and maintained.

Sequencer: Recording and playing back MIDI data requires the use of a sequencer—a computer program that is basically a cross between a tape recorder and player-piano roll. Sequencers allow a musician to record a performance into the computer just as if he were recording his performance upon, say, a cassette tape. There is no tape involved, however, and the sequencer records MIDI messages instead of the actual sounds. The messages are stored in the computer during recording, and later saved to a hard drive or writeable CD for permanent storage. Then, upon playback, the sequencer plays the instrument (that you just did) by electronically recreating all of your gestures.

Unlike a simple player-piano mechanism or tape recording, the original MIDI data may be edited extensively once it is stored in such a program (i.e., transposed, inverted, played backwards, "mistake-proofed," reorchestrated, remixed, made faster or slower without changing the original pitch, made louder or softer, etc.). In addition, almost all sequencer applications boast individual specialties; staff notation, real-time effects editing, algorithmic note generation ("composing" programs), etc.

Just as important as are the features is the quality of the user/software interface—how easy is the program to learn and implement? How long does it take the program to locate and begin playing a point near the end of a lengthy composition? How easily does it perform basic tasks—how many keystrokes, secondary windows, and screen redraws get between you and the desired command? And, very importantly, when you need help, how many hours a day are a company's technical support representatives available to answer questions? The choice of a sequencer program is difficult; many variables must be taken into account. Composers who spend a great deal of time in front of a computer must be able to work comfortably and efficiently with whichever program they choose. (The sequencer is a "blank sheet of paper"—their creative arena—and should fit like a glove.) Examples of sequencer software are Cakewalk, Cubase, Logic, and Mark of the Unicorn. There are many such programs, as sequencers are perhaps the most often used tools in music production and constitute the MIDI musician's ultimate "Word Processors."

Increasingly, music notation programs (e.g., Finale, Sibelius, Notion) contain built-in sequencer functions allowing step-by-step input and playback of complex multipart (multitimbral) musical scores.

These and other software applications allow the interconnection of synthesizers, samplers, mixers, and outboard processors; storage and cataloguing of patch changes; multichannel recording and editing of musical data; automated mixdown; and publication-quality transcription of score and parts.

Two recommendations: (1) Don't purchase more complexity than is required; music software is expensive. Just as with word processor applications, most people only use a fraction of the capabilities of any notation or sequencer program. If you won't ever need to publish complex orchestral scores, a simplified "stripped down" version of the software may prove adequate. (2) Regardless of the software package in question, work (or at least dabble) with a program before buying it; once immersed, consumers tend to remain loyal to a familiar product rather than learn another, albeit more "user-friendly," program.

There are a few companies that specialize in the "MIDI-fication" of existing pipe organs. In fact, any type of organ (electronic or pipe) may now be retrofitted so that its keyboards, pedals, expression shoes, and combination action may be used to control externally connected synthesizers, samplers, and effects devices. Organists may then sequence both organ and synthesizer improvisations for eventual transcription. Seated anywhere in the building, recitalists may "try out" their programs as the organ faithfully reproduces their performance, replete with expression changes, registration changes—and mistakes!

This begs momentarily imagining the indolent organist, who (after a leisurely 8:58 wake-up) reaches for his telephone and, via the Internet, instructs his parish's computer—and organ—to begin the playover of Hyfrydol at precisely 9:00 A.M. The organist presumably catches another twenty winks.

Keyboard Controllers: There is a plethora of keyboard controllers to choose from, and their specifications are constantly changing. The "feel" of a keyboard is so subjective that a recommendation is pointless. Those who are used to a firm, weighted piano action will find keyboards manufactured by Yamaha or Roland excellent choices. Those keyboardists coming from a background of harpsichord or organ playing may prefer a lighter action. Kurzweil and Kawai products generally feature lighter actions and polyphonic aftertouch—an extremely useful tool for producing expressive, independent lines.

A visit to the local "high-tech" music store—in person, or online—or a perusal of the advertisements in a magazine like *Keyboard* or *Electronic Musician* evinces a mind-boggling array of keyboards as well as outboard "black boxes" known as signal processors. Normally bolted one atop the other into steel-framed utility cabinets, these metal boxes inspired their more familiar moniker—"rackmount." In the last few years a quantum leap has taken place in the development of these processors—digital filters, equalizers, "reverb" units, delays, chorusing units, flangers, compressors, expanders, and noise reduction units. A top-of-the-line digital reverb unit purchased just ten years ago sounds noisy and unrealistic compared with any number of current units costing half as much.

More recently, these formerly outboard devices are being included as part of the sequencer and notation applications themselves and are called "plug-ins." Although they tax heavily the available power of a computer's processor, as computers become ever faster, the need for outboard gear is being obviated by all-in-one applications.

One thing is certain: electronic music produced without some type of added reverberation can and usually does sound terribly antiseptic. Further modification of the sound before it reaches the listener may be desirable (e.g., delaying, detuning, or equalizing a synthesizer's output). But by far the most useful piece of external signal-processing equipment (or internal plug-in application) is that which produces some form of digital reverberation. So-called "convolution" plug-ins are now available that run silently inside MIDI applications and mimic the reverb "signatures" of famous halls and cathedrals. You can actually purchase the "sound characteristics" of Carnegie Hall, St. John the Divine, or the Taj Mahal, and, using their acoustic properties, produce your music within these spaces.

Third-party plug-ins, as well as the capabilities of outboard effects processors, are constantly being updated, upgraded, and refined as future software developments become available, thus avoiding costly trade-ins. You simply download the new revisions to the computer or unit rather than purchasing a whole new software application or device. As with virtually all electronic-music equipment, there is no price limit for those willing to pay for "cutting-edge" technology—the highest price effects units and software can cost thousands of dollars.

If you've decided to simply play back music you've previously programmed into a sequencer application that is controlling a digital organ (or MIDI-controlled pipe organ), you're all set. If, however, you wish to play back music you've programmed into a computer that, in turn, is controlling a number of synthesizers or sound modules, you'll need to combine these "virtual tracks" into a final performance, which can then be sent to amplifiers and loudspeakers.

Mixer: A "mixer" combines many input signals electrically into a smaller number of outputs and lets you balance the relative levels of these input signals. When combining anything more complex than a single synthesizer and effects device, a mixer is essential. How many inputs are necessary? Count on more than you think you'll need; your system will expand, but your mixer won't.

Fully automated, digital mixers once costing tens of thousands of dollars are now readily affordable by the average consumer. They not only record how far you move a volume slider or turn a knob, but also physically replicate the moves—in ghostlike fashion—during mixdown. Editing is simple; just move a volume slider (or "fader") to a new position, and the change is digitally recorded along with the musical performance. The Yamaha DMP 7 ($3,995) was a pioneer in 1988 with its eight channels of computer-controlled motorized faders, MIDI control of nearly every mixer parameter, built-in effects, and completely digital signal path. Today, for less than $500, these same capabilities are available as part of most sequencer and musical notation programs.

The technique of combining prerecorded analog tape with live performance has had a successful history (q.v., works by Felciano, Pinkham, King, etc.). Yet it is astonishing how few of these works from the '70s and '80s are even performable today; reel-to-reel tape players and cassette recorders are antiques and increasingly hard to find and maintain.

Works written using cutting-edge technology by Pierre Boulez and his students at IRCAM (*Institut de Recherche et Coordination Acoustique/Musique*) just a few years ago are relegated to archival performance on CD, as the sophisticated computers and devices that produced these works are no longer in production and no longer supported.

Composers writing works for a specific model synthesizer would do well to include a CD recording of the desired sounds along with the printed score so that future generations have at least a chance at replicating the intended effects and sonorities!

Completely digital hard-disk audio recording—once available to only a few major record labels—is now available and affordable to anyone with a laptop computer. All edits are nondestructive. If you replace a section of music by "splicing-in" a new one, subsequently deciding to revisit the first version, restoration is effortless as both the new and original materials remain stored in the computer. Even computer memory is cheap compared with just a few years ago. A six-minute stereo digital recording devours sixty megabytes of disk space, and yet you can now walk around with a hundred times that amount of memory— six gigabytes—on a flash memory no bigger than a lipstick.

Combining Electronic and Acoustic: Whether prerecorded or live, the combination of electronic and acoustic instruments requires tuning homogeneity. Technicians controlling prerecorded digital recordings, or synthesists who can't accurately match the reference pitch of their acoustic collaborators run the risk of perpetrating a painful offense! Even hybrid organs composed of acoustic pipes and digital sound generators need to be checked carefully before they are used together in performance. The acoustic always wins. As temperature and humidity can wreak havoc on pianos, organs, harpsichords, and other instruments that are not easily or quickly tuned, it is, therefore, imperative to assure tuning uniformity immediately before a service or recital, as it is sometimes awkward or impossible to do this once a performance has begun.

Amplifier and Speakers: Regardless of method, the reproduction of any digital recording or live performance requires an amplifier and speakers. The amount of amplification required to fill a particular space with sound (expressed in watts) can be likened to the amount of wind pressure necessary in a pipe organ. The size and rating of a speaker can be compared to pipe scalings. A Gothic cathedral and a tiny parish church have vastly different requirements; no one formula for assessing the number of watts per person, given a particular enclosed space, is sufficient. The Bryston, NAD, Carver, Crown, and Hafler companies manufacture high-quality amplifiers that are capable of faithfully reproducing electronic music in both small and large rooms. Each of these designs may be "bridged" from stereo to monophonic format, more than doubling its available power. A separate monophonic amp may then be used to drive each individual channel, if required. Many designs feature a power reserve. When a short burst of high energy is needed (cymbal crashes, percussion bursts, etc.), the amplifier "kicks into overdrive," supplies the necessary temporary power, and then resumes normal operation in a matter of milliseconds.

Amplifier selection, as with the selection of other components, is a highly subjective matter, best resolved by listening to available products. Always "audition" a piece of equipment in its final location if at all possible before completing any purchase.

Without question, loudspeakers are the most critical component in any audio system. While other components process electrical signals, loudspeakers are transducers; they transform one type of energy into another (in this case, electrical into mechanical—the opposite of a microphone). Obviously, the speakers one would place on bookshelves in a home would be grossly inadequate in a large hall or stadium. Yet perhaps surprisingly, the formidable speaker and horn combinations used in public address systems are not designed to accurately reproduce music.

A loudspeaker system is made up of three parts: the drivers (tweeter, mid-range—now commonly used as a noun—and woofer), the crossover network that divides incoming electrical frequencies into two or three separate bands (which are then sent to the appropriate driver), and the enclosure itself. Analogous to a pipe organ's case, this acoustic box contains the drivers themselves and (in most designs) plays a vital role in the overall sound of the speaker.

There are four basic approaches to speaker design: acoustic suspension, bass reflex, electrostatics, and satellite/subwoofer systems.

Acoustic suspension was pioneered by the AR Company in the 1950s. In this design the drivers are mounted in completely sealed and airtight enclosures. Since any inward (negative) movement of a driver is absorbed and attenuated by the enclosure, the only sound emanating into the room is produced solely by the forward movement of the speaker cone. While this generally provides an accurate ("tight" not "booming") reproduction of low frequencies, it is not without trade-offs. Acoustic suspension speakers tend not to be very efficient, that is, they require more amplifier power than most other designs to produce the same volume level. Additional very large enclosures are required to reproduce, say, the lowest tones of a pipe organ or bass drum.

The standard bass reflex design (e.g., JBL, Klipsch, Kef, B&W) incorporates an opening in its otherwise sealed enclosure that is tuned to a specific frequency. This "bass port" causes the loudspeaker to resonate at that frequency, thus enhancing the speaker's bass response. Furthermore, since both the woofer's outward and inward motions are channeled through this opening, there is a substantial increase in the speaker's efficiency—a bass reflex speaker will play more loudly than an acoustic suspension design using the same amount of power. Once again, however, there is a trade-off; control and accuracy are sacrificed for the added "punch." These speakers are the most common choice for sound reinforcement applications (i.e., rock concerts, outdoor symphony concerts, etc.) where high fidelity is less of a concern than high decibel level.

Electrostatic speakers (e.g., Magnepan Inc.'s "Magneplanars") are physically the largest (some models look like Japanese shoji screens) but also the least efficient speaker designs. They require a great deal of power to produce high fidelity even at moderate listening levels. The advantage of this design is difficult to explain, but is easily heard. A thin sheet or diaphragm of magnetically chargeable material is waffled between two metal plates. As the incoming current charges first one side of this plate and then the other, the metallic sheet is drawn alternately between the two, producing the same audible pressure waves as a conventional speaker cone. Because this diaphragm's surface area can be as large as that of a refrigerator, sound no longer emanates from a single locatable source—it seems to emerge from the walls themselves. These speakers are generally more expensive to produce than the aforementioned designs. Because of their delicate construction, "electrostatics" are found more often in the homes of avid high-fidelity buffs than in busy recording studios or sound reinforcement applications.

The latest trend in speaker design is represented by Satellite/Subwoofer Systems (e.g., Bose, Genelec, M&K, Velodyne, JBL). In this design, small enclosures are combined with a separate specially designed woofer enclosure. There are definite advantages to this design. The onus is no longer on the satellite enclosures to produce the bass tones; thus these smaller speakers can provide an improved three-dimensional stereo image. Subwoofers produce only very low, monophonic, and nondirectional frequencies. Thus, in applications where speakers will be appreciated more when heard and not seen, the larger subwoofer enclosure may be placed practically anywhere in a church (in an organ loft or under a pew, altar, lectern, pulpit, and so on) without compromising the sanctuary's esthetic integrity.

Your ears are the best guides when choosing loudspeakers, given the requirements of a particular space. As always, insist that you be allowed to "audition" any prospective loudspeakers in their eventual locations before purchasing. It is senseless to spend $10,000 on state-of-the-art synthesizers only to have their sound reproduced by an antiquated and/or woefully inadequate PA system; it is also foolish to purchase more equipment than a space requires.

The question of how many speakers are necessary is interesting. Two-channel stereo imaging (left and right) has remained the norm, even though a four-channel quadraphonic format was designed to replace it in the '70s. Stereo speakers placed left and right in front of a listener result in two-dimensional sound. In order to simulate depth of field, the quadraphonic premise required that an additional pair of stereo speakers be placed to the rear of the listener. Furthermore, it was discovered that the illusion of a large hall could be achieved by slightly delaying the audio signal being sent to the rear speakers. Thus, it was believed that seated in the midst of a quadraphonic configuration, a listener could perceive sound waves traveling front to back as well as side to side.

For reasons related more to marketing than design, the four-channel idea was a commercial failure. With electronic music, however, the effect of four-channel "wrap-around-sound" is very appealing. Sounds may seemingly "spin" around the listener or "shoot" diagonally from front-left to rear-right, etc.

Over the past few years, the development of the 5.1 "surround sound" format has become standardized. Essentially the same as "quad," the only difference is the addition of a center loudspeaker for spoken dialog, and a subwoofer in order to reproduce the lowest frequencies. Though originally designed to enhance the experience of watching films and videos, the 5.1 configuration works very well when listening to music. (The center speaker is generally unused in this case.) A single 5.1 amplifier, with built-in digital delays and all necessary speaker connections, simplifies wiring hookup and replicates the effect of sitting in a large movie theater. This is an exciting format that readily lends itself to the realization and reproduction of electronic media.

What of the Future?

An on-going development that deserves mention is "artificial intelligence." Computers are peerless when it comes to storing and retrieving data. They successfully process and formulate information. Compare the simultaneous emotional, intellectual, and physical demands on the human brain while performing any major concerto from memory, and we appreciate how much faster the brain processes data. Computers don't "learn" very efficiently . . . yet. Breaking down esthetics into a series of binary data is quite a challenge! Yet there is research by Harvard's Robert Levin and others to support the claim that if a computer could "learn" what is "Mozart" about Mozart, and was programmed to be fluent in the harmonic idiom of eighteenth-century Vienna, the same computer could "compose" like the master himself. Farfetched as it may sound, computers have been remarkably successful in generating possible solutions to missing phrases in otherwise complete compositions.

Ethical Questions:
Do I, Can I, Just "Phone It In"? Does This Put Musicians Out of Work?

Commercially available sampled sounds are not going to put the great singers, instrumentalists, orchestras, and choirs of the world out of business. But for television, movie, and especially for commercial sound tracks, sample players are now used extensively. Unfortunately, samplers have put some studio musicians out of work, but they have also created a whole new field of music-making and breed of musician—the synthesist. Although the fidelity of sample libraries is amazingly real—and ever increasingly so—should we really be trying to convince our congregation that there is actually a brass quintet up in the organ loft playing Gabrielli when there isn't? Do you really want your congregation to believe that you can play the accompaniment to "For Unto Us a Child Is Born" if you can't? The time it takes, often, to program a sequencer to produce automated passages of music, would be far more efficaciously spent actually practicing the passage in question. Why would anyone want to misrepresent his or her handbell or children's choir as being better than it really is? Would it really be prudent for any choirmaster to attempt a performance of Brahms's *Requiem* with eleven voices and a computer "filling out the sound" with sampled "Ooohs" and "Ahhs"? Is taking "the easy way out" ever the goal?

Tomorrow's church musicians must be as educated, talented, inspired, informed, and hard-working as the conservatory-trained organists of yesteryear. In the entire history of church music, the pipe organ—so often considered de rigueur for "proper" liturgical celebration—is a relative latecomer, especially in this country. The idea that *any* instrument (with the exception of the human voice) is a liturgical sine qua non is a stifling notion indeed.

Today, many musically gifted young people, who are growing up with computers in their classrooms, are drawn to the musical applications of technology, and are able to control a cornucopia of sound with their own two hands. Surely this is one possible way to attract young people back into the field of sacred music.

Conclusion: The Purity of the Future?

Every ten years witnesses a tenfold reduction in the cost of music-related technology, as well as the development and availability of hardware and software that would have been previously unimaginable. In 1987 when I bought my first Macintosh computer, it contained 20 megabytes of memory. Today, twenty years later, I can carry 200 times that amount of memory on a little device that clips to my keychain—while the average Macintosh laptop contains 2,000 times that amount!

I hope musicians will explore these new technologies, availing themselves of their sonic possibilities. Those who say synthesizers have no place in our worship exhibit the same narrow-minded mentality as those who protested the introduction of pipe organ music in the American churches of the 1800s. Let's face it; no one in his or her right mind has extensive dental work done without the benefit of anesthesia anymore! Are you somehow more of a "real person" or a "better person" if because of some bizarre notion of purity, you force yourself to experience root canal or tooth extraction without a painkiller? Do we object to the electric lights on the music rack, do we eschew the heat in winter or air conditioning in summer? Does the hot water from the sink or cold iced tea in the refrigerator annoy us? Do we refuse to use plastic wrap to keep our food from spoiling? Why then, do we, using a historical temperament that only favors compositions in the key of F major, superciliously claim our artistry is somehow possessed of greater integrity when we insist on a hand-pumped bellows supplying air to a tracker organ—which only resonates to the music of Sweelinck and his contemporaries? Can we really hear the difference between that hand-pumped bellows and a motor-driven one—with 60 decibels of twenty-first-century traffic noise intruding through the windows?

I believe excellence and beauty in the electronic medium is as possible and attainable as virtuosity on any acoustic instrument. We are in a great and timeless procession to the foot of the throne of God—to lay down our new gifts of worship beside those of Palestrina, Bach, Stravinsky, Ellington, and all who have come before. Let us have confidence that while humans live we shall ever yearn to create and perfect the offerings of our time to lay at the feet of the same one God. For we know in the words of F. Pratt Green—

How often, making music, we have found
A new dimension in the world of sound,
As worship moved us to a more profound Alleluia!

Owen Burdick is the seventeenth organist and director of music at historic Trinity Church on Broadway at Wall Street in the city of New York, an Episcopal parish chartered in 1697. Burdick is in international demand as a composer, conductor, and clinician. His compositions have been performed in major venues in New York, London, Paris, Los Angeles, and Reims. He has composed the scores for numerous documentaries and films, and his 1988 oratorio, *Paschal Triptych: A King Portrait*, was nominated for a New York Emmy Award. The Tribeca Film Festival has invited Burdick and the Trinity Choir to perform Arvo Pärt's *Passio* in a mixed-media collaboration with Paolo Cherchi Usai's film of the same name.

Owen has been commissioned by the Episcopal church to compose music for four General Conventions, most recently in 2006, and by the American Guild of Organists where, at their national convention in 2006, he appeared as a guest soloist on the Marshall & Ogletree Virtual Pipe Organ, and presented his Trinity Choir in William Albright's *A Song to David*. He has recorded for the NAXOS, Hänssler Classic, Nonesuch, Summit, Gothic, and Centaur labels and is represented by CCS International.

What About Handbells?

JUDITH C. DODGE

The twentieth-century English poet, F. Pratt Green wrote,

> When in our music God is glorified,
> and adoration leaves no room for pride,
> it is as though the whole creation cried Alleluia!
>
> How often, making music, we have found
> a new dimension in the world of sound,
> as worship moved us to a more profound Alleluia!

My reading of Mr. Green's beautiful hymn text, found in The Hymnal 1982, no. 420, implies that there are a multitude of ways to make music in the worship of God, the purpose of which, of course, is to glorify God. Handbells can add mightily to that glorification. This same hymn text refers to the Gospel's reporting that at Christ's Last Supper with his disciples, Jesus and his friends sang a hymn; they made music together before they left for the Mount of Olives. My sense of this story, as reported in Matthew 26:30, is that in community, gathering at the Lord's table and making music with our friends spiritually enhances the occasion. For those who are unable to sing, or who feel inadequate singing, musical instruments, including handbells, can become their voices and provide a sought-after spiritual enhancement of the experience, the eucharistic experience, as a community gathers at table. Mr. Green continues:

> Let every instrument be tuned for praise!
> Let all rejoice who have a voice to raise!
> And may God give us faith to sing always Alleluia!

In corporate worship, God draws praise from us. We enjoy God's presence by lifting our hearts. Worshiping communities do this in a variety of ways, some of which are customs that are hundreds of years old, while others are new and innovative. Interestingly, handbells can at once be thought of as both traditional and experimental, a conservative mode of religious expression and a very progressive way to make music part of our spiritual expression. Handbells are a powerful liturgical tool if used well. They are unique harbingers of a season if thoughtfully programmed; bells are messengers to a community if rung in ritual or in a regular routine; bells can bring up deeply held feelings or help express profound emotions marking important life passages. An old rhyme from an unknown source tells us:

> To call the fold to church in time,
> We chime.
> When joy and mirth are on the wing,
> We ring.
> When we lament a departed soul,
> We toll.

History

Tower bells have long been associated with Christian churches and often have been placed in special buildings adjacent to the church structure or in towers reaching skyward above the churches themselves. Ringing tower bells are often associated with proclamations of the great Christian festivals, Easter and Christmas, and the tolling of tower bells has traditionally announced events to the wider village, long before modern communication technologies. (Isn't it ironic that church towers are currently rented by cell phone companies for satellite tower installations?)

> I heard the bells on Christmas day
> Their old familiar carols play,
> And wild and sweet the words repeat
> Of peace on earth, good will to men.

In England, tower ringing developed its own peculiar style called change ringing. Hearing the peals of bells go through their mathematical changes is an awesome experience; one has to admire the concentration of ringers as they go through the number patterns. Interestingly, what was once solely an English art form has become an American venture in such disparate places as churches in Hendersonville, North Carolina; Washington, DC; Little Rock, Arkansas; and institutions of higher learning such as Kalamazoo College in Michigan, Smith College in Massachusetts, and the University of Chicago in Illinois. All have their own distinctive sound of change ringing.

Learning to ring changes is a difficult process. In order to practice, without using the large tower bells and ropes, English tower ringers long ago acquired tuned sets of handbells, from six to twelve to a set, and used them in the warmth of the church parlor instead of the drafty and often cold tower to rehearse the patterns of the changes.

Although tradition does connect the development of the English handbell to the training and practice of English tower ringers, in fact handbells have their own Christian history unrelated to tower ringing. Jane Yolen, in her book, *Ring out! A Book of Bells*, indicates that tune ringing goes far back in history. Yolen states that

> by the early Middle Ages, hand bells were rung by musicians through-out Europe. These bells, taken over from the monks and missionaries by wandering musicians, became very popular in royal courts. Companies of ringers were formed to play tunes, each ringer handling two bells. A leader would keep the ringers together, and many a merry tune was sounded upon those bells.

The modern handbell is rung with a clapper fixed with a spring that holds it away from the casting. Handbells made in England, by the Whitechapel Bell Foundry in London, have leather handles and leather clappers. American-made handbells, manufactured by the Schulmerich Bells foundry and the Malmark Bellcraftsmen foundry, both in Pennsylvania, use more modern plastic and rubber instead of leather to strike the casting. The overtones are a twelfth above the fundamental, with the manufacturer taking care to be sure all the bells cast in a set have a consistent harmonic profile. The largest handbell can weigh as much as 22 pounds, and the smallest, 4 ounces.

The development of contemporary English handbell tune ringing in the United States is a story that began in the mid-nineteenth century. Richard Proulx tells us in his small book, *Tintinnabulum,* that various handbell ringing groups from Europe toured America in the 1850s, but that it was P. T. Barnum who created a sensation in this country with the famous "Swiss Bell Ringers." The popularity of the English handbell, referring to a specific type of bell played in the hand and not its country of origin, was first evident in Boston, Massachusetts. Gradually, more people heard the bells, saw their potential, and started to develop handbell groups in New England, which led to the formation of the New England Guild of English Handbell Ringers in 1937. During the period immediately after World War II, the popularity of handbell ringing grew. Because the only maker of the English handbell was the Whitechapel foundry in London, many American travelers from churches visited Great Britain and brought back individual bells in their suitcases, accumulating one, two, and sometimes three octaves of tuned bells over time. (One can imagine the difficulty they would have now bringing the bells in their luggage through today's security checkpoints!) In fact, the handbells that I first learned to play in the early 1950s in Santa Fe, New Mexico, were collected in this manner. Bell choirs were formed in scattered churches across America. Eventually these churches and some schools throughout the country united to expand the original New England Guild constituting the American Guild of English Handbell Ringers (AGEHR) in 1954. With a strong organization, musicians could pursue common questions, solve common problems, enjoy their mutual interests, standardize compositional and ringing techniques, and give impetus to building a common repertory for handbell ringers by encouraging composers to write original music for this unique "instrument." Indeed, finding music was a challenge. In the early days of handbell choirs, many directors had their ringers read music directly out of hymnals or from octavo copies of anthems.

Music and Music Education departments of colleges and universities were slow to respond but were becoming more aware of the demand for trained handbell ringers and teachers. Westminster Choir College, now part of Ryder University in Princeton, New Jersey, was one of the first institutions to hire a handbell teacher, Donald Allured, already well-known in ringing circles as a fine director, teacher, and composer. Westminster realized the need to train church musicians to be proficient in handbell ringing as well as the more traditional subjects of organ and choral directing that the traditional school produced. Allured was also keen to work with church musicians throughout the country at ringing conferences and workshops to develop new ringing techniques and encourage the composition of new music especially for handbells. Music publishers likewise began to realize the potential profitability of making handbell music widely available. Handbell music composers themselves developed standards and symbols for ringing techniques for the industry. In addition to AGEHR's sponsoring composers and publishing music, other publishers began to create a modest albeit important repertoire of music for handbells. In other words, a "literature" for the instrument was at last being created. Publishing houses such as GIA, Choristers Guild, and Lorenz began to include handbell music in their catalogs. That list of publishers has grown to include others such as Augsburg Fortress, Theodore Presser, Selah, Art Masters Studios, Beckenhorst Press, Hope Publishing, Cantabile Press, and Agape.

Handbell Usage Today—Pro and Con

Liturgical churches in general and Episcopal and Lutheran churches in particular have also been slow to develop handbell-ringing groups. In fact, many music directors are outright hostile to incorporating handbells in their music programs except as accompaniment to sung plainsong. Some argue that there is no scriptural basis for handbells in the liturgy. Others sense that their congregations are too resistant to change even though handbell ringing would expand musical expression in worship. Many feel that the equipment needed in the nave for a handbell choir to play—tables, pads, music stands, music notebooks—take up far too much room, cannot possibly fit into an already crowded space, and are distracting. This argument also extends to the need for rehearsal and storage space for the equipment, not to mention the cost and the need for maintenance. Handbells are expensive, as are most fine instruments. Musicians frequently have no training in ringing, are hesitant to attempt to teach or direct handbell choirs, and are reluctant to delve into the technical information about the mechanical aspects of the bells. There is also concern at both academic institutions that train musicians, and churches with fine well-established music programs, about the quality of literature available for handbells. Too many college deans and church music directors have assumed that there is not a body of literature for English handbells because it is a relatively "new" instrument.

Just as there are good arguments against having handbell programs in the church, especially those with traditional liturgical worship, there are likewise splendid arguments for such programs. Oftentimes the hostile attitude toward bell choirs changes when directors themselves actually learn how to play the instruments; discover some of the high-quality literature available, composed specifically for handbells; and see the interest develop in their congregations, especially among young people. When the handbell program began in 1974 at St. Columba's Episcopal Church in Washington, DC, it was intentionally and specifically directed at high school age young people. There was no organized youth program at the time, but there was a successful and excellent Boy Choir and Girl Choir; there was nothing in music for the older grades. With hand-bell ringing established for boys as their voices changed, and for girls as they moved into high school, there was now an organized and recognized program for them to join that had integrity and importance in the liturgy. Eventually, three choirs for children and youth developed: the first, the Genesis Ringers for fifth grade and up; the Gallery Ringers, an intermediate group; and the St. Columba Ringers, the advanced group with most of the youngsters in high school. Concurrently, adults began requesting to learn bell-ringing skills, and three choirs were soon established to accommodate them. Over the years, many of the youngsters have returned to ringing handbells as adults. They find ringing a musical and social diversion from a variety of demanding professions. They have found playing with a bell choir to be a deeply satisfying way of making music with other people.

Inexperienced directors are often surprised and curious to see handbell programs develop in the churches of their more imaginative and creative friends and colleagues. Music educators and church music directors themselves are often stunned at the music-reading skills that develop among their handbell ringers, enhancing their sight-singing skills and general music-making abilities. Many colleges and universities that train musicians and music educators now have handbell ringing in their curricula. Excellent training is also offered by The American Guild of English Handbell Ringers (AGEHR) through a widespread program of conferences, seminars, and conventions as well as through their journal, *Overtones*. The repertoire is vast and original, from very simple anthems for one to two octaves of bells, to sophisticated compositions for upwards of four, five, and even six octaves of bells. More composers of note have incorporated handbells in their compositions or written for bells only. Bells have been included in symphonic works by composers such as Daniel Pinkham, Benjamin Britten, John Tavener, and John Rutter. They have been effectively woven into the fabric of choral anthems by composers such as David Hurd, Alfred Fedak, Peter Hallock, Jayson Engquist, and Libby Larson.

Incorporating handbells in a specific liturgy in the lectionary is no longer the great problem it was at one time. Ringing can be done throughout the liturgical year; music can be found for almost all occasions. No longer is bell ringing centered only on the Christmas season. A very large repertoire of increasing sophistication includes psalms, hymn arrangements, anthem accompaniments, descants, and original compositions, although there also continues to be a large share of secular and popular song.

Benefits

The values that a bell program adds to a church's music program are considerable. Ringing gives a "voice" in making music for the nonsinger as well as the singer. This can be a person of any age, from an elementary school student to a retiree. These varied ages can ring happily in the same bell choir. Both children and adults can learn together from scratch, and they can all ring in the liturgy, contributing to "the work of the people." Many ringers themselves have expressed to me the profound personal joy of being able to play bells at important services during the church year. One ringer has spoken movingly of the significance to her of ringing at the annual Advent Lessons and Carols service. The experience creates for her a way to open herself to the self-study and reflection recommended for the Advent season. A bell choir also can give variety and diversity to the usual instrumental preludes and communion repertoire found in the church, as well as add aural "color" and visual enhancement to a plainsong chant or a descant.

The first time I heard handbells as accents with chant in procession, it opened my ears to chant as nothing else had ever done. The occasion I shall always remember was at a compline service in the Cathedral of St. Mark in Seattle when the men's choir moved in procession through the darkening building, singing the psalm, with the handbells punctuating the sung text. The sound made the movement and the liturgy mysterious, a moment that was richly spiritual and profoundly moving. Peter Hallock, then music director at St. Mark's, was one of the first Episcopal musicians to thoughtfully and richly use handbells for chant and in his own compositions. The creative and imaginative Richard Proulx also recognized very early the possibilities of generating increased mystery in chant through his use of bells. His collection, *Tinntinnabulum* (mentioned above), has been extremely valuable over the years to church musicians. Musicians and clergy planning services of Lessons and Carols at Advent and Christmas as well as Lent have effectively used handbells to enhance the expression of text. And many churches have imaginatively used handbells to illuminate the spirit of a feast day service. A number of years ago at the end of a beautiful candlelight Christmas Eve service in the Arizona desert church of St. Philip's-In-the-Hills in Tucson, a teenage handbell choir quietly began the well-known "Carol of the Bells" by Nikolai Leontovich, playing in the dark from memory the single melody line. As the teens played with increasing energy and sound, there was no doubting the great sense of the joy and excitement of the incarnation celebration that night.

How to Begin

A typical ensemble or choir of handbell ringers is made up of eight or more players, but smaller groups can also be formed for descants or psalm accompaniments or for compline or Taizé services. The ensembles or choirs formed can also provide an invaluable function as an outreach tool in the community, truly performing and entertaining others in a nonchurch setting. Their ringing has an enormous value as an evangelistic tool to bring people into the church. Ringers realize that each of them contributes his or her gifts, which ultimately build up the church (1 Cor 14:26–27).

There is no end to the variations of ringing groups, from youngsters just learning to read music, with bells enhancing that skill, to retirees ringing for the sheer joy of getting together to make music. Over the last two decades, making music on English handbells has had such an enthusiastic following that professional and community handbell choirs have developed throughout the United States, most of whose ringers got their start in church choirs or in high school and college bell programs. Some of the groups are well-known, touring and making high-quality recordings. These include Sonos in San Francisco; The Raleigh Ringers in North Carolina; the Chicago area's Agape Ringers; Bells of the Cascades in Portland, Oregon; Bells of the Lakes in Minnesota; and the Westminster Concert Bell Choir of Princeton, New Jersey. They are available for concerts and offer excellent recordings to the public. Some have even been hired to play for television commercials!

So, what about handbells? Is it worth the time and effort? Where does one begin? Here are the basic considerations:

1. Begin with a vision and a real desire to have handbell ringing in the music program. The music director/organist must want to have handbells. There must also be the tacit agreement of the rector or pastor of the church to develop a program. If the musician in place is desirous but not trained, she or he can find a ways to learn, or can advertise to find a ringer and director with teaching skills, offering appropriate compensation.

2. Find interest in the congregation, because it is often parish enthusiasm that provides the initial fund-raising to purchase the bells and equipment. This core group will need to buy or rent at least two octaves of bells as a beginning.

3. Find and set aside rehearsal and storage space for the bells. Two 5-foot banquet tables can be used for two octaves of bells, or special tables may be purchased. Four-inch thick foam pads with covers for the tables can be purchased as well. Special self-standing notebooks

for the music are available. Some institutions have a room dedicated to handbells so they can remain set up in place between rehearsals.

4. Join AGEHR and locate others in the community who are members. Fellow ringers will be valuable resources for questions that will inevitably arise.

5. Consider purchasing choir chimes as well, or even having chimes as the initial investment. Malmark makes Choirchime®, Suzuki makes ToneChimes, while Schulmerich Bells make the Melody Chime®. Made of tubular aluminum with clapper heads, the chimes are quite durable and can be used with very young children. They also add a new color to already existing handbell choirs.

6. Anticipate being surprised at the delights of ringing, and the pleasures of directing handbell rehearsals.

It is important to be ready for both success and failure. Beginning can be slow. Assume success, but don't be afraid of failing. Some of our finest learnings as musicians come through our failures. Program levels will be varied, but can always be fun and interesting, albeit at times, frustrating. Assume excellence in training at the outset with a dedication to high quality in both ringing and in repertoire. The music does not have to be difficult to be interesting. Bell music should be selected with the same standards that are used by the musician for choir anthems and organ voluntaries. Bells should always be rung musically. As in anything else of value worth doing, handbell choirs demand patience, attention, focus, and dedication to research—all qualities that are central to the development of a good music program in any church. And again it must be stressed that the music director and the clergyperson be convinced of the value of handbells in the overall music program and the value of their contribution to the liturgy, or the effort will be less than successful. In addition, care must be taken not to overuse the bells in the liturgy, and to be certain that they are used appropriately.

Once a decision has been made to develop a program, contact one of two bell manufactures in the United States: Schulmerich or Malmark. The Whitechapel bells are available from England. These three manufacturers have compatible bells that can play together, although the Whitechapel sound is more distinctive than that of the American-made bells. The English-style handbells have a strong fundamental sound; this is favored by American handbell choirs. Pettit and Fritsen bells from the Royal Dutch Bellfoundry have a different rich overtone sound and so are incompatible with the American bells unless used as a distinctive solo line. They can be effective for accompanying plainsong because of a medieval sound quality. There is a Flemish-style bell, made in Holland, but not frequently seen among bell choirs in the United States.

Schulmerich has a rental program available for one year with the rental fees applicable to purchase. A church might also consider beginning with choir chimes, which are less expensive than handbells, and then moving to handbells once a program is established.

Hundreds of directors have found success with these instruments. Handbell choirs throughout the country continue to develop and grow, so explore and experiment. Liturgies are enhanced, and that "new dimension in the world of sound" that F. Pratt Green wrote about opens up worlds of spiritual growth and vitality. As St. Paul reminds us:

> [B]e filled with the Spirit, as you sing psalms and hymns and spiritual songs among yourselves, singing and making melody to the Lord in your hearts, giving thanks to God the Father at all times and for everything in the name of our Lord Jesus Christ.
>
> *Ephesians 5:18–20*

Resources

Handbell Manufacturers

Malmark Inc. Bellcraftsmen
Bell Crest Park
5712 Easton Rd.
PO Box 1200
Plumsteadville, PA 18949
800-426-3235
malmark@voicenet.com
www.malmark.com

Schulmerich Bells
PO Box 903
Carillon Hill
Sellersville, PA 18960-0903
800-772-3557
www.schulmerichbells.com

Handbell Resources

AGEHR Inc.
American Guild of English
   Handbell Ringers
1055 East Centerville Station Rd.
Centerville, OH 45459
313-278-7387
www.agehr.org

Handbell World
www.handbellworld.com

Handbell Services Inc.
1213 Mason Street
Dearborn, MI 48124
313-278-7387
www.handbellservices.com

Articles and Publications

Allured, Donald, et al. *A Guide to Handbell Assignment*. AGEHR, 1995.
   www.agehr.com
Berry, Susan. *Bell Basics*. Hope Publishing. www.hopepublishing.com
———. *Healthy Ringing*. Hope Publishing.

Breneman, Judy. "Essay on Bells." *Association of Anglican Musicians Journal,* December 1994.

Cischke, Kevin. "Building and Maintaining a Bell Choir." *The American Organist,* September 2006.

Frazier, James. *Handbells in the Liturgy.* Concordia, 1994. www.cph.org

Hager, Alan. *Time for Bells.* Sweet Pipes Publishing, 23 Scholar Lane, Levittown, NY 11756. (516) 796–2229

Honoré, Jeffrey. *Handbells in Catholic Liturgy.* Hope Publishing, 1999. www.hopepublishing.com

Ivey, Robert. *Handbell Assignment Book.* Agape, 1993. (Agape is an imprint of Hope Publishing, see Web site above.)

———. *Learning, Teaching, Performing.* Agape.

Jennings, Trevor S. *Handbells.* York: Shire Publications, 1989. www.shirebooks.co.uk

Keller, Michael R. *Developing More Advanced Coordination and Technical Skills in Handbell Choirs.* AGEHR, 1996. (See Web site above.)

———. *Rehearsal Planning, Techniques, and Procedure.* AGEHR.

———. *Score Study Techniques.* AGEHR.

MacGorman, Venita. *Basic Training for Bells.* Lorenz Publishing. www.lorenz.com

Parsons, Thomas E. *Bass Bell Techniques.* Top Publishing, 2006. www.fromthetopmusic.com

Proulx, Richard. *Tintinnabulum: The Liturgical Use of Handbells.* GIA Publications, 1997. www.giamusic.com

Thompson, Martha Lynn. *Handbell Helper: A Guide for Beginning Directors and Choirs.* Nashville: Abingdon Press, 1996. www.cokesbury.com

VanValey, Janet, and Susan Berry. *Learning to Ring Series.* Lorenz Publications, 1988. www.lorenz.com

Yolen, Jane. *Ring Out! A Book of Bells,* illustrated by Richard Cuffari. Clarion Books (Houghton Mifflin), 1974. OUT OF PRINT, ISBN 0-8164-3127-2 (available used from www.amazon.com).

Judith Dodge is the director of music/organist at St. Columba's Episcopal Church in Washington, DC, where she coordinates the largest music program in the diocese, directs the choral program, oversees the Concerts at St. Columba, and conducts one of four handbell choirs. She is past president of the Association of Anglican Musicians and a former member of the Standing Commission on Liturgy and Music. She has served on the faculties of both the Evergreen and Mississippi Conferences on Liturgy and Music. She holds a degree in Music Education from the University of Colorado, and a Master of Arts from San Francisco State University and recently received an honorary Doctorate of Humane Letters from Virginia Theological Seminary.

What About Electronic Music?

ISAAC EVERETT

When Episcopalians think about church music, they tend to think along two lines. On one hand, there are organs, cathedral choirs, Thomas Tallis, and The Hymnal 1982. On the other, there are acoustic guitars, shakers, Steven Curtis Chapman, and church camp songbooks. There is a vibrant community of church-goers, however, who identify with neither the traditional music of previous centuries nor the folk music of previous decades. Those things make good music, but it's not *our* music. It's not the music we hear on the radio, the music we dance to in clubs, or the music that we put on our iPods when we go to the gym.

It's often said that music is a language—a claim that has been made by folks as diverse as Shakira and Susanne Langer—and I believe it to be true. Music is more than one language, though; music is languages from all over the world, languages from different social classes, and languages from different generations. This is why iTunes offers over 2 million songs, and satellite radio has hundreds of stations, each sorted by subgenre; and it is why a growing number of Christians are trying to incorporate electronic music into church. This movement, sometimes called "alt worship" and often associated with the emerging church, is made up of people simply trying to worship God in their own language.

The term "electronic music" is a bit ambiguous. For some people, the term conjures memories of a certain type of strident, experimental art music from the '60s and '70s. Others will associate the term with electronica[1] and other kinds of urban dance music. Technically speaking, any time a musician plugs an instrument into a wall outlet, he or she is making "electronic music."

For our purposes the term will be loosely defined as music that is produced and performed with the assistance of computers; this broad definition includes electronica, hip-hop, and most types of popular music. Although electronic music pervades pop culture and everyday life, most people will never hear it in church. Electronic music is also somewhat mysterious; although a nonmusician can listen to Bob Dylan play an acoustic guitar and understand what's going on, most people have no idea how pop, hip-hop, and electronica are made. This chapter, therefore, will engage not only the reasons why electronic music is being used in churches but also the myriad ways in which it is being used.

The Need for Pentecost

Shortly after Christ's resurrection, the Holy Spirit came to the apostles and inspired them to preach to the nations.[2] Notably, the Holy Spirit did *not* ask the apostles to teach the assembled crowds Aramaic and Greek so that they could understand what was being said; instead, the Spirit enabled the apostles to preach in languages the gathered people could already understand.

Over time, the gospels were written down and translated into Coptic, Latin, German, English, and eventually at least 2,100 other languages. The church didn't limit itself to learning verbal languages, however; it also skillfully adopted new and changing cultural languages. When storytelling was the primary conduit of information, the church used parables and legends to proclaim the gospel. When the printing press was invented, the gospel was taken to the people in written form. When the arts were capturing the public's imagination, the gospel was spread through magnificent paintings, sculptures, and architecture, and when rationalism and the Enlightenment challenged the church's hold on Western thought, the gospel was proclaimed through social justice, activism, and charity. In this tradition, I believe that each generation of Christians needs to retranslate the gospel into its own cultural language.

Unfortunately, as a professional musician in New York City who works in both sacred and secular music, I feel as though the gospel has yet to be translated into the language of my generation. The disconnect between the modes of communication used by the sacred and secular worlds is startling. In the secular world, I have become used to electronic media, nonlinear narrative, and polyfocality. I am disappointed if a concert does not boast spectacular visuals. I not only expect to hear ambient audio when I'm at a restaurant or a store, I expect to see ambient video when I'm dancing at a club.

In church, however, I am used to other things. I am accustomed to following a linear service as it progresses through a book. I expect to hear organs, cantors, and chorales. I am used to acoustic guitars, shakers, and "Peter, Paul, and Mary" harmonies. Even "contemporary" Christian music has very little to do with what I hear on the radio, on television, or in dance clubs. Contemporary worship music seems to draw its aesthetic from Vietnam-era folk music rather than from Generation Y sensibilities.

I'm not suggesting that the church abandon its traditions but I am suggesting that the church be aware of the fact that those traditions can sometimes be a barrier to communication. When young people experience worship in church,

I want them to come away brimming with thoughts of truth, justice, and the transforming power of God's love. I don't want them trying to puzzle their way through a cultural language for which they have no context.

The challenge in this pursuit is that being revolutionary is not difficult; throwing out traditions and abandoning the imagery of our predecessors is extraordinarily easy to do. What is challenging, however, is being revolutionary in a theologically sound way that is a natural extension of centuries of Christian experience.

As parishes wonder what they can do to attract young adults—and the Episcopal church has boldly decided to double church attendance in the next fifteen years—we need to realize that most people who love organ music, plainsong, praise music, and camp songs are already in the Episcopal community. There are not thousands of cradle Episcopalians in the world waiting to be discovered by the 20/20 Project; and if we're going to double the size of our church, we're going to become a different church in the process.

Today's Musical Language

So what is the musical language of today? Spend an hour to two listening to a Top 40 radio station and think about what you hear.[3] Odds are, you'll hear drum loops,[4] synthesizers, sampling, and digital signal processing.[5] The vast majority of hip-hop and R&B is created with samples[6] rather than with a live band, and with the exception of rock and country, most pop and dance music synthesizes the drum track rather than recording a live drummer.

Electronic music production is even more prevalent in advertising because it is much cheaper to create music with a computer than with a band. Original music created for television shows, corporate training videos, and the music you hear when you're put on hold rely heavily on these techniques. In other words, Americans are constantly immersed in electronic music whether they realize it or not.

Purchased Music

By far the easiest and most common way of incorporating electronic music into a service is by playing MP3s of established artists. At Sanctuary,[7] an alternative worship service I help produce in Manhattan, we have a full band and so we're more likely to play the song ourselves than use a recording, but I've seen both used effectively.

In my experience, the best time to do this sort of thing is before the service begins, in lieu of a prelude. Sitting and listening to music is a very passive experience and I try to discourage passivity during worship. As a prelude, however, it can help congregation members make the transition from the outside world into the worship space. People are less likely to have conversations if there's music playing and they're more likely to sit and think about what they're hearing, thumb through the bulletin, or read the preparation for worship.

Ambient Music

Another possibility is the ambient/trance music, most of which is pretty subtle and doesn't have lyrics. A lot of creative services use this kind of music in the way that traditional services use silence. Since this genre of music tends to be unobtrusive, it can even be played underneath spoken text, a technique that gives the liturgy forward momentum. Putting an ambient track underneath the eucharistic prayer brings up the energy of the service tremendously. Additionally, playing music during the prayers of the people makes extended periods of silence more comfortable. You've probably seen readers zoom over the "add your own petitions" moments as if they didn't exist; music can prevent that.

Ambient electronica also tends to be very repetitive, often using only one or two chords. At Grace,[8] a church in London, Jonny Baker uses this to his advantage by writing simple settings of the liturgy that can be sung over preexisting music. It would be hard to sing an entire mass this way, but inventing little melodies for responses like "Lord, hear our prayer," or an *Agnus Dei* is very doable. This method makes the music participatory without requiring the church to produce original music.

At some point, however, you're going to want to start creating your own music. This isn't as hard or as expensive as you might think.

Samples and Loops

Samples are short bits of music, usually two or four bars in length, which you can use to construct original music. Making music with samples is more like building with Legos® than it is like writing music in the traditional sense, but it allows a nonspecialist to make something that sounds pretty good in a relatively short amount of time. The somewhat recent explosion of Apple's Garage Band[9] is a testament to this; suddenly music lovers everywhere can amaze their friends with great sounding music they have "created."

Although you'll eventually want the flexibility that comes with creating your own samples, purchasing samples is an easy to way to incorporate new sounds into your worship. Most sampling programs, such as Garage Band, Sony Acid Pro,[10] and Cakewalk Sonar[11] come bundled with a large library of samples and loops, and many companies sell license-free specialized sample libraries (Sony's is particularly extensive).

It's also possible to make samples out of commercially available music (although it is illegal to distribute such samples). Once, at Church of the Apostles,[12] Lacey Brown sampled the chorus of "Come Together" as an antiphon for the 133rd Psalm. A subtle electronic loop was played below the reading of the psalm, but when it came time for the refrain the congregation found themselves singing along with John Lennon.

Sound Effects

Music is not the only thing that can be sampled—anything that makes noise can be recorded and played back during a service.[13] Dafna Naphtali,[14] a New York–based musician and sound artist, once led a ritual at Union Theological Seminary that included a twenty-minute backdrop of sounds she'd recorded out of her apartment window, including a mockingbird, a car alarm, and the voices of passing pedestrians. At Sanctuary, we supplemented a Good Friday reading of the Passion with the sounds of rioting crowds, roosters, and nails being driven into wood.

One of the most effective uses of sound effects I've ever seen was in a memorial service for the bombing of Manchester. Morph,[15] an Ipswich house church in the United Kingdom, layered snippets of angry voices yelling at God as a meditation. Although it was impossible to make out complete sentences or thoughts, the emotional character of the voices was moving and the extreme volume created a sense of privacy; worshipers were able to pray, cry, and yell without feeling exposed.

Backing Tracks for Live Musicians

Once sampling has been mastered, the next step is to make backing tracks for songs your congregation already knows. For example, if your congregation is used to following a song leader with a guitar, it can be easy to find a drum loop that will fit with the music and give the song more energy. If you're comfortable with a sequencer, add a bass line to lend weight and support. There is an entire genre of electronic music that uses nothing but drum and bass loops (called, not-so-surprisingly, "drum-n-bass"), so even if this is all you do it will still be impressive.

The next step would be to sequence some textural layers, which could be harmonic pads, rhythm parts, or countermelodies. At this point the backing track will really start sounding like music. Once you start adding layers it can be tempting to keep adding more and more until the music is extremely thick and complex, but be careful to leave some room for the live instruments. This method of combining live musicians with prerecorded samples is how I usually work.

Backing tracks allow for a greatly increased musical vocabulary, including sounds from hip-hop, club electronica, and sound effects while live musicians make the music spontaneous, responsive, and fun to watch. Although the live musicians are adding color and energy, the basic architecture of the music is not reliant on any of them. If a musician has an emergency (or flakes out), the service can go on relatively unhindered; if a musician messes up, gets lost, or breaks a string, he or she can quietly fade into the background without the song suffering too much.

Furthermore, musicians can be swapped out at random without the entire band suffering. My band at Sanctuary usually consists of an electric guitarist, a drummer, and me on piano, which is a nice balance to a backing track, but I have also worked with a band consisting of an oud, a doumbek, and a didjeridu and had the same songs work just fine. This does not mean that you shouldn't have a tight, well-rehearsed band. Laptops can crash, important cables can go missing, and power outages can occur so it is important that a band be able to play without a backing track.

Backing Tracks without Live Musicians

As you move from drum loops to full-blown backing tracks, the next obvious step is a track so complete that live musicians aren't necessary at all. You might be on a budget, you might not have any available musicians who can improvise well, or you might not have space for a band to set up. I do a lot of my out-of-town gigs this way when the churches in which I'm playing can't afford to fly out more than one person. Performing electronic music without live musicians isn't a significantly different process from using backing tracks; you'll just want to make sure that your track is complex enough to stand on its own and you'll want to have a few variations to throw in to keep the music from getting boring.

It is vital that the congregation be able to sing along; it doesn't matter how brilliant a backing track you've put together if the worshipers feel left behind. Use musical cues to make it clear when a new verse is starting. Add an unornamented melody line to the track and put low in the mix. Best of all, have a strong musician serve as a cantor. Even if there isn't a band, a live singer helps the congregation find the melody, shows where to join in, gives them something to look at, and generally humanizes the music.

Prearrangement vs. Live Mixing

A frequent criticism of electronic music in a live setting is that it's lifeless and unresponsive. A live musician can switch songs on the fly, repeat a chorus a few times if the congregation is into it, and vamp underneath a procession or communion. There are ways to accomplish these things electronically, but they involve being able to mix samples spontaneously.

Most music software, such as Acid Pro or Garage Band, requires you to lay out the entire piece of music, start to finish, and then press play. Although you can do a lot of creative things with this sort of software, you have to plan everything out ahead of time. There is music software designed for mixing on the fly, however, the most widely used being Ableton Live[16] and Reason.[17]

These programs open up many possibilities. If you are singing a psalm antiphonally, you can have your music vamp underneath the reader and then cue the antiphon whenever the reader is finished reading. The reader can read the selection as quickly or as slowly as he or she likes and the antiphon will always come in right on time.

At Sanctuary we play music underneath the eucharistic prayer but given the length of the prayer, it's unreasonable to ask a priest to consistently arrive at the *Sanctus* at the same moment. When mixing live, however, it's possible to have a constant undercurrent of music throughout the entire eucharistic liturgy, seamlessly shifting back and forth from a quiet musical undercurrent to the *Sanctus*, memorial acclamation, or *Agnus Dei* and back again. By mixing live, we get the best of both worlds: the unique sound of electronic music and the flexibility of a live musicianship.

Most liturgical musicians who mix live do so on a laptop, but there are even more organic alternatives. At Revelation,[18] an emergent church in Bristol, James Bragg uses a lot of the same liturgical tricks that other electronic musicians use: creating backing tracks for songs the congregation already knows, playing ambient music behind text, and spinning instrumental music for dancing, all of which he plays off of his laptop. What makes James different from a lot of church musicians is that, like many retro DJs, he uses a set of turntables. A program called Final Scratch[19] allows him to control the playback of digital music with a set of vinyl records pressed with digital timecode. This has several advantages, the most obvious being that a laptop can hold tens of thousands of songs and is significantly lighter than a case of records.

Watching a DJ spin vinyl is significantly more interesting than watching someone clicking on a laptop. Although a lot of DJs in New York have switched to laptops (and even iPods), vinyl is still considered to be more organic, more versatile, and hipper. With a setup like James's, you can create original music for every service and still get scratching effects.

The Trajectory of Sound

At this point it's worth stepping back to consider how music is used in liturgy. With the exception of ultrahigh churches in which the entire liturgy is sung, the majority of worship services follow the Broadway musical model: a great deal of text occasionally interrupted by a musical number. Now in a good musical (*West Side Story, Rent*), the songs are important to the narrative and advance either the plot, the characterization, or both. In a not-quite-so-good musical (*Crazy for You, Babes in Arms*), on the other hand, individual songs having little to do with the plot are included simply because they are popular.

The use of hymns is similar. Every song should either advance the emotional arc of the service or advance the message of the service; mere reinforcement is not enough. Each hymn should be chosen and placed based on what it says, what it sounds like, and how it will make the congregation feel. Most good worship planners today put a good deal of thought into the hymns they choose to use.

Although Broadway shows are still alive and well, they are no longer a central component of American entertainment. The next generation has moved on to film, which treats music very differently than does theater. As in theater, film music serves the emotional needs of the narrative but in a far more pervasive and subtle way. Although an average film will have music for about a third of its length, it's extremely rare for the music to be in the foreground. This doesn't mean that film music fulfills a less important function than theater music; a great deal of narrative information is packed into a film score. A good composer will make the tense scenes tenser, the thrilling scenes more thrilling, and the moving scenes more moving.

Church music can function in the same way. The amount of music in a service can be dramatically increased without the liturgy feeling crowded. Rather than merely asking, "What hymn would be appropriate here?" ask yourself, "How should this liturgical moment feel and what music will help accomplish that?" Creeds can be inspiring, psalms can be haunting, confessions can be wrenching, and celebrations of the Eucharist can be celebratory; music can make that happen.

What Songs to Sing?

Learning all about electronic music production and incidental music to support the liturgy won't necessarily help you in picking hymns. Most music in worship falls into four categories, all of which are both viable and useful in different situations. Fortunately, since an average service will have at least three or four hymns per week, it is not necessary to pick among them. I believe it's important for a worship planner to remain open to as many options as possible.

Secular Music: People like to hear songs that they know, and hearing a song in church that you are used to hearing in dance clubs can make you experience the song in an entirely new way. At Sanctuary we've used U2's "Still Haven't Found What I'm Looking For" for the book of Ecclesiastes, and we've used "Can't Buy Me Love" by the Beatles for the story in which the rich man is unwilling to give his possessions to the poor.[20] We've used Elvis's "Stranger in My Own Hometown" for the moment in which Jesus returns to Nazareth[21] and "Use Me" by Bill Withers for services about stewardship. Church of the Apostles has used Suzanne Vega's "Penitence" as a prayer of confession and Storahtelling.[22] A Jewish Ritual Theater group in New York has used Damien Rice's "Cold Water" to tell the story of Jonah.

Coming up with the perfect pop song for a service can be difficult, but most congregations are more than eager to introduce you to music. In the back of the worship space at Church of the Apostles, there's a large sheet of paper on which people list songs that are meaningful to them. Members of Sanctuary occasionally post song suggestions to the church blog. Not only does encouraging the congregation to suggest music make the worship planner's job easier, it also keeps the worship rooted in the context of the community.

Taizé, Contemporary Christian, and Praise Music: Lumping Taizé in the same category as praise music isn't intuitive, but the two share a lot of qualities, including simple melodies, repetition, and an appeal to emotions. These qualities bring a lot of advantages with them. Simple, repetitious melodies are easy to sing and are easily picked up by ear. This music rarely uses complex harmonies, which makes the songs much easier to play as well as making it much easier to create backing tracks. Furthermore, the emotional quality of the lyrics leads the singer to meditation and prayer rather than to theological reflection.

There is nothing wrong with theological reflection, of course, but it is more useful at some points of the service than others. In my experience, thought-provoking music is best used during the liturgy of the word, when scripture is being read, sermons are being preached, and the congregation is worshiping God with their minds. Meditative and prayerful music, on the other hand, is called for at the end of a service when the congregation is praying, sharing communion, and worshiping God with their hearts.

Taizé chants have the advantage of being very diatonic; unlike many traditional hymns, Taizé can be sung over a drone or a single, unchanging chord. This makes it very easy to combine Taizé chants with backing tracks or even other songs. At Sanctuary we've combined "Bless The Lord, My Soul" with "Let All Mortal Flesh Keep Silence" into a medley, singing both over a dynamic backing track, a didjeridu, and the lowest pedal on the church's pipe organ. Church of the Apostles has sampled Arvo Pärt's "*Veni, Sancte Spiritus*,"[23] layered in an ambient bass and drum track, and mixed the entire thing with the Taizé chant of the same name.

Both praise music and Taizé chants have ardent supporters as well as critics and in fact, the emergent/alternative worship movements largely grew out of a dissatisfaction with praise music and "contemporary worship." Nevertheless, Taizé and praise music have created powerful experiences for many people and should always be an option.

Traditional Hymns: There is no reason for a musician specializing in electronic music to be afraid of the hymnal. The Hymnal 1982 is a treasure trove of beautiful melodies and spectacular imagery. That said, the hymnal also sports hymns with archaic, limited language and dull, plodding melodies (Anglicans sure love their quarter notes). Flipping through the hymnal is like panning for gold; it's in there, but sometimes it takes a bit of work to bring it out.

When using a traditional hymn, the easiest option is simply to play the hymn as it is, without embellishment and without electronics. This often overlooked option can be extremely powerful. I once planned a worship service centered on reconciliation. The majority of the service was my usual electronic blend of trip-hop, acid jazz, and reggaeton, but at the very end of the service I turned off the laptop, signaled the band to be quiet, and led the church in "The Church's One Foundation" on an acoustic piano. Several people told me that it was the most moving part of the service.

Playing it straight isn't the only option (and there are a lot of organists in the world who can play hymns straight a lot better than I can). Many of these old melodies are amazing and playing around with the accompaniments won't change that. People love to sing familiar hymns and even emergent types who are looking outside of traditional church can be moved by singing a song they remember from childhood. Using familiar music also has a more immediate benefit: since people know the tune they'll be less likely to be thrown off by whatever electronic magic you've conjured that week.

Some traditional hymns, in fact, are incredibly popular in the emergent world. "Let All Mortal Flesh Keep Silence," for example, which is a translation of the second-century Liturgy of St. James set to a French carol from the Renaissance, has been recorded and released by Church of the Apostles in Seattle, Visions[24] in York (United Kingdom), and myself[25] in the styles of alt rock, ambient trance, and IDM (sometimes referred to as "downtempo," but literally, Intelligent Dance Music), respectively. Jonny Baker[26] has released an entire album of "old hymns in dub." Other popular hymns in the emergent world include "Humbly I Adore Thee" and "O Sacred Head, Sore Wounded," which still speak to us though they have startlingly archaic language.

That said, some hymns are better candidates for electronic treatment than others. Some melodies are simply too square while others are simply too overdone. I don't think I'll ever hear a contemporary version of "Hark! The Herald Angels Sing" that doesn't make me break out into hives, no matter how masterful the artist. As amazing as it can be to reclaim our traditions and make them our own, sometimes it really is just better to play them straight.

Electronic Service Music: Finally, there is music that is composed specifically for Eucharists, which can include psalm and canticle antiphons, congregational responses, and eucharistic prayers. Jonny Baker has an influential Eucharist album out, and a Russian Orthodox *"Kyrie"* from *A Musical Offering*[27] made the rounds in the British emergent scene, but for the most part this type of music hasn't been recorded. That, combined with the fact that there are no psalters being printed by the emergent community (although a few of us are working on them), means that the majority of service music is either written in the churches using them or passed around between friends.

Conclusion

I once had a friend tell me, "You don't change the Eucharist, the Eucharist changes you." Although I appreciate the spirit of what he was saying, if the earthly church ignores the sweeping tides of cultural change it will become more and more irrelevant. Keeping in mind the story of Pentecost, we should endeavor to teach ourselves the languages spoken outside the church. We should listen to the radio, we should go to music venues, and we should dance at clubs. We should ask our young church members what music they love and what they love about it. We should encourage young musicians to give their talents to their communities. Just as the Logos came and pitched its tent among us,[28] speaking our languages and sharing our experiences, we must pitch our tent in the world, taking seriously the pluralist, postmodern, and media-savvy culture in which we live.

Notes

1. "Electronica" is a loose term that refers to a variety of styles of dance music, including jungle, glitch, IDM, trip-hop, drum-n-bass, and other similar genres.

2. Acts 2:1–13.

3. The best place to find out what's currently popular is http://www.billboard.com.

4. That is, short bits of drum track, usually between one and four bars in length, that are capable of being repeated continuously.

5. That is, using excessive pitch correction, delays, reverb, and other processes to produce unique vocal sounds.

6. A sample is a short bit of audio such as a horn line or a drum break that is taken from a preexisting recording and inserted into a new song.

7. See http://www.sanctuaryny.org.

8. See http://www.freshworship.org.

9. See http://www.apple.com/ilife/garageband/.

10. See http://www.sonymediasoftware.com/products/acidfamily.asp.

11. See http://www.cakewalk.com.

12. See http://www.apostleschurch.org.

13. Sound effects and other samples are also available in online libraries like http://www.sonomic.com and http://www.sounddogs.com.

14. See http://www.dafna.info/.

15. See http://www.morphcommunity.info/.

16. See http://www.ableton.com.

17. See http://www.propellerheads.se/.

18. See http://www.fernforest.co.uk.

19. See http://www.stantondj.com.

20. See Mark 10:17–31.

21. See Matthew 13:54–58.

22. See http://www.storahtelling.org.

23. This is the fifth movement from his *Te Deum*.

24. See http://www.visions-york.org/visions.html.

25. See http://cdbaby.com/isaaceverett.

26. See http://www.proost.co.uk.

27. See http://www.episcopalchurch.org/50071_53236_ENG_HTM.htm.

28. See John 1:14.

Isaac Everett (http://www.isaaceverett.com) is a New York City-based pianist, composer, and liturgical iconoclast. His music has been called "exquisite and evocative" by NewYorkTheatre.com, "compassionate and brusquely humorous" by *New York Press*; and he has been dubbed a "way cool dude worth checking out" by *The Turning Magazine*. He recently released his debut album, *Rotation*, which became the most sold item at General Convention 2006 (http://cdbaby. com/isaaceverett).

Isaac has a bachelor of music in jazz composition from NYU and a master of arts in ritual studies from Union Theological Seminary. He is the founder of Transmission, an emerging church in Manhattan; a company member of Storahtelling: Jewish Ritual Theater Revived; and the artist in residence at the Church of the Epiphany (Manhattan).

What About Contemporary Ensembles?

MARK GLAESER

About fifteen years ago, my world was shaken when I was asked by my senior pastor to come up with a contemporary worship service for our suburban Lutheran congregation. Being classically trained as an organist/choirmaster, I was immediately threatened and challenged far outside my comfort zone. Being a baby boomer born between the years of 1946 and 1960, however, I was also raised on the music of the Beatles and the Bee Gees. While I intimately knew the church music of Beethoven and Brahms, I was now being asked to develop the other side of the musical equation.

Rationale and History

Our pastor was firmly convinced that people would be interested in coming to a service where people heard music that sounded more like what they heard on their radios, televisions, and stereos than what they had heard in the typical church for the last 150 years. Moreover, he argued, Martin Luther himself worked diligently to put the liturgy and hymns of the worship service in a popular and accessible style. The framers of the Protestant Reformation stated in article 7 of the Augsburg Confession:

> The church is the assembly of saints in which the Gospel is taught purely and the sacraments are administered rightly. For the true unity of the church it is enough to agree concerning the teaching of the Gospel and the administration of the sacraments. It is not necessary that human traditions or rites and ceremonies, instituted by [people], be alike everywhere.[1]

Language, he continued, is an ever-changing, evolving subject. New words and phrases are added to dictionaries on an annual basis. My pastor was telling me that, at least for our upcoming contemporary service at Christ Church, music would be needed to convey a different language than that which people had heard as a congregation largely unchanged from the 1950s.

In my parish, this meant music in our contemporary worship service was going to emphasize a strongly accented rhythm, orally conceived melodies, with roots reaching back to African-American spiritual and Appalachian folk traditions. Accompaniment styles would now emphasize the guitar and rhythm sections of a band rather than the pipes of an organ. This now blew my world right out of the balcony and into the realm of the band.

It turned out that my pastor was right: people in our congregation were attracted to this form of music and began coming to our new contemporary service. The funny thing is that they didn't stop coming to our traditional service. That attendance number maintained itself. Sure, some people drifted to the contemporary service, but slowly people started attending our new service option (more about this later) and, more importantly, began to invite their friends. Today one-third of our worshiping congregation worships at a traditional service and two-thirds worship at a contemporary service.

In addition, the average age of our congregation has dropped from fifty-two to thirty-two in the course of fourteen years. I am not advocating that contemporary worship is the new savior of the church, but I will gently remind you that the Episcopal and Lutheran churches (and their other Protestant mainline friends) are dying. There are less of us each year. The average age of their membership is increasing each year—for Episcopal churches, the age is sixty-three as compared with fifty-six in Lutheran churches. Since the Evangelical Lutheran Church in America was formed in 1988, each and every year we have had fewer members, less overall numbers of congregations, and fewer pastors to serve them. In any other organization, the CFO and governing board would be looking for the answers to the downturn. In the church we look the other way and feel like we are selling out to the culture if we resemble the culture. I once commented that I feel like we (the church) are standing around on the deck of the *Titanic*, playing kick ball with the chunks of ice on the deck, muttering about the cold dark night, ignoring the listing of the ship, and confident that our ship will never sink. I can't help feeling someone should at least consider grabbing a life jacket or maybe moving toward a lifeboat.

For the purposes of this chapter, we will confine ourselves to discussing creating and sustaining a contemporary worship service, led by a contemporary instrumental and vocal ensemble, perhaps directed by you or another person in your congregation. In practice and in treatment here, I do not consider the pipe organ good and the saxophone bad. It is simply music, whether read from a score by George Frideric Handel or a lead sheet penned by Handt Hanson. The purpose of music is to "cradle the word," in the words of Martin Luther. Is there good music and bad music? As a matter of taste, yes. As a vehicle for worship, yes. And I have worshiped in congregations where traditional music is quite bad. And I have worshiped in congregations where contemporary music is quite excellent. Our standards for quality church music must never be lowered; they must remain as high as ever.

Following are some basic criteria for song selection:

- Does the text of the song articulate a biblical view of reality?
- Does the music match and edify the overall tone of the text?
- Is the music easy enough for a congregation to learn after singing one or two verses?
- Is the music interesting enough to motivate the congregation to learn it in the first place?
- Is the music durable enough to be sung several times over the course of a year?

General Recommendations

I would recommend the following guidelines if you find yourself venturing into the contemporary arena of church music:

- Visit other congregations in your vicinity and see/hear what they are doing in worship.
- Begin with a small ensemble (guitar, keyboard, drums or percussion, and a vocalist or two) and grow as you are able or feel led. This enables you to grow into the job as leader, while also reducing your need for music scores in the beginning other than a piano part with chord symbols for the guitarist.
- As opportunities for growth present themselves (in order of preference, which is certainly not always reality), first add a bass player, then an electric guitarist, then a solo instrumentalist (sax, flute, violin), and finally another keyboardist (a synthesizer or two).
- Contemporary music features two voice parts above all others: alto and tenor. If possible begin with these two first. Then add a soprano and bass to provide the flexibility of a quartet. If the ability to increase size presents itself, add more women (up to three to a voice part) and men (two or three to a voice part). An important thing to note here is that the higher voice parts are more easily heard above the sound of the band. A bass singer will often be lost if singing just the bass line throughout the service. If the full ensemble is playing, and the congregation is singing, the vocalists should sing unison. Consider adding vocal parts when the instruments play softer or the musical texture is more spare.
- When you have the presence of percussion in your ensemble, you are typically looking at the need to mike the singers (and even some of the

other instruments) to be heard over the drums. There are many articles out there about the pros and cons of mikes (check out *Technologies for Worship* magazine at www.tfwm.com), but if you are emulating a style of music that resembles today's popular music, you will need to use mikes. Your singers and their vocal cords will thank you. If you truly understand and accept the fact that this music is rhythmically driven, you are dealing with amplified sound on some level.

- Audition all members of your group. If you are amplifying their sound, the congregation is hearing more of it—good and bad! I have a built-in three-month trial for all new musicians because of experiences with those whose skills were not up to par. It can be most unpleasant, especially for the volunteer, to be removed from service later on.
- Immediately tune the radio in your car to a contemporary Christian music station or two (it is the fastest growing genre in the music industry) and educate yourself to the sound of contemporary music. You will hear a variety of styles of instrumentation and a variety of ensembles. Listen carefully to the instrumentation—who is playing the melody, what are the drums and bass playing, and who is filling in the harmonies, etc.) Listen to the vocal pop style, much of which may not be written on the page. Where does the vocalist make use of vibrato, straight tone, etc.? Take note of the artist and group names. Much of their music is available at your local Christian bookstore and sometimes online.
- Subscribe to a few choral clubs that feature this kind of music. A list of my favorites is included at the end of this chapter in the Contemporary Worship Resources.

Required Resources Before You Begin

You are going to need some initial resources in this venture.

- **Music**—The major sources publishing contemporary praise and worship music at this time include: Maranatha! Music; Word/Integrity Music; and Vineyard Music Group. GIA and Oregon Catholic Press offer contemporary liturgical music, including hymns, psalm settings, and liturgical settings. In addition to individual pieces, these publishers offer collections by composers or artists as well as CDs. I always purchase the CDs in order to educate my ear and the ears of my musicians. Many musicians drawn to this genre are quite familiar with hearing and playing by ear. Remember, this form of music comes from an aural tradition. Ask your musicians to emulate the singing/playing style on the CD. This will provide you with a whole new vocabulary for use in talking with your musicians. Subscribe to *Worship Leader's Song DISCovery*. Published bimonthly, it includes a CD and digital lead sheet for songs they consider to be the best of current contemporary Christian music. Our congregation is quite liturgical and I found the music of David Haas to be particularly helpful in the beginning stages of our contemporary worship service. His music is accessible, liturgically appropriate, and melodically engaging for the congregation. His CDs that accompany his collections—recorded by top-notch musicians—provided me with the tools I needed to develop my instrumentalists and singers. My favorite collections of his are noted in the appendix.

- **A Band**—Start small and grow it from there. We began quite successfully with a piano, an acoustic guitar, and a singer. Here is an outline of your needs in order as opportunity for growth presents itself :

  - For the foundation of your sound, you need a good keyboardist and/ or an acoustic guitarist. If you cannot find the guitarist, you should ask around, *but you must hear him or her play.* My experience tells me that the acoustic guitarist—the most represented sound in this genre—is most important to the sound of the band and probably easier to find than an electric guitarist. Reading chord symbols is a must. Strum patterns or picked arpeggios provide the sound that undergirds the rest of the ensemble.

  - Next you need a bass player. An upright bass is fine, but an electric is more flexible and adaptable in the long run. If you cannot find a bass player, you might be able to convert a trombone or tuba player who is familiar with reading bass clef. You could also have a second keyboard player that can play a bass part on a synthesizer. Our congregation had to buy a used bass instrument in order to add this musician to our group.

  - Drummers are also intrinsic to this sound. I had a real phobia against drums in the sanctuary. It took me a while to realize this, but if you start listening closely to contemporary music, you will note the constant presence of percussion. Drummers can be challenging in that they often love to play loudly, especially if they come from a rock band background. Sometimes, players with jazz band or nightclub experience know better than solo artists how to be a part of the group.

  - I have had great success recruiting all of these musicians from among the teens in my congregation over the years. When I have been desperate to cover a part, I have asked them for the names of their school friends. I have also received the names of new musicians as I have become friendly with a few of the high school choral and instrumental conductors in my town. I've also been known to place a "want ad" in our church's bulletin and newsletter.

  - Talent also begets talent. Each new musician has added much to our group over the years. Each has pushed our envelope further toward excellence, and pushed the envelope of our repertoire. Each has helped us attract better players and musicians over the years. Take advantage of this naturally occurring phenomenon and you will be grateful.

- **Singers or a Choir**—Recruit first from within your other choir(s) and ensembles in the congregation, encouraging favorite singers to up their commitment by adding a new group to their life. They should possess the ability to produce a straight tone and control their vibrato. Of course, the ability to read music is a plus, and I will assume that they have a great sense of pitch. As mentioned earlier, a lot of contemporary music features a soloist, and the genre overall favors altos and tenors. Our group progressed from one soloist at inception, progressed quickly to a duo, then a quartet, and evolved into a double quartet. I am aware of congregations that successfully break their groups into smaller teams that rotate in their leadership. I subscribe to the more-the-merrier school of philosophy so I have a large group to work with on most Sundays. SpiritSong, as we call ourselves, has now grown into a group of twenty-six singers that divide between two contemporary services. Some of the best musicians through the years, quick to emulate the sounds and style intrinsic to this genre, have been my high school students and their friends. I appreciate the vitality and vibrancy they bring to our sound and group dynamics.
- **Sound Technician(s)**—Our congregation had none of these. I begged and recruited until I found a warm body who was willing to learn. I sent her to another church for three weeks to closely follow their team of technicians. I bought her a video and a book to educate herself (see resource list at the end). Our congregation even rented a consultant for the weekend to come listen to our group, watch our sound person mix sound, and participate in our worship service. My local band/instrument store provided me with the name of the consultant. This turned out to be the best $300 ever spent in this venture.
- **Sound System**—This includes a sound board, an amplifier, speakers, microphones and mike stands, cables and cords, and more. Ask your local music store for help on this one. A reputable dealer, hopeful of winning a sale, will often bring a system out for you to try in your church before you invest in one.
- **Rehearsal Space**—I recommend rehearsing in the room where the worship service will be held, each and every week. You cannot replicate amplified sound in any other space than where it is to be heard. There are too many variables with room acoustics, instrument sound levels, and more. Take my word on this one!
- **Instruments**—Our congregation purchased a synthesizer for my use, and over the years it has even been upgraded. In addition to our electric bass,

we even now own a couple of sets of drums, every percussion instrument imaginable, and a soprano saxophone. Luckily, if you are on a tight budget, most drummers can bring their own drums. This is a huge commitment on their part in terms of lugging drum cases and stands, and the time necessary to set up. A local drum manufacturer gave us a great set of used drums a couple of years into our venture, which really saved my drummer from burn out.

Does all this sound like a lot of money to you? It can be. I'll bet your congregation's pipe organ or quality piano was expensive, too. Does all this sound like a lot of work? It can be. My life was far simpler when I was alone in the balcony and not keeping up with a cadre of musicians and their music. For our congregation, this was not going to be an experiment—it was going to be a quality experience to which we were committed. If we were going to do this, we would do it well. I naively and fearfully told my pastor that I would accept this challenge under several conditions. I thought of as many conditions as I could, half hoping to discourage him or buy myself more time! My conditions were:

- Church council/parish board support. The burden would not just fall to the music department to create this alternative service. No one should risk this alone. Our constitution as a congregation of the ELCA (Evangelical Lutheran Church in America) lists as our statement of purpose that "To participate in God's mission, this congregation shall worship God in proclamation of the Word and administration of the sacraments and through lives of prayer, praise, thanksgiving, witness, service (statement of purpose, chapter 4, C4.02)." This language clearly states that worship is the most important thing we exist to do as a church. Yes, our governing body was going to need to stand squarely behind this decision.
- A dollar commitment needed to be reflected in the church budget. I was not going to be expected to pull this type of music for a worship service out of a hat without the outlay of money. I needed resources like a sound system, perhaps a synthesizer, some training, CDs of sample music, and music publications. I knew that if worship was the most important thing we existed to do as a church, then our budget could and should reflect that.
- The evangelism team would need to share in the support of this venture. This team, thankfully, got involved in this process and called and invited our neighborhood and community to our first contemporary worship service, which was to be held on Transfiguration Sunday, 1992. I realize this sounds more like what your Baptist friends do at their churches than what you might do at your church. But I challenge you to imagine a Lutheran or Episcopal church where people invite someone to church more frequently than once every twenty years! We decided to try to put

the Great Commission into practice in our own backyard. In fact, we rented a bank of twenty phones and temporarily installed them in the church basement. We recruited callers, drafted a script from which they could refer, had the youth group provide the callers with refreshments, dialed up folks at dinner time to be sure people were home (just like those persistent churches in your area), and sent materials to those who would let us. Is this a numbers game? It sure is—a 1 percent return is what the experts told us we would have. And we did. We called 20,000 people or households, 2,000 let us stay on the telephone line and agreed to let us send them some materials about our congregation, and 200 showed up for worship on Transfiguration Sunday that year (our kickoff Sunday). Two hundred! Talk about a kick start for our worship attendance numbers. I was moved beyond words when I watched 82 people (children *and adults*) receive the sacrament of holy baptism later that same spring at our Easter Vigil service. "Go therefore and teach all nations, baptizing them. . . ." Lest we think ours is the first church to play the numbers game, don't forget that Jesus fed 5,000 after one of his sermons and the first Pentecost was celebrated by 3,000 people joining the church that day.

- We as a staff and a leadership team made a pledge not to give preference to one service type over the other. We decided to view all worship as worship, and not as good versus bad, traditional versus contemporary, organ versus band, handbells versus saxophone. We intentionally decided we would not let members of the church or members of our musical ensembles corner us and have them ask us what our *truly* favorite service was. Our worship schedule simply included an early service that was traditional and a later service that was contemporary. Perhaps you, too, already have a divided congregation, but I hope it is divided by worship times and not worship styles. Good worship is good worship regardless of worship *times* or worship accompaniment *styles*.

In retrospect, I know my list of needs, made out of fear and ignorance, was one of the single best things I ever did. Be bold. Ask for more than I did!

Some Helpful Resources

There are four publications I believe could be very helpful to you as you begin this endeavor. All three can be found in the resources list that follows. The first is *Leading the Church's Song,* which like this book offers different chapters on various emerging genres of music being embraced by churches today. I coauthored the chapter on contemporary music with Richard Webb and it goes into much greater detail on the subgroups within the contemporary area such as praise and worship, alternative, contemporary liturgical, rock 'n roll, etc.

The second is *Contemporary Music Styles: The Worship Band's Guide to Excellence.* Bob Barrett of the highly successful Saddleback Church in Lake Forest, California, authors this book. In addition to covering subgroups like gospel, latin, and country, he covers in great detail the nuts and bolts behind creating and performing effective up-tempo pieces and ballads, as well as the retooling of old hymns. Bob also breaks apart the rhythm section of the band and provides you with examples and concrete tools for success. It is written with the inexperienced church musician in mind.

The third is *Instrumentation and the Liturgical Ensemble* by Marty Haugen. Marty does an excellent job of helping the novice learn how to think about the band, the sounds that each instrument makes, how to add layers of sound, and how to orchestrate the overall product so that everyone doesn't play everything all the time. Being an organist myself, one of the most helpful images that Marty discusses is how the various instruments in the ensemble relate to different stops on the organ. The electric bass serves the same function in leading congregational song, as do the 16-foot pipes in the pedal. It provides the harmonic foundation and often propels the piece forward, while being easily heard by the congregation because its notes lie well below the range of where people are singing. In the same way, a descant instrument such as a soprano saxophone is like adding a mixture stop on the organ. Its notes lie well above the range of the congregational singing, and yet, like a mixture stop, would be boring if played on every verse of every song. To be even more helpful, Marty's resource comes with an accompaniment CD or cassette tape with examples of his illustrations. He begins small, and then illustrates what to do if you have one instrument but lack another.

A fourth resource discusses the selection of music. As I have traveled around the United States talking about contemporary worship for the last dozen years or so, I have frequently encountered the concern that contemporary music often has shallow or "I"-centered language. While this can certainly be found in the contemporary genre, I must assume that your striving for excellence will propel you to look further for texts that edify and engage. A great little resource for this area is *Choosing Contemporary Music,* published by Augsburg Fortress. Be careful: The "I" or "me" language is a double-edged sword. Personal pronouns are just as readily found in traditional music with hymns like "I Know That My Redeemer Lives," "My Song Is Love Unknown," the *"Magnificat,"* or "I Love to Tell the Story." My theory is that the newer texts are more scrutinized simply because they are new. Our ear has fallen deaf to the language of the familiar and timeworn but we notice every syllable in the new. One of our most important jobs as cantors and ministers of music must be the discernment of what we select to be sung by the congregation. I don't select every hymn in the hymnal just because it got into the book. In the same way, we must weed through new music to find great texts.

Conclusion

Overall, I would have to say that our contemporary worship experience has been a great success. Surely, in terms of attendance numbers, that is true. Personally, I would also tell you that I am a better director of music as a result of this service. I'm a better musician because I have learned to listen more—to recordings, to suggestions from the group, to suggestions from my congregation as well as my coworkers on staff. Even more, I have learned how to share. I mentioned earlier that playing the organ by myself in the balcony was quite comfortable and familiar to me (I got on the bench in fourth grade and haven't gotten off yet). I will tell you that learning to share has been extremely rewarding for me. I have seven instrumentalists and twenty-four singers on a weekly basis who really view their volunteer church job much as I do mine: leading the congregation's song. They know which music is appropriate and which is not. They know the difference between music that cradles the Word and music that is self-serving. And they tell me. All the time. "We need to do this song here," and "We need to look for a piece that does this," and "Why can't we do this?" have become all too familiar conversations. SpiritSong feels good about their role of telling the Good News through music. Their attendance and commitment tells me that the Holy Spirit has transformed their willingness to be in a band into being a servant of the Word.

Note

1. The *Book of Concord*, trans. and ed. by Theodore Tappert (Augsburg Fortress), p. 32.

Resources

Favorite Alternative Liturgies

GIA Publications: 1-800-GIA-1358; www.giamusic.com
> *Mass for the Life of the World*, David Haas: Full Score G-3889FS; Vocal Edition G-3889
>
> *Mass of Light,* from *Creating God,* David Haas: Full Score G-3341FS; Vocal Edition G-3341
>
> *Do This in Memory of Me,* David Haas: G-5433
>
> *Mass of the Angels and Saints,* Steven Janco: Full Score G-4442FS

Hymnody

GIA Publications: 1-800-GIA-1358; www.giamusic.com
> *Gather:* Pew Edition G-3260H; Choir Edition G-3260C; Keyboard Edition
> G-3260 A; Guitar Edition G-3260G (2 vols.)
> *Gather Comprehensive:* Pew Edition G-4200H; Choir Edition G-4200C;
> Keyboard Edition G-4200KL (2 vols.); Guitar Edition G-4200GL (2 vols.)

Augsburg Fortress Publications: 1-800-535-3858; www.renewingworship.org
> *Worship and Praise Songbook: Words and Melodies,* ISBN 0-8066-3850-8;
> *Keyboard/Guitar Score,* ISBN 0-8066-3851-6
> *New Hymns and Songs,* ISBN 0-8066-7050-9

Word Music: 1-888-324-9673; www.wordmusic.com
> *Hymns for Praise and Worship,* editions available: choir/worship team, wor-
> ship planner, keyboard, various instrumental parts, conductors score,
> 0 80689 35217 1

Praise Choruses

Integrity Music Direct: 1-800-533-6912; www.integritymusic.com
> *Hosanna Music,* CD or cassette and pamphlet-style booklet

Worship Leader's Song DISCovery: 1-800-286-8099; www.worshipleader.com
> Published every two months; comes with *Worship Leader* magazine, CD, and
> pamphlet-style songbook for instruments and singers

Word Music: 1-888-324-9673; www.wordmusic.com
> *Songs for Praise and Worship:* Pew Edition; Singer's Edition; Worship Planner's
> Edition; Keyboard Edition.
> *Best of Contemporary Christian (WORD and Hal Leonard),* ISBN 0-634-
> 01590-7 (over 400 songs—fake book)

Fellowship Publications: 1-480-838-8500
> *The Best of the Best:* Pew Edition with full music or lyrics only, diskette available

Brentwood-Benson Music Publishing: 1-800-846-7664
> *The Praise and Worship Fake Book* 45757-0714-7 (over 500 songs)

"How-To" Manuals

GIA Publications: 1-800-GIA-1358; www.giamusic.com
> *Instrumentation and the Liturgical Ensemble,* Marty Haugen: Book and two
> cassettes G-3674
> *Beyond Strumming: A Liturgical Guitar Method Series,* Petrunak and Felong:
> Book 1 and CD G-4756, Book 2 and CD G-4770

Augsburg Fortress: 1-800-328-4648; www.augsburgfortress.org

Sound Decisions: Evaluating Contemporary Music for Lutheran Worship, Collins and Weidler: 69-2339
  Leading the Church's Song, several editors, including Glaeser: 3-402
  Choosing Contemporary Music, Bocklund, McLean, and Glover: 3-450
Taylor Made Music: 1-714-457-1892
  Contemporary Music Styles: The Worship Band's Guide to Excellence, 96-90235
Concordia Publishing House: 1-800-325-3040
  Let the People Sing, Cherwien: 99-1666

Anthems

Word Choral Club: 1-888-324-9673; www.wordmusic.com
  Octavos, Musicals, Collections: With CDs or cassettes
GIA Publications: 1-800-GIA-1358; www.giamusic.com
  Favorite David Haas Collections: Where the River Flows; Glory Day; No Longer Strangers; Star Child; Before I Was Born
Integrity Music Direct: 1-800-533-6912
  Hosanna! Music Series: CD and softcover book for singers and instrumentalists

Alternate Text Resources (Prayers, Confessions)

Augsburg Fortress: 1-800-328-4648; www.augsburgfortress.org
  Sundays and Seasons, Cycles A, B, C, Frank Stoldt, general editor: 3-1203
  Renewing Worship (Principles for Worship; Holy Baptism; Holy Communion and Related Rites; Life Passages)
  Revised Common Lectionary Prayers, ISBN 0-80063-484-1
Liturgy Training Publications: 1-800-933-1800
  Prayers for Sundays and Seasons, Cycles A, B, C, Peter J. Scagnelli: 1-56854-212-7, PRAYSC

Copyright Release Information

Christian Copyright Licensing International (CCLI): 1-800-234-2446
  Fee depends on size
OneLicense.net; 1-800-663-1501
  Fee depends on size
John Ylvisaker Copyright Contract: 1-319-352-4396
  $75/year flat fee

Video Projection

Worship Image Gallery: 1-800-805-8001; www.goodsalt.com
   1,000 images for worship

Presenter's Toolkit: 1-800-525-2203, www.digitaljuice.com
   6 DVDs, 4,500 photos, 3,200 video clips, 6,700 illustrations, 4,500 graphic
   backgrounds

Mark Glaeser is minister of music at Christ Lutheran Church in Charlotte, North Carolina, where he directs a diverse program of over twenty-five choirs and ensembles, including choral (children's, youth, and adult), handbells and choir chimes, a recorder consort, instrumental ensembles (brass, strings, and winds), and two contemporary music ensembles. He is a registered music therapist in addition to being a rostered associate in ministry in the Evangelical Lutheran Church in America (ELCA).

Mark has served the Association of Lutheran Church Musicians as Region II past president and is active in planning regional and national conferences. In addition to directing the Lutheridge School of Worship and Church Music, Mark is active as a workshop clinician for contemporary worship, Orff ensembles, handbell clinics, choral reading sessions, and implementing change in worship without alienating the congregation. He was involved with the ELCA in the publication of *With One Voice* and *Worship and Praise Songbook* and most recently served on the task force for *Renewing Worship* and the new hymnal, *Evangelical Lutheran Worship*.

What About Instrumentalists?

Young and Amateur Musicians

CYNTHIA HOLDEN

A professional jazz pianist, percussionist, and clarinetist rehearsed with several elementary and middle school instrumentalists to play "When the Saints Go Marching In" at the start of the Eucharist on the Feast of All Saints. The Sunday school children paraded down the church aisles carrying pictures of various saints they had learned about in previous weeks. It was a festive procession; upbeat, joyous, and yes, a bit out of tune. Many parishioners responded positively to the presence and participation of both "pros" and the amateur musicians. One individual stated that he did not come to church to hear an elementary school band.

Certainly one could challenge the theological depth in the text; one could also commend: the enthusiastic participation; the intergenerational involvement; the cooperative efforts among the clergy, Sunday school, and musicians; and the attention to the liturgical calendar. So, was that an appropriate use of instrumental musicians in church?

Should There Be Instruments in Church at All?

At the exodus of Israel from Egypt we have the first recorded song in scripture. In Exodus 15:20 we read that Miriam took a tambourine and sang to the Lord. Psalm 33, in its opening verses, bids us to "Sing joyfully to the LORD . . . Praise the LORD with the harp; make music to him on the ten-stringed lyre. Sing to him a new song; play skillfully, and shout for joy." Psalm 150:3–6 calls us to praise the Lord "with the sounding of the trumpet, praise him with the harp and lyre, praise him with tambourine and dancing, praise him with strings and flute, praise him with the clash of cymbals, praise him with resounding cymbals. Let everything that has breath praise the LORD."

King David, passing the throne to his son, Solomon, set apart certain of the Levites to supervise the work of the temple of the Lord. "Four thousand are to praise the LORD with the musical instruments I have provided for that purpose" (1 Chron 23:5). As Solomon had the Ark brought to the temple, "all the Levites who were musicians—Asaph, Heman, Jeduthun and their sons and relatives— stood on the east side of the altar, dressed in fine linen and playing cymbals, harps and lyres. They were accompanied by 120 priests sounding trumpets. The trumpeters and singers joined in unison, as with one voice, to give praise and thanks to the LORD. Accompanied by trumpets, cymbals and other instru- ments, they raised their voices in praise to the LORD and sang: 'He is good; his love endures forever.' Then the temple of the LORD was filled with a cloud, and the priests could not perform their service because of the cloud, for the glory of the LORD filled the temple of God" (2 Chron 5:12–14).[1]

Despite scriptural affirmation of the use of instruments in worship, one would be hard pressed to set a precedent for or against instrumental music in church, based on the history of music. The early church attempted to steer clear of all things with pagan associations, so, at least for a time, instruments were not used. Little is known about the practice during the Middle Ages; however instruments were banished from churches in the Pre-Reformation movement in Bohemia under Jan Hus (1373–1415), indicating that they had found their way in. As the Lutheran chorale developed in the sixteenth century, it expanded into larger forms utilizing instruments that continued through the Baroque period. Today there are churches rarely without instrumental music and those whose worship includes only the unaccompanied human voice. Either option, as well as many between the two, is permissible and neither is sacrilege. Determining whether and which instruments are appropriate for a given congregation requires one to ask further questions.

Is the Addition of Young and/or Amateur Instrumentalists Right for *Your* Parish?

- Is your parish receptive to instruments being used in church?
- Would adding your violinist to the hymns on Christmas Eve be appropri- ate, or would it be perceived as someone showing off (whether or not that is the attitude of the player)?
- Does the parish have a reputation for presenting "only the best" in music, or is it receptive to involving the living saints with growing gifts?
- Do you have someone in your midst whose gifts might enrich the church's worship life?
- Is the musician capable and willing to play?
- Is the musician mature enough to be self-disciplined in worship?
- Are you able and willing to train that person to fill a music leadership role?
- Will use of the particular instrument under consideration enrich the worship life of the gathered community or distract from it? Remember that there are other places in the life of a church where talents can be shared outside of the principle services.

- Are there practical reasons for using instruments?
- Are they needed, perhaps, to accompany the liturgy in the absence of an organist or keyboard player?
- Do you want to make a difference in the lives of those you are called to serve as a parish musician?

Pastoral and Musical Rationale

For the musician: Is the reason for your faith not best shared one on one? Is the most intimate of musical sharing, vulnerability, and challenge not between two people—each a soloist, yet each also working in sync with another human being equally exposed?

There is little room for "masks" or hiding in music making. One must prepare well and live into those preparations. One must be "real"—and ready to forgive and cover the "sins" of the other, if at all possible, for the good of the music. In the context of the divine service, the desire to give the music one's best efforts increases. At the same time pressure is eliminated in the knowledge that the gifts come from our Creator. They are intended for our well being, the good of the community, and, specifically perhaps, one's faith community.

To share one's instrumental gifts, one must first recognize them, be encouraged in their pursuit, and then nurture them—perhaps for many years. In time, however, the gift must be shared—or one finds oneself in nothing more than a selfish and self-serving endeavor.

I got stuck there—for nearly ten years. For me, the immobility was nerve related. I don't like being in front of people; I don't like embarrassing myself. I'm not perfect, but I want to look like I am, so, given the hopelessness of the facts, I chose not to share the gift I had after a particularly uncomfortable recital experience. I loved to play—for myself. If no one else heard me, no one would know what I could do and, as a result, try to force me into yet another potentially traumatizing situation.

That all made perfectly logical sense to me until God confronted me with the parable of the talents on the morning I nearly severed a finger by accident with a butcher's knife.

Recall Matthew 25 and the servant given one talent. He chose to hide it in the dirt out of fear. The master, on return, demanded an accounting and in response to the servant's cowardice, declared him wicked and lazy, and took the talent from him. God had not, up to that point in my life, ever been quite so direct with me. I had been troubled at the time with a seeming lack of progress—better stated as an obvious regress—in my playing. The confrontation with the word of the Almighty terrified me; it also offered an open door to a new place if I was willing to take a step in faith. The greatest thing about such steps is that our Lord has promised that we never take them alone.

At age twenty-three, my serious studies in organ and church music commenced that week; first with private study, then trial by fire as a substitute, then as organist in a parish; later the opportunity came to pursue an advanced degree while continuing parish work. God also blessed me with a musician husband—a patient teacher and encourager who agreed to direct the choirs in that first church we served (which was new territory for a clarinetist).

There were children in that church. Many of them liked to sing and had been "on stage" in musicals during a previous director's tenure. Seeking guidance, my husband took a course with Helen Kemp in working with children's choirs that transformed his approach to the choir and, as a result, shyness about making music in the presence of others was rarely a problem. One boy took nearly two years to match pitch—but it didn't keep him from singing, though there were days it nearly drove us mad! When he finally did channel in, he knew it, the other singers knew it, and his confidence soared amid great rejoicing.

Though this chapter is not about singing, the choral environment gave birth to instrumentalists. "May I bring in my recorder?" asked a chorister, who, it turned out, had a wonderful musical aptitude. She played a simple piece and soon added her recorder to the voices of the children's choir. She began flute study and played solos and descants as part of the congregation's worship. Another flutist also wanted to play. She and my husband decided on a duet. Rex is one inch over six feet, Anne was approaching four feet. We have a photo of a rehearsal with Rex on his knees so that Anne could stand and the two could share a music stand. Anne kept at it, playing for church, in solo festivals, in school, at her sister's wedding, her grandmother's funeral, and through the tough time of losing her mother to cancer. Music provided a link, a way through those especially difficult moments, an outlet for emotion, an occasion for dialogue and tears, for shared experience—a time for ministering, if you will.

A fine pianist was to be married and wanted a portion of the Bach Cantata 197 at her wedding. A cellist friend would participate, as would a vocal soloist. My recollection of the wedding is faint—but the rehearsal? What pleasure in the playing! The bride, with her abundant talent, coached the music. We did as we were told and basked in the joy of the music-making art.

Conversation with an acquaintance in a choral ensemble turned to instrumental music. Flo stated that she played flute. We read through some scores together and I asked if she would play a voluntary for church. Before long both she and her husband joined the parish choir; they got involved in the church, and a friendship developed, abundant with sharing of our faith, our fears, compositions, chamber music, singing, and vacations where entertainment is always touched by our own music making—be it a lofting flute played on the rim of the Grand Canyon, quartets sung at a café in Turin, rehearsal in an airport en route to England, or strains of music sung around a picnic basket in the desert.

These are but a few of the many means God has used both in church and outside of it to inspire and feed a musician who, in turn, was moved to exercise her own gift for the people of God in the divine service of our Lord and Maker.

Music touches people beyond words. Instruments serve the functional role of supporting congregational song, but the instrumentalist and the melody also impart far more than that, engaging the mind, the emotions, and even the soul. Can such a gift be misused? Of course it can, especially in the hands of sinful human beings. Music can be used manipulatively. Egos can command attention to the person rather than the Creator or the divine service. Nerves can shatter confidence to a point where the resulting sounds are not edifying. Poorly chosen music can be inappropriate for worship.

There are pitfalls. With prayer, work, and determination, however, relationships develop, individuals grow in confidence, avenues for musical service are provided, and the body of Christ in the church is strengthened.

Factors Leading to the Use of Instruments at Saint John's

When I arrived at Saint John's, a music survey was taken that yielded unexpected results. There appeared to be more interest in instrumental music than choral music. While my contractual task was to build a choir program, I noted those interested in playing and called on them as I was able.

The parish has five weekly services. A goal was to have music leadership, in addition to the organ, regularly. Several singing and two handbell choirs have been developed. We also use instrumentalists to play voluntaries and add their instrumental "voices" to that of the congregation in a manner that is different than the "voice" of a choir—be it in addition to or instead of the choral ensemble.

The combination pipe-electronic organ has also encouraged pursuit of instrumentalists because the organ is limited and rather nondescript in sound, and the acoustics are dry—which, together, encourages neither the singer nor the organist, but does lend clarity of sound for instruments that greatly enrich the accompaniment for congregational song.

There was a history of using brass for holidays. As talents were discovered and the current ensemble assembled, involvement was expanded from Christmas and Easter to also include Rally Day, Reformation Sunday, and/or All Saints, Thanksgiving Eve, Christ the King, Epiphany, Transfiguration, Palm Sunday, Ascension, and Pentecost, highlighting key points in the church year and parish life.

An abundance of flutes lent itself to using two at a time in unison, or on duets and descants—a useful approach for those who are challenged by nerves. With several teenaged clarinetists, trios or quartets are possible, as is having each player learn the same solo, with each taking a different weekend service so as to not require the organist to prepare multiple voluntaries for any one weekend. Middle school percussionists find their place amid anthems and hymns; a bassoonist happily plays a solo line or doubles a continuo part. Saxophones and strings add their voices; pianists of varied abilities contribute solos and duets, and a young musician with good counting skills plays timpani parts on a synthesizer in hymn concertatos given our limited chancel space, which does not allow for kettle drums.

The parish decided to hire a full-time director/organist and use only volunteers in the music program. This limits what we do to the gifts of those we have available or can find. The approach demands persuasiveness and creativity as one embraces the gifts that are present, and encourages the further sharing of talent and dedication of time. We have found that we can do far more than we could hope to pay for, were there an instrumental music budget, while building up people in the process.

Additionally, as we anticipate the day when the facilities will be expanded and a pipe organ added, we have a team of people already in place to assist in accompanying congregational song during such time as we are without an organ.

Guidelines for Implementing the Use of Instrumentalists in Worship

Beginning instrumentalists are proud of the fact that they play an instrument. You can tell by the way they talk, how they carry their instrument case, the way they bring it to choir rehearsal so you can hear them play, how they dress for their school concert, and the way they volunteer to play for "anything you need me for." That enthusiasm is fantastic and it is to be encouraged—carefully.

Meet with Your Prospective Musicians

Whether you seek to begin with one musician or a host of them, get to know each individually. Meet with the person and request that he or she bring his instrument and a piece of music to play. Keep a record of the date; the person's name; parents' names, if applicable; contact information; age, grade, and the school attended (especially if your church has children from a variety of school districts). Also note the instrument, years of study, private teacher (if any), choral experience, and any other instrument the individual plays. Indicate extenuating circumstances you need to keep in mind, such as the person or parents' work schedules, custody issues resulting in the person not always being available, and other conflicting obligations (church-related as well as scouts, dance, sports, tutoring, etc.).

For the music interview, clap rhythms in various meters, and have the person clap them back. Have the individual clap several rhythms that are written out. Sing a short passage and have it repeated. Ask the musician to "warm- up" on a scale and tune with the piano or organ. Does the person have the ear to do this well? Listen to the prepared piece, noting strengths and weaknesses such as tone, breath support or handling of the bow, and general musicality. Have the person sight-read a hymn or short passage of music. Does he or she have command of the rhythm, key signature, notes, phrasing, and musical affect? Can the person follow a conductor? Depending on the instrument, determine which clefs the person knows and can use. Is he or she able to transpose at sight (not likely for a beginner, but possible for an advancing player)? Are there apparent improvisational abilities? This meeting will help the music director determine how best to use the talents of the individual successfully.

Young Players

Some children will not be ready to play for a church service. Be affirming, but be honest. Encourage continued study and practice; tell them you would like to hear them again; perhaps even set a date several months away. Give them a hymn melody to learn to play—maybe even a simple melody they could learn to play for (and with?) their Sunday school class. Thank them for meeting with you; remember their names; and call them by name when you see them. Don't feel guilty for making a wise call.

If you believe that the individual is mature enough musically and personally to play in church, select something that will be perceived by the player as "easy" but not insultingly simply for the first assignment; perhaps use two or three players together, playing in unison, to build confidence. Have the budding musician play something with just the keyboard or organ so that you will see how the person responds under pressure before using them in ensemble or with the choir where, should they have trouble, it will be a greater challenge to cover it and keep everyone together.

In preparation for rehearsal, know what you want the person to play. Mark each score so that finding one's place is easy. Communicate times and places for rehearsal and arrival before the service to both the child and his parent—in writing, if possible. Ask the parent to stay for the rehearsal so that he or she knows what is expected of the child. This also avoids a situation where you are alone with the child—something to be very careful about.

Rehearse everything you expect the child to play, including repeats and page turns. Work in the worship space with the accompanying instrument. Anticipate nervousness and talk openly about it. Apprehension is normal. Focus on breathing, careful preparation, and how the child fits into the larger whole of the liturgy. Don't forget prayer.

Thoughts will flood the young artist's mind. Where should I (the instrumentalist) sit? When do I stand? Where should I go to play? Where do I put my instrument when I'm not playing? What about my case? When do I go to communion? When does "my part" happen? Will you give me the tempo? How will I know when to come in? What do I do when I am done?

Cover the logistics so the questions do not overwhelm the player and the attention can be on the service rather than the self. Communicate confidence beforehand and appreciation afterwards. Show it; speak it; write it. Encourage the child every way you can—again, be honest with him. Highlight what went well and address areas to work on so that the child can grow from the experience. Forgive mistakes, if need be. They will happen.

Advancing Players

Instrumental parts abound in choral anthems and add another color to the choir's sound. Rehearse the instrumentalist first with just the accompanist. Prepare the choir and then put everyone together.

Some players are able to open a hymnal and sight-read. While you may trust them to do so, still plan a "road map" for the hymn so that the director, key-boardist, and instrumentalist know how it will be introduced and who will play what and when. This avoids potentially embarrassing moments that should not disrupt the liturgy—and need not do so if all are prepared.

Consider using advancing players to assist younger ones playing the same instrument; have them tactfully offer some tips or play together upon occasion. The less advanced players will tend to play better and more confidently as they follow the more experienced person's lead. This can also build intergenerational relationships that can benefit the church for years to come.

Ensembles

Identify a voluntary to be played by several players. Arrange rehearsals and set a date to play the piece. If all goes well, the players will want to do more. Have the group play one or two hymns in a service; add them to a psalm antiphon. Have goals in mind and be a taskmaster as necessary to get things going and keep rehearsal focused, but also permit the group to gel as the players get to know one another.

Include prayer in your rehearsal. It can be short, but it has the effect of binding together hearts and putting the reason for coming together before each participant.

As the group finds its identity, allow members to determine rehearsal time, if possible. Communicate your needs and desires for the group, but be open to hearing theirs as well.

Would they like to play more (or less) often? Is there a piece they want to do that would be a good challenge? Do they feel overloaded? Four services on Christmas Eve may have sounded doable in September, but come Advent, with family, church, school, and social responsibilities, you will find yourself in the midst of some pretty stressed out people—one of whom will be you as people are backing out of playing.

Can the advancing ensemble run without the music director being present? Especially as instrumental programs grow, it is not always feasible or necessary for the director to be at all rehearsals. In our brass ensemble, a "point person" guides the group's rehearsal, conveys necessary instructions, and keeps the communication lines open—but much of the preparation is done by the players alone, with the organist coming in either near the end of the rehearsal, or for a single rehearsal just prior to the next time the brass play.

Find an "Expert"

I have found it immensely helpful to have an "expert" come in a few times a year and coach our brass. The group comprises men and a high school student. These are dedicated, wonderful people who, except the teenager, had all put their instruments away. They were, like the beginning students, proud of the fact that they play an instrument, but were sometimes insecure in how they played. A member of our parish plays professionally and is gifted at teaching. His various commitments prohibit him from playing regularly with the ensemble, but he gladly responded to a request for help. He gave the group exercises to aid in tuning and tips for playing their particular instruments that an organist wouldn't necessarily know; he also helped teach them how to teach themselves and help one another. The results amazed all of us and spurred the group on to far greater musical heights than we had imagined.

If such a person is among those in your congregation, tap into the resource. Also refuse to let yourself be frustrated by the fact that the individual may not be on board as a player. Such a decision on his or her part may be about ego and not wanting to play with those less advanced, but often it is far more about a whole host of other things—and having his or her support as he or she is able to provide it will reap far greater benefits than allowing animosity or resentment to grow. Prayer can be helpful here; so can patience as you wait on God to provide for what is needed to accomplish his purposes for the music in your church.

What about Advanced Volunteers?

You will find some people who play confidently and well. They are dependable and are delighted to do almost anything you ask. Rejoice in this! Be on the lookout for music you can do with them that will enhance the worship in your church. Write music for them; commission music with them in mind, if opportunity avails itself. Encourage them to share music they discover. Be careful to not take advantage of any one individual; go out of your way to express your appreciation, encourage their gift—and enjoy it!

Some Practical Pointers

- For services where the instrumentalists are doing a great deal of playing, put the music in a binder in the order in which it will be played.
- Purchase music that grants permission to copy the instrumentalists' parts. This keeps the church within the copyright law, and it avoids having to reorder parts, should someone lose his or her music or neglect to return it.
- Communicate "what, when, and where" carefully. Stress dependability. Allow ample time for rehearsal; realize that it sometimes won't be enough, which will necessitate postponing the individual's playing, or cutting back on the music.

- Teach musicianship, but accept that sometimes you will need to teach by rote in order to be ready for the upcoming service.
- Prepare yourself to be let down occasionally. An instrument will be left in a school locker. A ride will fall through; a game will go into overtime; things happen. Be patient, be understanding, and be especially careful when scheduling that person in the future. If dependability continues to be a problem that ought to be within the individual's control, do your best to help teach it. If you are successful, everyone wins. If not, let it go without hard feelings, but do not continue to subject yourself to that person's lack of consideration for *your* time and effort. If the player wants to know why you have not called to ask him or her to play in recent weeks or months, be honest.
- Keep a record of who plays when, so that volunteers do not get inadvertently overlooked.
- Musicians of all ages must, when participating in worship, demonstrate respect for the sacred space and the liturgy in which they participate. Be sure to communicate the church's expectations. Should someone refuse to comply, he or she should not be asked to fill a music leadership role in the service.

Required Resources

What is most needed is time, talent, and a heart for the ministry of music—for recruitment, preparation, planning, ordering, writing music as necessary, rehearsing, and doing follow-up calls and notes.

Beyond that, one needs:

- space for rehearsal, if other than the worship space
- room for playing in the worship space with

  - clear sightlines between the instrumentalists, the conductor, and the organist/pianist
  - good lighting
  - consideration of acoustics and the ability of individuals and ensembles to hear each other
  - access to electricity for instruments requiring it
  - music stand(s) and chairs
  - a metronome—to establish or determine tempos
  - a recording device

    - to make a practice recording for players, as necessary
    - to record a rehearsal in order to "step back and hear it"

- a music writing program such as Finale® or Sibelius®
- staff paper and pencils
- music, including

  - hymnals
  - repertoire pieces
  - collections of instrumental descants
  - instrumental supplement for the hymnal in use at the parish, if available

- space for maintaining and filing instrumental music
- instruments—many people have their own instruments; investing in percussion, or maintaining instruments that may have been donated and are in good condition may enable participation from someone who might not otherwise be able to do so. Inquiring as to the availability of an instrument can sometimes turn up what is needed.

Recruitment

Treat recruitment as a way of life. Make it a matter of prayer.

A music survey placed in the weekly service leaflet, passed out in Sunday school and youth group, and mailed in a newsletter or a direct mailing is a worthwhile endeavor each spring as people think about the fall, and at summer's end as the school year gets underway. Post a copy on the church bulletin board and Web site where it might catch the eye of someone looking to get involved.

List the opportunities available in your church for musicians. These might include choir(s), handbell choir, instrumental ensembles, instrumentalists, a praise band, soloists, etc., whatever it is that you have or seek to develop. Have people indicate areas of interest and provide contact information. Meet with all who respond to assess their interest and skill level. Be forewarned, most people will not fill out or return the survey—even those who intend to.

"One on one" is the best way to recruit. Coffee hour is a good place to talk to people and find out what their interests are. If you are the music director, it almost guarantees that in time, if an individual has any music background, it will come out in conversation. When it comes up, ask, "Are you doing any playing (singing)?" Note the response. If someone wants to get on board, ask him or her to meet with you to find an appropriate way to use the person's gifts; then offer the musician an opportunity to play something that is guaranteed to work well, allowing plenty of rehearsal time in case it is needed.

If you are rebuffed, do not take it personally. Should you sense interest, bring it up at an opportune moment in a future conversation and see what the response is. It often takes building a relationship before a person will trust you enough to *willingly* put himself or herself in a situation—like playing for people—that makes a person feel vulnerable. If someone is not interested, let it rest. If you aren't sure, offer another opportunity sometime later. Each time you do, a seed is planted. Some will take root, and others you will know to leave alone.

 Does your pastor know of a hidden talent? Talk to the church office staff, Sunday school teachers, youth leaders, and choir members for leads. If the desired forces are not at hand, extend the search. Attend local school concerts, talent shows, community orchestra and chamber music performances, and note the players. Who is teaching privately? Be clear about the volunteer aspect of your request, and ask if they know of someone capable and interested in playing. You might get a name, a promise of a return call; the individual might decide that she would like to do it—or it could yield nothing—but that "worst case" is no further behind than you would have been had you not inquired at all—and, best case, you might have a fine player on board.

Ask your present musicians if they have friends who play; befriend your local music teacher and ask for recommendations. Many schools encourage students to do community service; playing their instrument in church often qualifies. Remind the students to report their playing so they receive credit and thank the teacher for any help provided.

When making contact with a recommended, but unknown student, contact the parents, introduce yourself, tell them where you are from, how you obtained their child's name, what you would like them to do, and what the commitment entails. This gives the parents the opportunity to ask questions or express concerns. It also enlists their support. They will often come along to the service with their child and you may, in time, find the family becoming active in the church, as you have already established that there is a place for their child to fit into the parish life and worship.

Consider inviting a friend to play a voluntary with you and share a meal after the service. You will get to catch up, you will have modeled what you are hoping to hear from others, and that person may be willing to come back. Only God knows when or how the Holy Spirit will work in someone's life, and an invitation to be part of a service puts the individual in a place where the Word will be present. As we share our faith and lives with others, there is no law saying that fellow musicians are off limits!

Finally, take care not to overlook adults already in your midst who may have set their instruments aside. Music might be just the outlet that business person, the stay-at-home parent, or a newly retired person needs, and the adults can then be wonderful mentors for the young as intergenerational groups form. Ease these people in slowly. Give them time to get the dust off the instrument and prepare, as it has probably been quite some time since they picked up their horn or fiddle. Then take delight in seeing how they blossom as musicians and find a new niche in the church!

Refer back to your lists. Many of those musicians will have continued to study and some will have had great musical breakthroughs since you last met with them. The additional study might make them very capable of handling that which you would like to do. Patience and gentle persistence will yield results in God's time.

Key Considerations

- Is there interest and a need for instrumentalists in your church?
- What are your church's liturgical goals?
- What instrumental music fits these goals?
- Who (or what) are your church's present instrumental resources?
- How can you build on those to meet the goals?
- Who will oversee the development of this part of the church's ministry?
- Who will encourage those who are enlisted to participate? *This is important and includes members of the congregation—not just the pastors and music staff!*
- What are the obstacles you expect to face—talent, space, finances, egos, other?
- In addition to prayer, how will you meet those challenges?
- Is the congregation willing to accept gifts of talent from youth or those outside your congregation?
- Would talents shared by "guests" be welcomed or perceived as threatening?
- Evaluate how committed you are to fostering musical growth among congregants; it takes time and energy.
- Go slow. Add instruments to adorn that which you already have in place, and do so sparingly so the sound is evident and welcomed—not tiring.
- Remember that you are dealing first with people, secondly with instruments. High musical aspirations are good, but always act in love and gratefully receive the gifts in individuals God sends you.
- Thank God for the gift of music; enjoy making it; take care not to miss those glorious moments when the music transcends time and space.

Unexpected Results

I asked a group of fellow church musicians to identify and describe a specific use of instrumentalists in the context of a liturgy that they believed to have been particularly effective. Having asked such questions before, I should know better than to expect people to answer as I anticipate they will. A colleague responded by describing a Christmas Eve service in which a child who had recently lost a parent participated. The answer had nothing to do with what music was played, where it happened in the liturgy, what the instrument was, or if it was played well. It had everything to do with shared grief, love, and support as a hurting member of the family of God in that place worked through the healing process, enabled by the gift of music.

As one uses the gifts of young and amateur instrumentalists in worship, what one chooses to do is best dictated by the readings, the liturgy, and the accompanying and supporting hymnody so as to maintain the integrity of the service. Carefully consider the ability of the individual players as music is selected or written for them to play so that they will be able to do it well and the resulting music will enhance the liturgy and edify the congregation.

Keeping that in mind, what specifically is done will not matter near so much as that the family of God took time to notice who was in their midst, invited people into the fellowship, nurtured the musical gifts of those people, and incorporated them into the life of the family of God. The prayerful sacrifice of time and energy in the mentoring will aid the building up of those "living stones" into God's temple where the many and varied sounds of his praise resonate now and into eternity.

Note

1. Scripture taken from the Holy Bible, New International Version (NIV). Copyright 1973, 1978, 1984 by International Bible Society. Used by permission of Zondervan Publishing House. All rights reserved.

Bibliography

Chiusano, Gerard, and M. D. Ridge, eds. *Liturgical Ensemble Basics*. Portland, Oregon: Pastoral Press, 2005. www.pastoralpress.com

Hopson, Hal H. *The Creative Use of Instruments in Worship*. Vol. 5, *The Creative Church Musician* series. Carol Stream, IL: Hope Publishing Company, 2000. www.hopepublishing.com

Kennan, Kent Wheeler. *The Technique of Orchestration*, 2nd ed. Englewood Cliffs, NJ: Prentice-Hall, Inc., 1970. http://vig.prenhall.com/catalog/academic/product/0,1144,0130771619,00.html

Resources

Augsburg Fortress: www.augsburgfortress.org
  Numerous resources including: Mark Albrecht, *Easy Timeless Tunes*, for solo instrument and keyboard in multiple volumes with solo options for a variety of instruments for each piece in the collections.
Church Publishing: www.churchpublishing.org
  Numerous resources including: Tedesco, Lorna, *Trumpet Descants for 101 Noteworthy Hymns.*
Concordia Publishing House: www.cph.org
  Numerous resources including: Donald A. Busarow, *Hymnal Supplement 98*, instrumental descant edition.

GIA Publications, Inc.: www.giamusic.com
   Numerous resources.
Hal Leonard Publishing Corporation: www.halleonard.com
   The catalog lists collections and pieces by instrument name.
Robert King Music: www.rkingmusic.com
   Fine editions for brass ensemble.

Cynthia Holden, AAGO, is director of music and organist at Saint John's Lutheran Church, Sayville, New York, where during the past four years she has developed a program involving four vocal choirs, two handbell choirs, and instrumentalists following a thirteen-year tenure as organist/choirmaster at Saint Peter's Episcopal Church in Bay Shore, New York. She was a coordinator and faculty member for the Leadership Program for Musicians at the George Mercer School of Theology in Garden City, Long Island, New York. Cindy has served the Association of Anglican Musicians and the American Guild of Organists on convention committees, as a presenter, as education coordinator, dean, and Committee on Educational Resources member. She is currently Region I president of the Association of Lutheran Church Musicians.

What About Instrumentalists?

Using Professionals in Worship

JOHN MARSH

Your choir is singing excerpts from Handel's *Messiah* for the Christmas concert. You have been rehearsing your volunteer instrumentalists at the church to accompany the performance. A few critical parts in the chamber orchestra are still not covered, however, and are causing concern. Time is running out and those "holes" need to be filled soon.

The acoustic guitarist for your contemporary ensemble has been transferred to a new job in a different city. The departing musician is not only a fine player, but also a leader to everyone in the group. His shoes are hard to fill and none of your other guitarists is able to lead.

It's ten days before Easter and the lead trumpet for your volunteer brass group has come down with an illness that will keep him from playing for several weeks.

All of these situations can occur—if they have not already—in your church. You like to use your "homegrown" volunteer musicians, but faced with an emergency, a decision must be made: shall I hire a professional musician to fill the need?

It's not an easy question to answer. The implications of your decision can be long lasting. Will it offend the volunteers? How much will it cost? How do I find the right musician(s) to hire? Will the vestry approve the expenditure? Once I've used professional musicians, will I ever feel the same about my volunteers? Will I want to hire professionals all the time? How do I successfully integrate the professionals with the volunteers? Will the pros understand the challenges (and rewards!) of working with volunteers? How can I make the situation work to everyone's advantage? How can I structure the rehearsals to take into account the differences in approach between volunteer and professional musicians? How do I find music that will work with both professionals and my volunteers?

Using professional musicians in your church can be both fulfilling and challenging. They are used to higher musical expectations, more polished results, tighter rehearsals, and more demanding leadership than are your volunteers. It is important to understand the implications of using them before making a decision.

This article is about using professionals in largely volunteer church music situations. It is not intended to look at purely volunteer situations, or those churches that hire only professional instrumentalists or choirs.

The large picture of our work as church musicians involves not only musical considerations, but pastoral ones as well. Newcomers should be welcomed into our parish life (whether they are volunteer or professional) and, if they do not already have a church home, be encouraged to remain as active members of your church. Involving them in a way that makes them want to be part of your group is critical. As directors, we need to set a standard for excellence that keeps our people interested and committed to our common goal. As Clay Morris says in his book, *Holy Hospitality*, "[I]t is important to retain a commitment to quality. In the same way that attention to the food and drink we serve reflects an aura of abundance, the music we listen to and sing should be the best we can afford.[1]

Will It Offend the Volunteers to Hire Professionals? Volunteers want to present the best musical offering possible. Not only *Soli Deo Gloria,* to the glory of God, but also to help them give their best efforts. Usually they will welcome anyone who helps them raise the level of their performance. By all means, tell them a professional is joining the group. If you don't, they'll figure it out on their own. Let them know what's going on. Share the need and they will respect your decision. For any emergency situation, they will already understand the need is there.

How Much Will It Cost? How Do I Find the Right Musician to Hire? Costs can vary widely from city to city. There's no standardized fee structure for musicians in church, but organizations such as the American Guild of Organists[2] often have guidelines. The local musicians union will also have fee guidelines, but be certain to ask for the church scale (which is less expensive than regular scale). When hiring professional musicians, you can do it in one of two ways:

1. Get a "jobber" to contract the musicians you need; remember, however, that the contractor will charge a fee for this service.
2. Hire musicians directly yourself. You'll save money this way, but it will take time to get things arranged and keep up with details.

If you do the contracting, tell the instrumentalists up front how much you can pay. Professional musicians already know that churches don't pay top salaries. If they balk at what you offer, ask them how much they want. Maybe you can find a halfway point that satisfies everyone. One important point to remember: professional musicians are honor-bound to abide by union rules regarding pay so they may not have much flexibility. The musicians you hire today may want to play a job next week that requires union membership. If they flout union rules, other union contractors will be reluctant to hire them.

Pay all the professional musicians the same. When they find out that someone else is being paid more than they are (and they *always* find out!), you'll have an insurrection on your hands.

As far as paying for the expense, you can usually find the funds to cover the expense if it's an emergency situation. If the music budget won't bear the expense, ask to make an announcement about the need at services. People will often give financial support you need if you ask for help. Does your church have rules that prohibit raising money outside the budget? If you are not certain, find out before making an appeal for help.

Finding the right guest musician to meet your need can be tricky. I have always kept my own personal list of musicians of all kinds (vocal and instrumental) with as much contact information as possible. It's not that I hired all the people on the list. I just jot down names when I hear colleagues speak about them. Others on the list have worked for me before. You never know when the information may come in handy!

Talk to other church musicians and see who they have hired. Recommendations can provide invaluable insight. The local musicians union also has names. If you know a union member, ask for help with names and phone numbers from the union handbook. School or college band or orchestra directors or teachers also can give you names. Sometimes, the directors or teachers may be interested in playing for you.

How Do I Successfully Integrate the Professionals with the Volunteers? In the same way it's wise to be honest up front about pay, it's also wise to do the same about your situation. Tell them about your ensemble. Let them know what they'll be playing and the abilities of the volunteer players. Tell them how often you have been rehearsing with the others. Most professionals will have had students on the same level of ability as your volunteers. Tell them it's important for everyone to work well together in a spirit of cooperation, mutual support, and working toward the same goal—a successful performance.

Will the Church Governing Body Approve the Expenditure? If you are hiring a musician due to an emergency, I doubt that any treasurer would veto your expenditure. Besides, it's likely that you'll have enough in your budget to cover it. If you don't have the money budgeted, try making an appeal to the congregation and convince your church governing body that the situation represents an emergency—not poor planning on your part. In most instances, an "angel" will offer to help. Keep the names of individuals who have contributed to your music program. You may need the names again later. Make certain you put the donor names in the program and send them a thank you note! Then they will be more willing to help you out next time.

I have often found a designated account (memorial account, special music fund, concert series, etc.) to be a good way to keep funds donated for special needs separate from the regular music budget (if your church allows such designated accounts). It can act as a kind of emergency fund when these special needs occur.

Once I've Used Professional Musicians, Will I Ever Feel the Same about My Volunteers? Will I Want to Hire Professionals All the Time? If you love what you do and believe in a pastoral music ministry, you will always want your ministry to be about volunteers. When we work with volunteers, we help build the body of Christ and help fulfill the Great Commission. The pros get you through difficult situations. Yes, having professional musicians can make some things easier, but it can also be a lot more work having them around all the time (think payroll, egos, absences, etc.).

How Do I Get the Most Out of My Rehearsals with Volunteers and Professionals Combined? If you are hiring professionals to fill a last-minute "hole" in your instrumental ensemble, you already have the music chosen. So there's no decision to be made about what music to use. But there are several things you can do to be certain that both the professionals and your volunteers enjoy the experience of working together.

Thoroughly plan the rehearsal. Have a rehearsal plan with clear goals and know the order of music to be rehearsed. What would you like to accomplish in the rehearsal? What sections of the music will need the most rehearsal? Plan to rehearse difficult sections of music before rehearsing the entire piece start to finish, and do it early in the rehearsal when the musicians are freshest. Easier sections won't require as much rehearsal. Consider starting with an easier piece or section to get the rehearsal started in a confident, positive way. Remember to alternate easy and difficult sections, loud and soft pieces/sections so you pace the rehearsal. Don't tire them out in the first thirty minutes! If certain passages require more time than you anticipated, be prepared to make a quick decision about what music to do in your remaining time.

Be organized. You know from experience that your volunteers will not learn their music as quickly as the pros. So that means you need to be organized. Have the music picked out with adequate copies for everyone. Music should be marked in advance of the first rehearsal with necessary information (breath marks, tacets, dynamics, articulations, rehearsal letters, cue notes—or cue words from the text if the music involves choir, etc.). Don't waste valuable rehearsal time marking music with vital details. Everyone will respect you more as a leader when you know what you want and express it clearly.

Plan enough rehearsal time. If you know in advance that you will be combining pros and volunteers, plan enough rehearsal time with your volunteers ahead of rehearsing with the pros. Volunteers will need more rehearsal to master the music. Set them up to play confidently and the result will be satisfying to everyone—performers and congregation alike.

My sister is a violist in a professional orchestra in a large city. When she plays for churches, she often has horror stories to report about what a bad experience it was for everyone involved. "The director had not marked the music, couldn't answer our questions since he obviously didn't know the music very well, and wasted our time." Though I have come to the aid of my church music colleagues by telling her what it's like "on the other side," she is often right. The director did not do his homework ahead of time.

Study your score. Would you take a test without knowing the material? So why have a rehearsal when you don't know the music? Study your score thoroughly. Mark the score with information you'll need to communicate to the musicians. Anticipate their questions. Don't try to impress the professional musicians with your knowledge of their instrument if you don't know what you are saying. For example, a string player will know when you say something incorrect about his or her bowing. Don't say something to impress your choir and wind up having the professional musician lose respect for you. It's best to give more general suggestions for what you want in a passage: "Play less legato here—can you give this passage more articulation?" This is part of preparing for your rehearsal: know something about the instruments you use. There are many texts that give such information. Marty Haugen's book, *Instrumentation and the Liturgical Ensemble*,[3] is a good place to start for church musicians with little experience in this area.

Respect all musicians. If the rehearsal involves choir with instruments, warm up the choir in a space apart from the rehearsal area with the instruments. Don't make the instrumentalists sit there while you use the scheduled rehearsal time warming up the choir. Let them get set up while you do the warm up or have someone else help you with this task. Since the pros and volunteers will likely not know each other, take a few moments at the beginning to welcome the newcomers and introduce them to the group. Name tags can help build community among your musicians.

Start and end on time. Professional musicians are hired for their time. Don't expect them to rehearse for three hours when you are paying them for one and a half hours. Respecting people's valuable time is important whether you are working with volunteers or professionals. It inspires confidence when you know what you are doing and are on time. If you are rehearsing longer than two hours, consider a short break. Let them know how long the break will be before you let them go. Offer refreshments during this time (or after rehearsal) to give everyone an opportunity to meet and greet. Remember that union rules require a break after one and one-half hours of rehearsal. If you are close to the end, however, ask the musicians if they mind staying a few minutes. They may want to work another few minutes and finish the rehearsal rather than taking a break and coming back.

Communicate. Let the musicians know your plan for the rehearsal, and rehearse sections with all the instruments early. Often, some instruments don't play except for large portions of the score. So don't make brass players sit through your entire rehearsal if they are only needed for a small portion of the accompaniment. Rehearse them early and then let them go. They will appreciate your consideration. As a conductor, be certain you know how to communicate with your musicians. Your choir may be familiar with an emphasis in your conducting on text stresses over beat patterns, but instrumentalists need a clear and consistent downbeat.

And communicate again. Rehearsal time is precious. Leave an information sheet on the stands with important information in case you run late: performance time and call, what to wear, where to leave instrument cases, etc. It's often helpful to put this information in a three-ring binder along with the music so the musicians don't lose it. If instrumentalists wants to see their music ahead of the rehearsal, make them copies of the music in their folder, but don't give them the folder with the originals. If they forget the original, you'll have a big problem when they arrive for rehearsal.

Rehearse where you'll perform. Since you will have your musicians for a limited amount of time, hold your rehearsal in the space where the performance will take place. If you are holding multiple rehearsals and some of them must be held elsewhere, make certain the rehearsal space has good lighting, proper temperature control, adequate ventilation, reasonable acoustics, and enough room for the musicians whether they are seated or walking around. Have the rehearsal space set up the way you want before instrumentalists arrive.

Manage the logistics. Choose a seating arrangement for your ensemble ahead of the rehearsal, and communicate clearly where you want everyone to sit. That means you have to have given the matter your full consideration earlier. An easy way to let players know where you want them to sit is to leave an index card with their name on it on their chair. Don't let pros and volunteers huddle with their friends. Mix them up so you get more experienced musicians helping others by the example they set. Of course if you have only one or two musicians per part, there may be only one way to seat them, but plan to get the most out of the pros. The volunteers will learn from them even if they are playing a different instrument. If things don't seem to be working well at the beginning, consider moving musicians around to help improve the sound. Remember this important point of etiquette: sit the professional first chair and your volunteer second chair. The pro, who will still wind up leading the section wherever he or she sits, will appreciate this consideration.

Keep the rehearsal moving. Be clear when you stop to rehearse a part or section: give page number, line, measure, beat as necessary, and they'll learn to stay with you and keep the energy of the rehearsal alive. Likewise, give any announcements clearly and quickly. The musicians didn't come to hear you talk. If one part is having difficulty with a passage, plan a separate time to rehearse the part. Don't hold up the entire rehearsal. Keep it moving. End your rehearsal by thanking the musicians and telling them something positive they've done. Nothing succeeds like confidence.

Expect professionalism. Don't tolerate a bad attitude from the professional musician. There are too many other musicians who will welcome the opportunity to play for you. Hire someone else next time and let your fellow church musicians know of your experience when they ask for a recommendation. You can expect your hired musicians to be respectful of your worship customs, but don't expect them to participate in the worship. Some of them may be of other faiths. It is not appropriate to ask a Jew to take communion!

How Do I Find Music That Will Work with Both Professionals and My Volunteers? Only you know the abilities of your volunteers. So pick music that challenges them, but is within their reach. If you are experienced arranging music for instruments yourself, this can be the best way to get music to match their abilities. Start with hymns before branching out to more difficult arrangements. The St. James Music Press has a collection of hymn arrangements (with descants) for various instrumental combinations and transpositions.[4] This publication can offer guidelines for doing your own arrangements of other hymns. Start looking for the music you need early!

Another source of instrumental music is Live Oak House[5] in Austin, Texas. Dale Elmshaeuser, founder of Live Oak House, began publishing his own compositions for instrumental ensembles in worship services. As with many other church musicians, he had been frustrated in his efforts to find suitable music that was playable by church instrumentalists of many ages and abilities. His solution was to write music for the instrumental groups he was directing. He now publishes music by other composers. The Live Oak catalog includes compositions for strings, brass, woodwinds, orchestral ensembles, and choral arrangements with instruments.

Ask fellow church musicians for ideas of appropriate instrumental music. Benefit from their experience and it will save you a lot of time as you plan your service or concert.

When choosing music, remember that it's better to have slightly easier music played well than to have difficult music played badly. Trumpet players don't want to play high and fast for too long. If you have a professional trumpet player, he may ask for more money!

Many instruments are transposing. Learn the necessary transpositions for the instruments you have. (See the book by Marty Haugen in the bibliography at the end of this article.) When you are preparing your hymn arrangements, who will do the transposition? Though most professionals can transpose at sight, amateurs usually cannot. Finding out that certain instrumental parts are in the wrong key during rehearsal is a big problem. Do your homework on this ahead of time.

Many choir anthems come with instrumental obbligato parts. Using a professional musician for the instrumental part can often give the anthem a more polished sound.

If you are hiring a small group of musicians (i.e., quintet, quartet, trio, etc.), try to find an ensemble that plays together regularly. They will know how to work with each other and you will benefit from their common experience. Such groups often have a large repertory of music they play for events (weddings, receptions, etc.). Ask them to play a prelude, offertory, or postlude for you. They won't need rehearsal for this music and may forego an additional fee since they are already at your church to play with your choir.

Likewise, you can ask these same musicians to play along with the hymns. If you do so, it is important to copy and enlarge the hymns for ease of reading. If you are using instruments that transpose, be prepared to offer the musicians parts in their transposition. Brass instruments balance well with the organ, but other instruments do not. It may be wise to let a group (such as string players) play an introduction alone where they can be heard.

You can also ask a solo instrumentalist about playing for your services while at your church. Remember that professionals don't always have access to an accompanist without paying for one. Offer to have your organist accompany them for a musical offering during your program. They may welcome the opportunity. Make this offer only if you have a highly competent organist.

So Why Go to All This Trouble? Ultimately, it's about giving our best gifts to God. If you are preparing a musical offering for worship, you want it to be the best possible offering. It honors God and gives your flock a positive experience that reinforces their commitment to the music ministry of your church. If they have a bad experience and the performance is not good, it undermines their confidence and they won't want to continue in the choir or ensemble. The memory of a bad performance is a difficult memory to erase. A good memory makes musicians want to do even better next time. Yes, it does mean a bit more work for you as the director, but that extra effort pays off when you see the look on your choir's faces. That extra effort is small in comparison with the results it produces.

Likewise, the professional musicians will see that you are serious about not wasting their time, about producing a satisfying musical experience for all, about being prepared, about considering their needs. They will want to come back and work with you again. The professional musicians I use have been with me for years, and they enjoy the experience of performing in our church.

Notes

1. Clayton L. Morris, *Holy Hospitality* (New York: Church Publishing Inc., 2005).

2. Take a look at the American Guild of Organists' Web site www.agohq.org/profession/indexsalary.html for information on salary and employment guidelines. Although much of the information pertains to organists and choir directors, there are some guidelines for substitute musicians and following IRS guidelines.

3. Marty Haugen, *Instrumentation and the Liturgical Ensemble* (Chicago: GIA Publications, Inc., 1991).

4. *Instrumental Transpositions for 150 Hymn Tunes* (parts for B-flat and C Instruments—descants; B-flat Instruments—soprano and alto; E-flat Instruments—alto; F Instruments—alto and tenor; B-flat Instruments—tenor; C Instruments (organ)—soprano, alto, tenor, bass) (Hopkinsville, KY: St. James Music Press, 1991). www.sjmp.com

5. *Instrumental Music for Worship* (Austin, TX: Live Oak House). Phone: 512-282-3397, dale@liveoakhouse.com

Bibliography

Bibliography of Useful Resources for the Church Musician (compiled from a survey of the AAM membership). Produced by Margaret A. Neilson and Alan C. Reed. E-mail *cr273@aol.com* for this publication, or write: AAM Communications Office, PO Box 7530, Little Rock, AR 72217.

Collins, Dori Erwin, and Scott C. Weidler. *Sound Decisions: Evaluating Contemporary Music for Lutheran Worship.* Chicago: Augsburg Fortress, 1997.

Farlee, Robert Buckley, ed. *Leading the Church's Song.* Minneapolis: Augsburg Fortress, 1998.

Haugen, Marty. *Instrumentation and the Liturgical Ensemble.* Chicago: GIA Publications, Inc., 1991.

Lawrence, Joy E., and John A. Ferguson. *A Musician's Guide to Church Music.* New York: Pilgrim Press, 1981.

Morris, Clayton L. *Holy Hospitality.* New York: Church Publishing Inc., 2005.

Ode, James. *Brass Instruments in Church Services.* Minneapolis: Augsburg Fortress, 1970.

Routley, Erik. *Music Leadership in the Church.* Nashville: Abingdon Press, 1967.

Stickland, Thomas, ed. *The Leadership Program for Musicians* curriculum. Copyright by the Standing Commission on Worship, the Episcopal church, and the Division for Congregational Ministries, the Evangelical Lutheran Church in America, 1995, 1999.

Westermeyer, Paul. *The Church Musician,* rev. ed. Minneapolis: Augsburg Fortress, 1997.

John Marsh serves as director of worship and arts at Kinsmen Lutheran Church, Houston, Texas, where he leads musical ensembles and supervises worship guilds. Having previously served Episcopal churches, he is a former chair of the Church Music Commission of the Diocese of Texas who began the diocesan Children's Choir Camp and the Leadership Program for Musicians (LPM). John is a member of the adjunct faculty at North Harris College. He serves as coordinator and faculty member for LPM in east Texas as well as vice-chair of the national LPM Board.

What About Guitars?

ROBERT C. LAIRD

In the summer of 2002 young people from across the Episcopal church took up residence in Laramie on the campus of the University of Wyoming. The plenary group of nearly 1,600 people celebrated the Holy Eucharist twice. It was, in both cases, a cocktail of equal parts liturgical tradition and rock concert. Shaken, not stirred.

The liturgies worked. They really worked. I was the guitarist at those liturgies, and was privileged enough to see the reaction of the congregation during the worship services themselves. The crowd engaged the Eucharist, the music, the divine, in a way that only happens when liturgy is planned and prayed carefully and joyfully. It was nearly miraculous.

One of the many reasons those liturgies really connected was the combination of the musical sounds from the congregation's secular lives (guitars and drums, pop music forms) mixed with the liturgy of the church. This mixing of liturgical and popular is exactly what musicians have been doing since music first appeared in churches centuries ago. Guitars provide a point of access into liturgy for people who don't connect with more traditional hymnody and accompaniment in the church (organs and choirs, for instance).

In many situations, the guitar can be the ideal instrument for accompanying singing in worship. Its use in popular music makes it especially well suited for pop song forms in the church. Additionally, much of the traditional music of early America and even the Victorian hymnody of our tradition use harmonic progressions that can be played quite effectively on the guitar. Lots of music currently being written has the guitar in mind as a worship instrument. Many music publishers are putting out hymnal editions specifically for guitarists. Guitar players have dominated the youth ministry world for over forty years now. Guitars have claimed a place in the hearts of worshiping Christians, and contribute to the praise of God in the church.

In this way of praying, there are three parts of worship leadership: the music, the guitar, and the guitarist. Each of these parts contributes differently and so must be addressed individually. Combined, they can create an experience of music in worship that can bring a congregation to revelations of the holy. They have to be combined artfully, though, or it may be the guitarist that people are focused on, and not God.

Music

The amount of music available today for worship in the church is staggering. The Episcopal church's collections of music alone are enough to satisfy many congregations' needs. *The Hymnal 1982; Wonder, Love, and Praise; Lift Every Voice and Sing II; Voices Found;* and *My Heart Sings Out* each offer different genres and forms of music for worship, and many are available with guitar chords. But the music offered by the Episcopal church (or, indeed, any single denomination or publisher) is as a grain of sand on a beach compared with how much is out there in general, and there's no need to confine oneself to a single publisher or denomination when looking for music. I'm going to go even further in speaking to Episcopalians for just a second: there is nothing in the rubrics of the Book of Common Prayer or canons of the Episcopal church that says that one must use music published in the hymn collections of the church for worship. At all. And anyone who tells you differently is wrong. Now, rectors are ultimately responsible for worship, and they may prefer that music come from a hymnal of the church, but that is their preference and not a rule or law of the church. Thank you for indulging me.

The music that is especially well suited for guitars is of several genres. The folk music tradition from the United States in the 1950s and 1960s has left a body of music that is used and cherished in the church. Most, if not all, of the music in the praise and worship genre is guitar-based and comes directly from pop and rock styles. Also, the guitar can lead much of the hymnody in denominational hymnals if the chords are available. One collection that addresses this need is *Tell Out My Soul: Lead Sheets for The Hymnal 1982*, from Church Publishing (which I helped write, in the interest of full disclosure).

Almost any music can be led by the guitar, depending on the skill of the guitarist and the level of difficulty of the music. The two things that make a song more difficult to play on the guitar are issues of meter and harmony. Many hymns are written in an open meter, changing the number of beats in a measure without warning. This is very difficult for guitarists, because they generally accompany rhythmically and not melodically. Harmony can be challenging because many chords are beyond the abilities of amateur guitarists. The hymns in most denominational hymnals are voiced and harmonized for keyboard. Such voice leading can make for harrying chords for the guitarist. Fingerboard theory combined with the fact that guitar accompanying is rhythmically based creates challenges when keyboard and guitar play together. Fast harmonic movement may not be possible to play on guitar. Some chords may need to be simplified or respelled. For example if an F-sharp diminished chord is called for, a D7 chord, which is easier for guitars, may work.

Much of the music in *The Hymnal 1982* is easily adaptable for the guitar. Several of the hymns in the accompaniment edition were provided with guitar chords, if it was felt by the editors that the guitar would be an acceptable choice aesthetically for accompanying the hymn. Many of the tunes in the hymnal, like "Slane," "Land of Rest," and "Star in the East," are especially well-suited to guitar accompaniment. Many of the chorales can also be easily adapted for guitar, especially when the meter is standard and doesn't change from measure to measure.

The Roman Catholic world has already embraced the guitar by publishing guitar editions of the last several editions of their hymnals. GIA Publications has put out a number of different editions of *Gather,* their immensely popular "contemporary music" hymnals. Every arrangement in the hymnal is created with guitar accompaniment, published in its own guitar edition. In the *Gather Comprehensive* series, many traditional hymns are bound together with the newer material (much of which tends toward folk and world music).

In the larger world of Christian music, there are endless resources available for worship. Much of it, as with other song forms, is either crafted or performed poorly, and isn't necessarily useful in worship. Some of it, however, is brilliant, and works well for particular settings. In the rock genre, I have used the music of Chris Tomlin and Matt Redman most often. Both of them write really good music, and add texts that are accessible for a broad spectrum of theological viewpoints. Darlene Zschech also turns up a lot in my planning; she wrote one of the mainstays of praise and worship music, "Shout to the Lord." Of course, there are always new artists recording, and I couldn't be exhaustive if I wanted to. But this gives you an idea of where to start at the iTunes Store.

I tend to be a hard judge of songs, as anyone who has worked with me before will attest. Many people judge songs that are based in the individual experience of Christ and not the communal (the "we" songs as opposed to the "I" songs), but denominational hymnals are full of those songs, and it doesn't bother me. (For example, "I bind unto myself today"; "All my hope on God is founded"; "Humbly I adore thee, verity unseen"; "When I survey the wondrous cross." Enough said.) What really annoys me is love songs that are turned into Jesus songs, making the assumption that the "you" is really a "You." A friend of mine once referred to this genre of Christian song as "Jesus, be my boyfriend" music, and I think the term fits quite well. Some of my colleagues disagree with me vehemently on this point, arguing that if a song helps people connect with Jesus, and they like to sing it, one should lead it. I'll leave that decision to you, gentle reader.

Ultimately, the question is whether a congregation can easily sing a song, and whether or not they like it. I often lead songs that I don't particularly care for, but keep programming them because the groups I work with love them. I suspect you have had the same experience, and do the same thing.

The Guitar

The guitar is a stringed instrument that is plucked or strummed, the sound of which is amplified by either a wooden resonator box (acoustic) or electrically by using a speaker (electric). There are also guitars that are acoustic and have pickups to amplify the sound of the strings, which are generally called acoustic-electrics. This is because the sound of the strings is amplified the same way as with electric guitars, but the pickup is designed to sound like an acoustic guitar.

Guitars come in six- and twelve-string versions. A twelve-string guitar has the same strings as a six-string guitar, but the voices are doubled for the four lowest strings at one octave, and doubled at-pitch for the top two. This increases the volume of the instrument, and it gives the twelve-string a characteristic timbre.

There's really no right or wrong answer for choosing a guitar for worship. I personally play an acoustic guitar with a pickup, because I prefer the feel of the strings on an acoustic, and I like sitting on the porch with friends singing and playing (which is more easily done with an acoustic guitar). Many guitarists prefer playing electric guitars, which tend to have much lighter action than acoustic guitars ("action" is the distance the string rests from the fingerboard, indicating the amount of pressure required to play the string).

Unless you are playing for a small group of people or in an acoustically bright room, the guitar will need to be amplified for worship. Guitars are not loud instruments, and they can easily be drowned out by a group of forty joyful singers. Amplification can be accomplished one of three ways: a guitar amp, a microphone, or by plugging directly into the mixer of your sound system. But first, a word about amplification.

To amplify sound, you need three components: a mixer, to control the amount and quality of sound that you're amplifying; an amplifier, to make the sound loud enough to be heard; and speakers, so you can hear it. Every church's public address (PA) system has these three components, and they are always required. Sometimes companies sell amp and mixer combinations, which are very practical.

Back to the three ways to amplify a guitar in church. The first option is to use a guitar amplifier. A guitar amp has a mixer, amplifier, and speaker all built into one package. The guitarist can control the volume of the sound that comes out of the amp through controls on the guitar and the amp itself. This can be difficult in church settings because the sound only comes from the speaker, and so balance in the room can be difficult, but not impossible.

The second option is to use a microphone to amplify the guitar. In recording, this is the best method to capture the sound of an acoustic guitar. It can be tricky in live performance, though, because the guitarist has to stand in front of the mike for the guitar to be heard, and if the guitarist is also singing, that will likely be picked up by both the voice mike and the guitar mike, creating more balance problems.

The third option (which is my personal favorite) is to plug the guitar directly into the mixer for your church's PA. This separates the guitar sound from any amplified vocals the guitarist may be providing, and it provides a balanced sound throughout the room that you're playing in.

When including a guitar in your ensemble, there are some instruments that will naturally work better than others. I have not had much luck mixing the guitar with the organ in worship. The organ's sustained sound, and the timbre of the instrument itself, tends to drown out guitars. The piano is a better choice for pairing with a guitar, as their timbres tend to be more complimentary. A guitar could easily be added occasionally in a church accustomed to using the piano.

The Guitarist

Of the three components of leading worship, the guitarist is by far the most important. The guitarist is the one who convinces the congregation to sing. Without the guitarist, the music can't be appreciated. Without the guitarist, the guitar can't sing.

For congregational singing, the worship leader, whether a guitarist, an organist, a pianist, a cantor, or any other musician, must have the confidence to lead the congregation. Put another way, the most important part of leading worship with a guitar is the *leading,* not the *guitar.*

To illustrate my point, I will talk about how organists tend to lead with their instruments, and then show how guitarists can accomplish this on theirs. Organists, you may have noticed, accommodate and accompany singing in numerous ways. When playing an introduction, they will hold the last chord long enough for the congregation to take a breath and *feel* the end of the current stanza before continuing to the beginning of the next stanza. They can also pause between phrases in the hymn, allowing the congregation just enough time to breathe before continuing on. For instance, in the hymn "Amazing Grace" (671 in *The Hymnal 1982*), there is a fermata in the middle of the second line ("wretch like meeeeeee"). A good organist may decide that the fermata should be five beats long so that the next phrase begins on the final beat of a 3/4 measure. Guitarists can work with this because it matches the meter of the hymn. Sometimes, however, a keyboardist may not be disciplined about such specifics making it difficult for a guitar to honor its rhythmic contribution. Acoustics also play a role in how long final notes of a stanza are held. It may need to be different in a large, resonant space like a stone cathedral than in a small A-frame church with carpet. Whatever the environment, the keyboard and guitar must agree about such details for the best result.

Another aspect of the art of leading with a keyboard instrument (organ or piano) is that the instrumentalist usually plays the melody in such a way that the congregation can hear and follow it. This is what I mean in saying keyboard instruments lead melodically: they play the melody, at least enough that the congregation is able to hear and follow. Guitars usually can't do this. They play chords, which provide the harmonic foundation for the singing, even in parts, but they do not usually provide the melody. A guitar is not very good for leading by itself, for just this reason. The congregation is often unable to discern the melody, and if they are not strong singers on their own, they will stop singing.

Often, a singer or singing group is added to organ and piano hymn-leading, to assist the congregation with singing. The importance of choirs and cantors in this respect is being addressed elsewhere in this collection, and need not be taken up here. This does demonstrate, however, that instruments by themselves often need help to lead worship most effectively.

The guitar "sustains" sound by filling up the space with a strumming pattern, a series of arpeggios, or a picking pattern. There are many such patterns that are standard for each meter and for styles of music. The leaders' guide for *Wonder, Love, and Praise* (Church Publishing) suggests some simple picking or strumming patterns. *Leading the Church's Song* (Augsburg Fortress) is also helpful especially in chapter 8 about Latino rhythms. Various cultures depend on the guitar for accompanying congregational singing in church, especially Latino cultures: Mexico, Central and South America, Spain, Puerto Rico. Contemporary gospel music uses the electronic guitar extensively.

There are as many different kinds of guitarists as there are guitars, each with different skills. The majority of guitarists that I have worked with in my career have been amateurs who have taught themselves to play. These guitarists may be able to read music, but may not be able to read music on the guitar and play it. They will best be able to read chord symbols printed over the words of the song. Others may be able to read music and even play melodies. A jazz guitarist can likely read music or tablature (guitar notation), while some rock guitarists can only read tab, or sometimes they can't read anything but rather play extremely well by ear. There are so many people that have taught themselves to play the guitar that skills vary from guitarist to guitarist. Any guitarist should be able to read chords over words, and that may be enough for most of what your service will require.

The skills of guitarists differ greatly, and will dictate what is possible in your service. Determine what kind of role you want a guitarist to play—leader? Accompanist? If you're looking for a leader then your guitarist will need to be able to sing and accompany himself or herself. Interview a potential guitarist to find out his or her experience. One who is used to singing while accompanying himself or herself will be a different kind of asset from a guitarist who plays in a band. A band often has a lead guitar (plays melody solos and chords either electric or acoustic) and perhaps a bass guitar (supplies the foundation for the harmonic structure and rhythmic interest—electronic). If you're unsure of how you want the guitarist to play, don't be afraid to ask for his or her input. Most will be pleased to be asked.

Leading guitarists who accompany themselves should understand that they are not performing in the sense of being soloists to whom people come only to listen. You may want them to play that role on occasion, but you will usually want them to sing in a way that is helpful to the congregation, such as singing each verse the same way so that the congregation is sure of the rhythm, when to breathe, exactly how the tune goes, etc.

If you want the guitarist to play while you play the piano or a keyboard, work out how the two instruments can complement each other. Think of how you would combine stop sounds on the organ. Should the keyboard supply the bass line and melody while the guitar fills in the harmony? Can you trade off verses? If the guitarist can play a melody line (amplified), you could supply the harmony and rhythm.

FAQ

Why does some music say "guitar and keyboard should not sound together"?

Because the chord symbols above the keyboard part are not exactly the same as those for the keyboard. In such case the keyboard should improvise an accompaniment using the chord symbols. It does not mean that guitars and keyboards should not play together. There are many churches where the combination of instruments do so musically and imaginatively.

What is a capo and how does it work?

A capo is a device that creates an artificial nut (piece of bone at the top of the fingerboard) to raise the pitch of all strings at once. It is a transposing tool and is a necessity for all guitarists. Kyser makes a capo that can be changed quickly with one hand. It is of excellent quality, does not harm the guitar, and has replaceable parts. Shubb also makes a good capo which requires both hands to change, but is durable and dependable.

What are good keys for guitar?

Guitars can play in any key. The difference is that the capo is essential to accommodate those keys that push the limits of six strings and five fingers. Guitarists think in sharps and so the best keys are C, D, G, and A. The key of F is more challenging because it usually requires F and B-flat chords, both of which use only four of the six strings and sound thin. The key of G and its relative minor E minor are easy. To accommodate other keys the music leader needs to know that when the capo is placed at the first fret, it raises the key a half step and so on moving up the fingerboard. For example, for the key of E-flat, the guitarist could capo 1 (first fret=half-step up) and play in the key of D making the guitar sound in E-flat. Also for the key of C minor, the guitarist could capo 3 (third fret=1½ steps up) and play A minor. The rule is as the capo moves up by fret, the key played by the guitarist moves down by half-steps.

What is a "lead sheet"?

A "lead sheet" is a road map for musicians. It usually contains the melody and possibly lyrics with chord symbols indicating the harmony structure.

What if I have several guitarists who want to play together? What do I need to know?

There are some tricks to having multiple guitars performing together. Rather than have all guitars play at exactly the same pitch level, have one use the capo and play in another key. This will create the same harmonies, of course, but they will be voiced differently and so make the sound richer. For example, for the key of D, have one guitar play as usual and another capo 2 and play in C. Or for an interesting timbre have the second guitar capo 7 and play in G, which will add a higher octave to the sound.

The guitar is a viable addition to a church music program. Combining it with other instruments need only be limited by the creativity and open-mindedness of a leader who knows that the guitar primarily provides rhythm and harmony. Other instruments that add melody and more rhythm will be the most successful combinations. The average church musician will have access mostly to amateur guitarists rather than professional. The key is to find those who are committed and enthusiastic.

Robert C. Laird is a gifted young composer and an accomplished guitarist. He is the former precentor at the Episcopal cathedral in Minneapolis and a member of the Standing Commission on Liturgy and Music. He was a principal music planner and coordinator for the 2005 Episcopal Youth Event, and a member of the worship planning committee for the 2006 General Convention in Columbus, Ohio. Laird will enter General Theological Seminary in New York in the fall of 2007.

What About Cantors?

JOEL MARTINSON

Growing up in the 1970s in a musical and relatively by-the-book liturgical practice of an American Lutheran church congregation, my experience of musical
leadership in the service witnessed the pastor in the chancel while the organ and
choir in the rear gallery led the worshiping congregation in the nave. The pastor led the sung dialogues—primarily the *Kyrie* and *Sursum corda*, a number of
salutations and responses ("The Lord be with thee"—"And with thy spirit") pre-
ceding spoken collects; intoned the *Gloria*; and sang the Benediction (Blessing)
at the end of the service. The organist led the hymns and sang portions of the
liturgy supported by the choir, and one or more choirs (and they were of the
"singing" variety, no handbell choirs yet) presented a musical offering at some
time during the course of the liturgy.

From what I have gathered, musical leadership in the Episcopal church at the
time was somewhat similar, but varied more from place to place and between
various liturgical traditions—high, broad, and low. In any event, *The Hymnal
1940* did not provide music for the minor liturgical responses, and the choir often
took a larger part in singing portions of the service without the congregation.

With the advent of the *Lutheran Book of Worship* in the fall of 1978 and the
establishment of an "assisting minister" role, a place for lay solo musical leadership in the liturgy was born in late twentieth-century mainline Lutheran practice. The invocations in the *Kyrie*,[1] the intonation of the *Gloria* and, in some
settings, an intonation to the other hymn of praise ("*This Is the Feast*"), along
with spoken prayers, were designated for this individual.

Other than the presiding clergy's role in the liturgy or an occasional solo
passage in a choir anthem, there has generally been little place for the extended
use of a lay solo voice in the liturgical practice of the Western church in the past
1,000 years or so. The exception to this is concerted music during the Baroque
and Classical eras, which one might rightfully argue was *not* the best period
of liturgical practice to emulate today: the large mass settings in the Roman

Catholic church, elaborate anthems in the Church of England, and the cantatas of the Lutheran church in Germany. What twenty-first-century American congregation would survive a three-hour service each Sunday?

"Cantor"—A Diverse History

The term *cantor*, Latin for "one who sings," has at least three historical uses, each with a somewhat different meaning:

- The *hazzan* or *chazzan* in Jewish worship. This layperson (historically, a nonprofessional male) led the portions of the Hebrew liturgy that were in dialogue with the congregation. He was the *shaliach tzibbur* or "emissary of the congregation" who was chosen both for his knowledge of the prayers and for the ability to improvise music to them. In modern day Reformed Judaism practice, cantors often hold music degrees and are trained in an extensive five-year program including music, Hebrew, liturgical music and tradition, theology, pastoral care and counseling, among other areas.
- The *precentor* (Latin for "one who sings before") in the Roman Catholic tradition of the Middle Ages. This clergy member led the sung portions of the office in alternation with the choir (the *Schola Cantorum*, which was composed of monks or nuns in monastic communities); taught chant to the *Schola Cantorum*; started the chants of the services; and might also serve as rudimentary conductor. Later, the teaching responsibility was given over to a lay choirmaster. This practice continues in English cathedrals today. There and in the United States, the term precentor is now commonly used for the clergy member in charge of planning the liturgical services for cathedrals and major churches, equating a director of liturgy or director of worship in Roman Catholic practice, as well as to the one who leads chants in the offices.
- The *Kantor* in German Lutheran churches. The leader of song in an overall sense, this term covered the director of music for a church or group of churches within town council jurisdiction who served as choir director; teacher in the parish or choir school (often of Latin, at least); and conductor of concerted music provided by the choir and town musicians for services. The *Kantor* frequently was an organist, as well. The first position of *Kantor* is attributed to Johann Walter, musical collaborator of Martin Luther. J. S. Bach is perhaps the best known *Kantor* of all time. The term was reinstated in some late twentieth-century Lutheran churches in the United States. Paul Manz, "Cantor" of Mount Olive Lutheran Church in Minneapolis, was the first to my knowledge to reclaim use of the title. Paul Westermeyer, Lutheran pastor and musician, formerly the chaplain of the American Guild of Organists, has advocated in his writings and lectures recovering the term for use among those of us who serve

as "organist/choirmaster" or "director of music," as it more appropriately encompasses the whole leadership of the congregation's song, be it those participating from the pew, those singers trained in the gallery or chancel, or an organist's role leading from the organ.[2]

Song Leader

Throughout history, there have also been lay leaders in some Reformation faith traditions who led the congregation's singing of metrical psalmody and hymns, a precursor to the modern "song leader" that has often superseded the Vatican II-defined role of cantor in Roman Catholic parishes. In Calvinist congregations, which prohibited the use of organs and other instruments, there were clergy or lay leaders who began the singing of metrical psalms and later hymns. Known in the dissenting churches of England and the Presbyterian churches in Scotland as "*precentor*," a similar custom was observed in Congregational churches of New England. One unique and interesting practice in Norwegian Lutheran congregations, both in the mother country and in the New World, is the position of *klokker*. Originally a lay male employee of the Church of Norway, this official, whose title derives from the Norwegian word for "bell" (*klokke*), held multiple responsibilities in the local parish, including:

- ringing the bell, hence the title
- leading the congregational singing of liturgical music and hymns
- maintaining the church building (sexton)
- teaching at the school
- and, for periods of the nineteenth century, serving as scribe and keeper of duplicate parish records, in case of fire.

Sounds like the varied and busy life of the modern day church musician![3]

The Second Vatican Council and the Cantor

Perhaps the overriding goal of the documents produced during Vatican II (1962–1965) was the desire that all the faithful should be led to that fully conscious, and active participation in liturgical celebrations which is demanded by the very nature of the liturgy. Such participation by the Christian people as

"a chosen race, a royal priesthood, a holy nation, a redeemed people" (1 Peter 2:9; cf. 2:4–5, New American Bible), is their right and duty by reason of their baptism. In the restoration and promotion of the sacred liturgy, this full and active participation by all the people is the aim to be considered before all else; for it is the primary and indispensable source from which the faithful are to derive the true Christian spirit; and therefore pastors of souls must zealously strive to achieve it, by means of the necessary instruction, in all their pastoral work." (*Constitution on the Sacred Liturgy*—Sacrosanctum Concilium, 1963, article 14)[4]

Along with this call for renewal of the liturgy, the role of the various participants in the rite were reordered and redefined, and sometimes, restored. Contrary to popular belief, the *Constitution on the Sacred Liturgy* upheld the use of choirs (article 114), encouraged the continuation and fostering of Gregorian chant and polyphonic choral music (article 116), and gave the organ a place of "high esteem" in worship (article 120). The overriding goal, however, was to involve everyone in the service, and not to let the work of the entire body of worshipers—the "assembly"[5]—be abrogated to another group. The document *Music in Catholic Worship* produced by the United States Conference of Catholic Bishops in 1972 defines the role of the cantor thusly:

> While there is no place in the liturgy for display of virtuosity for its own sake, artistry is valued, and an individual singer can effectively lead the assembly, attractively proclaim the Word of God in the psalm sung between the readings, and take his or her part in other responsorial singing. Provision should be made for at least one or two properly trained singers, especially where there is no possibility of setting up even a small choir. The singer will present some simpler musical settings, with the people taking part, and can lead and support the faithful as far as is needed. The presence of such a singer is desirable even in churches which have a choir, for those celebrations in which the choir cannot take part but which may fittingly be performed with some solemnity and therefore with singing. Although a cantor cannot enhance the service of worship in the same way as a choir, a trained and competent cantor can perform an important ministry by leading the congregation in common sacred song and in responsorial singing (article 35).[6]

Experience with Cantors in the Roman Church

During my sixteen-year tenure as director of music ministries and organist at Saint Rita Catholic Community in Dallas, Texas, our cantors were volunteers, as were all our choristers. The majority of them had canted[7] at previous parishes, perhaps starting in college student congregations or in their home churches. A smaller number of them had music degrees, and a few of those had at one time held paid choral positions. The role of the cantor in the liturgical celebrations at Saint Rita was normally as follows:

- Invite the assembly to sing the entrance hymn (a welcome by a lector preceded this).
- Sing the invocations to the *Kyrie* in Advent and Lent.

- Intone the *Gloria* (in all seasons but Advent and Lent), if a choir was not present.
- Lead the singing of the "responsorial" psalm, clearly proclaiming the verses of the appointed text through music. This is the primary role of the cantor. Note: unlike Lutheran and Episcopal rubrics for the gradual psalm, the various Roman Catholic liturgy documents since Vatican II clearly state their preference for the responsorial method (antiphon—verse—antiphon—verse—antiphon, etc.) to be employed in the Mass. The only other method allowed is a setting of the text sung by the choir. Through-composed (direct) singing and psalm paraphrases (e.g., metrical psalmody) are allowed in the offices only. At Saint Rita, the cantor normally sang the psalm, though occasionally the choir sang choral verses instead to Anglican chant or something similar.
- Sing the gospel acclamation (*Alleluia*) verse, and intone the *Alleluia* refrain when a choir was not present.
- Announce the hymn during the preparation of the gifts, the offertory. Hymns were only sung here in the absence of an anthem by the choir, or if we were introducing a piece into our repertoire (a "hymn of the month").
- Gesture (bring in the assembly via hand and arm motions) the beginning of the *Sanctus*, the memorial acclamation, and the great amen.
- Sing the invocations to the *Agnus Dei*, or intone the first line, if it were a through-composed setting.
- Lead the singing of refrain-oriented songs (especially during the communion procession), when a choir was not present. Sometimes the cantor would sing the verses alone, if they were a dialogue with the people's refrain ("Here I Am, Lord") or if the verses were meant to be over an ostinato refrain, such as Jacques Berthier's "*Ubi caritas et amor.*"

The cantor was normally positioned at a podium specially designated for that use: a fairly large, wooden, pulpit-looking structure on the side of, and slightly ahead of, the choral risers that surrounded the organ in the front of the church. Over the years we debated the need for the cantor to gesture the assembly's entrance on the first stanza of hymns, and on acclamations intended to be sung by everyone. We also debated whether or not to announce hymns, since they were listed in the service leaflet. In the end, it seemed better to make the announcement and continue to invite the people to step up to the plate and fully participate. This was particularly important, if an offertory hymn was not very familiar. As we did not have a sound technician during the services, it was the cantor's responsibility to move into the microphone to sing his or her solo parts but to back away and sing lightly for anything that belonged to the assembly.

From time to time, either I or the cantor would lead a preliturgy rehearsal on a new liturgical setting. I usually took this role if I could rehearse the particular item *a cappella*. If an accompaniment was needed, I would begin the rehearsal at the ambo, then move to the organ and have the cantor gesture in the people at the appropriate time. At Saint Rita, this offered me the ability to directly communicate with the entire assembly by facing them (normally my back was to them as organist or choir director). Some cantors were willing to lead rehearsals, but even the best of them liked to prepare their spoken words ahead of time.

The choirs would sing one to two anthems each week—one at the preparation of the gifts (offertory), and another at the end of communion after the communion hymn. We strove for a balance between the participation of congregation, choir, cantor, organist, and other instrumentalists, and worked to explore and bring alive the vast heritage of sacred music from past through the present.

Prejudice, and Some Pitfalls of Poor Practice

To many musicians coming from Episcopal or Lutheran traditions, the idea of a solo song leader in *corporate worship* is anathema, particularly when the role of cantor is expanded to the all-too-prevalent "song leader," as it has been in a good number of smaller and less sophisticated RC parishes throughout the United States and elsewhere. As with the *klokker* of Norwegian Lutheran practice on the newly inhabited prairie of nineteenth-entury America, the need for a solo singer to lead congregational music may often imply the absence of or neglect of the role of choir and organ. The development of simpler, often unsophisticated, music since the 1960s, in which a solo voice sings verses, and the congregation sings refrains, combined with a rise in the use of amplification in services, and of nonorgan accompaniments—piano, guitar, string bass, and C-instruments at best, electronic keyboard/synthesizer, electric guitar, bass guitar, and drum set at worst—only compounds the gap between what many of us have valued as the best of sacred music and our worst fears about its future. In fact, my typing in "cantor in worship" into search engines on the Internet produced more hits on articles, blogs, and postings on how to reform or get rid of the cantor at Mass, than it did on Vatican II documents or other references to cantor in *Christian* worship. (There were quite a number of hits on the use of cantors in Jewish worship).

Often the practice of cantor/song leader has been reduced to the most base, misguided, and at times downright abusive side:

- A single miked voice dominating the assembly. And actually, a miked presider can do this, too, sometimes in an attempt to make up for absence of other musical leadership or for the lack of congregational response.
- The overuse of facial expressions ("mugging") by the cantor/song leader in front of the church.
- Unnecessary or improper gesturing. I have experienced cantors who look like they are flagging down an airplane or trying to serve as a goal post for a touchdown!
- The use or overuse of responsorial acclamations—"repeat after me: I sing A, you repeat A; I sing B, you sing B," etc.

- Descants and harmony sung by the cantor in a microphone over the people's music.
- An organist, whose gift might not be his/her voice, miked from the bench. When he or she is not visible, this produces a "disembodied voice" effect.

I once experienced a Trinity Sunday liturgy at a tiny RC parish in Central Texas in which a very earnest middle-aged female cantor, read "song leader," was accompanied by a young male bass guitarist. To the side of the duo, a relatively new, locked, electronic organ sat silent, due to the lack of anyone who could play it. (I later learned from the "cantor" that there were better church gigs in town—with the Lutherans!) The entrance hymn, "Holy, Holy, Holy!" was sung by the cantor's miked voice and by those of us in the meager congregation who gave it our best shot to overcome the carpeted room and her competition. To assist our singing, the bass guitarist played I, IV, and V chord roots under us. The service was not helped out any by the ancient Hungarian priest who served as presider in broken and unintelligible English—Latin would have been easier to understand! The final hymn, the well-known, nearly international anthem of the Roman Catholic church, "Holy God, We Praise Thy Name," ended the liturgy. Somewhere along the way we were treated to the cantor harmonizing over us—perhaps it was during the responsorial psalm?

Unfortunately, this poor practice is not helped, and may in fact seem to be supported by a statement in article 104 of another RC liturgical document, the 2003 edition of the *General Instruction to the Roman Missal* ("GIRM"):

> It is fitting that there be a cantor or a choir director to lead and sustain the people's singing. When in fact there is no choir, it is up to the cantor to lead the different chants, with the people taking part.

An accomplished musician with a clear voice trained in liturgy could serve the above function well. Most often, however, the absence of choir and solid accompaniment by an instrument intended to lead large groups of people in song (the organ) leaves the most untrained singer to his or her own devices. In this situation, the choir has lost its leadership role, and the assembly, who have grown increasingly dependent upon auditory and visual stimulation from the cantor, shirk the responsibility of initiating their participation. Once again, the "work of the people"[8] is by the few, but now is dominated by the nonprofessional, rather than a well-trained choir. The assembly reverts to listening, not actively participating.

Why Have Cantors?

After this troubling scenario, why should we as Episcopal and Lutheran church musicians, clergy, and worship/music/liturgy committees explore broadening our music ministry to include the cantor in its best sense of practice?

- We have seen from the historical section above that some leadership by a solo voice has been with us in Jewish and Christian liturgical practice of various kinds, be it from the clergy or the laity.
- Some music is best sung or best started by one voice. For example, it is most effective to have a single solo voice begin some elements of the liturgy, particularly plainsong. Set out by a cantor, a plainsong (Gregorian) psalm tone can be clearly repeated by the entire assembly—congregation and choir. The clarity that one voice naturally has in singing a gospel acclamation verse, takes a great deal of rehearsal time for a choir or semichorus of treble or bass voices to equal.
- Increasing the amount of sung elements in the liturgy, a goal of liturgical reform, sometimes calls for solo leadership from the laity, for example, singing the prayers of the people (intercessions).
- A cantor can assist in the restoration of singing as the normal "speech" of the liturgy, as is the case in the Eastern churches. Modern liturgical historians believe that Early Christians chanted everything, a practice that they inherited from the Jewish service. This returns life to the aberration of the spoken medieval low mass of the Western church, unfortunately still experienced in the "said services" of many Episcopal parishes around the country. The Sunday communal celebrations of the Eucharist should be sung! Psalms, the hymns of the Hebrew people, were not intended to be spoken, neither was the *Gloria* or the *Sanctus*, even in the "ordinary time" following Epiphany and Pentecost.
- Adding non-Sunday morning services to respond to the needs of changing cultures can require sung leadership without an available choir or organist. If the staff professional musicians are already taxed to the fullest by their current responsibilities, the presence of a strong (meaning professional and well-trained) cantor at a service can make sung participation possible.
- New repertoire has developed in the past forty years, some very worthy of inclusion in liturgical churches, which is designed for a single voice and congregation. Consider particularly:

  - Music from the Taizé Community.
  - Music from Africa, Latin America, and Asia, often featuring call-response procedure.
  - Music from non-European traditions in the United States, such as African-American spirituals, sometimes featuring call-response.

- New worship styles are developing that can add different dimensions to what is considered the usual Sunday service:

  - Meditative services and Eucharists using the music listed above, chant, and primarily unaccompanied song.

- In a culture bombarded by visual stimulation, it is important to explore that which can be sung easily, and "by heart," as well as from the printed page. The custom so common now in Episcopal and Lutheran parishes of printing the texts in the bulletin or service leaflet for absolutely everything in the liturgy that is read, prayed, or proclaimed does not help us in obtaining balance in this regard!

- Liturgical renewal, new words and music being created for the church (even in more traditional styles), and the exploration of earlier forms of music, such as plainsong, requires someone to help the congregation learn this repertoire. A good cantor can assist the director of music in this task:

  - Prior to worship services.
  - During Christian education classes—adults and children.
  - During children's chapel.
  - At social and organizational gatherings.

Who?

It is my belief that, like the *Kantor* of German Lutheranism, the chief musician of a parish (e.g., the director of music or organist/choirmaster), when possessing an appropriate singing voice (see qualifications below), should fulfill *some* of the roles of cantor when possible, particular the role of music teacher to the assembly. In presenting new liturgical music directly to the congregation in rehearsal, the people will know that their musician wants to do everything in his or her power to enable them to develop into full liturgical participants, and that singing is not only for those who attend the midweek choir rehearsal. A member of the clergy can also help in this regard, particularly if the musician is not willing or competent to assume this role. It is also appropriate for a director of music to intone *a cappella* portions of the service, such as a plainsong psalm or *Alleluia*, from time to time, particularly in the absence of a choir or cantor. Directors of music and musical clergy need to be cautious about taking on too many of the liturgical roles themselves, however, as was the case in the following example.

My recent experience has included a multiday conference of liturgists and musicians at which the priest and the organist played their roles as presider for the Eucharist and officiant at the daily offices, and accompanist, respectively, *and also* divided between themselves *all* the portions of the services normally assigned to a cantor or choir. Even in very small places with modest resources, one should have a third person to lead the congregation's song, a representative from and for the assembly itself. If it must be the organist, then find another accompanist, or mode of accompaniment (e.g., handbells or choir chimes), and sing more music *a cappella*. A presider should never assume a role given to the laity, unless there is *absolutely no one else* to carry it out.

The following are some important requirements of those who would be cantors, in order of importance:

1. Possess a pleasant singing voice—someone whom the majority of persons would agree they like to hear sing. A good cantor *may not necessarily* be the person who you would like to hear sing solo literature, though the *very best* cantors and the very best soloists I have had at my disposal in church positions have been one and the same.

2. Sing in the center of the pitch and have good intonation. It has been my experience that it is harder for certain voice categories and types, who make nice music otherwise, to serve as cantor, particularly sopranos with very high and airy voices, and altos whose notes above the break are not as solid, too fluty in character, and very different in timbre from their lower range. It seems that a good voice for canting requires a moderate amount of richness and weight (but not dark vowels) and generally needs to possess strength in the range at which the majority of congregational music is written. Second sopranos, first altos, baritones, and "bari-tenors" often have an easier time of fitting these requirements than their neighboring voice categories.

3. Be able to sing with a relatively straight*er* tone, not a lot of vibrato or a wide vibrato. It becomes very difficult to make out pitch or rhythm if there is a great deal of color in someone's voice. If you can only sing like an opera singer, you will not make a very good cantor.

4. Be a trained singer. Having at least some experience with voice lessons will not only make singers more comfortable with their vocal mechanism (and thus the music) but will also free them up to communicate better with the people: looking up and making eye contact, as well as singing the musical phrase and not just the notes. Being able to sing a wider range of pitches with ease will also help when canting at different times in the day.

5. Can be *heard* in the worship space. This is particularly important if a parish does not use amplification. Saint Rita's church building, though not an extremely large physical structure, seated roughly one thousand people. During my time there, I asked the cantors (and lectors, when I trained them) to project as if they were speaking *without amplification* to a large group of people.

6. Can be *understood* in the worship space. No amount of amplification will be able to make someone with poor enunciation intelligible. A cantor must know how to sing with clarity and break up legato lines in order to make consonants clearly understood, particularly the ones at the ends of syllables and words. Also, a cantor must sing at times with different rules of pronunciation than that of a choral singer or soloist, as certain practices (rolling "r"s, for one) will come off as affected.

7. It is helpful if a cantor is also an active member of the choir. My experience is that these singers were easier to use than those who were not, as they were able to learn new liturgical music or hymnody that was to be introduced into the service during the course of regular choir rehearsals. It is very important, however, to keep reminding oneself that the *cantor serving in the liturgy really belongs to the worshiping community* as its enabler (remember the role of the Jewish *hazzan*), *not* to the choir as its music emissary to the people. This does not mean that a cantor should be prohibited from singing anthems with the choir at the same liturgy where he or she cants, but it does mean that the cantor must fulfill his or her role completely, at all other times. For example, if the cantor is a soprano and stationed at the cantor stand during the *Gloria* to gesture the people, that cantor should not sing a descant at the stand or move away and join the choir in order to do so.

8. Be able to prepare music on one's own. Even with the best singer, I have sometimes had to teach notes in the warm-up period before a service. A good cantor should be responsible for learning the music in advance, and should ask for time from the organist to go through that piece at the weekly choir rehearsal or another prearranged time before Sunday. The congregation does not need to be experimented on or dragged through a poor sight-reading session during worship!

9. Be able to communicate through music, to be engaged in the liturgy and engage the assembly as a leader.

10. Be comfortable with being in front of people. Especially when leading a rehearsal. Some of the best cantors I know could sing anything in front of anyone, or read anything *written* in front of groups, but become very afraid when they have to make an announcement or rehearse the congregation. If these people are called on to lead a rehearsal, the director of music should prepare a carefully written script for them in advance.

11. Be responsible for arriving at the required time, and with a multiservice schedule as we had at Saint Rita, be able to find an appropriate substitute from the ranks of the Cantor Guild when necessary.

At The Episcopal Church of the Transfiguration, Dallas, where I have served as director of music since 2004, the cantor's role has generally been assigned to the paid section leaders. One exception to this has been in the office of compline sung by either the men's or women's *Schola Cantorum* in which the officiant (leader of the prayers) and cantor (beginner of the psalm) roles have been shared off and on between various members of the choir. After I arrived at the parish, the clergy and I introduced the singing of prayers of the people at the 11:15 Sunday service and at all the Holy Days during the Advent-Christmas and Lent-Easter cycles.

As we do not currently have a deacon, we have generally used adult and youth members of the parish who are recognized by, and therefore representatives of, the worshiping community. These intercessors also sing from the ambo at the front of the church, while the cantors sing from the gallery rail at the back.

One caution—it has been my experience that some of the persons most interested in being a cantor have the most problems successfully filling that role, and are perhaps looking to become a cantor for the wrong reasons. This ministry, just like the others in the liturgy, involves selfless service and humility. Of course, one's ego still must be present—if that were not the case, a person wouldn't be a model of Christ, either, embodying the human and the divine—but it is important to always keep in mind whom one is serving: the people of God.

What and When?

Psalmody is the chief responsibility of the cantor, whose role may take several forms:

- Intoning the first portion of the gradual psalm when it is sung in *unison* to a plainsong or modern tone. Though the historic practice is for the cantor to sing the first half of the tone with the choir joining on the second portion, our experience at Transfiguration is that the congregation does best when the cantor gives the example of the *entire* tone first, and the congregation and choirs begin singing on the next full verse. We usually precede the cantor's singing by playing the tone on the organ, unless the psalm is accompanied by handbells or choir chimes, when we give only the first few notes. I prefer that the plainsong psalms be sung without accompaniment by the organ.
- Singing the refrain, and then the verses during a psalm sung in a *responsorial* manner. It is important to give the singing of psalms a number of different treatments in the course of a liturgical year, both for variety itself, for the expression of a particular psalm in a particular celebration, and to heighten the character of a liturgical season or feast day. Responsorial psalm singing, though a new practice to Lutherans and Episcopalians, has spawned a great deal of excellent literature in and around its use in the Roman liturgy. The responsorial method involves singing an antiphon or refrain by the congregation, with the verses sung by a cantor or the choir. The normal procedure for anything sung in a responsorial manner with accompaniment is:

  - the organ or another instrument plays the refrain
  - the cantor (or choir) intones the refrain
  - all repeat the refrain
  - a verse (or set of verses, depending upon the setting) is sung by the cantor or choir

- all sing the refrain
- another verse (or set) is sung
- all sing the refrain
- etc.

It is possible to have the cantor sing the soprano lines of some Anglican chants, too, so they might serve as the musical material for the psalm verses.

- Singing verses *in alternation, or antiphonally* with the congregation. Though employed most often between the two sides of collegiate style seating (or divided chancel choirs) during daily offices, the practice of antiphonal psalmody can also be used between a cantor and the entire assembly. In this case the cantor would sing the entire first verse of a psalm alone, with the people answering with the second verse. This procedure continues with the cantor and people alternating the verses until the appointed passage has been completed. Note: though this procedure is called "antiphonal," it does not require an antiphon or refrain, as does the responsorial method. This procedure can work well with plainsong tones, simplified Anglican chant, or Anglican chant.

Gospel acclamations are the second most important place to use cantors. Though Lutheran practice has been to sing an *Alleluia* from a setting in the service book with the same general verse for each Sunday outside of Lent, it has increasingly become more widespread to adopt the Roman Catholic procedure of having cantor or choir chant the appointed verse to go with the proper lectionary readings for each Sunday or feast day (see *ELW* 168–175 for *Alleluias* and 176–177 for Lenten Acclamations, as well as those embedded in the ten holy communion settings). Episcopalians from low- and broad-church traditions have been accustomed to singing a sequence hymn before the gospel, as evidenced by the absence of any settings of *Alleluias* or Lenten acclamations in *The Hymnal 1982 (H82)* or its predecessors, with only a couple available in *Wonder, Love, and Praise (WLP)* (847 and 848). Appointed *Alleluias* and verses or tracts in Lent set to plainsong, however, are available in the volumes of *Gradual Psalms* from Church Publishing.

- The normal procedure for gospel acclamations, a term covering both the *Alleluia* and verse in non-Lenten seasons and the Lenten acclamation and verse, is similar to the first section of a responsorial psalm:

  - the organ plays the *Alleluia* refrain *unless it is long* and contains a shortened introduction[9]
  - the cantor or choir sings the refrain
  - all repeat the refrain
  - the cantor or choir sings the verse
  - all sing the refrain

Generally, I prefer to have either the treble (SA) or bass (TB) voices of the choir intone the *Alleluia* refrains, to give them more volume. Customarily, I ask the voices to intone who are in the same range as that day's cantor, who will then sing the verse alone. On festival days when brass and organ accompany the refrain, I like to have the entire choir sing the verse in harmony.

The third liturgical piece that a cantor might sing is the prayers of the people or intercessions, officially the role of the deacon. There are several formulas for singing the prayers of the people in *H82* (S106 to S109) and more in the appendix of the *Service Music Accompaniment Edition* (S362 and S363).

The last of the official service music for cantor is an *Agnus Dei* when sung in litany form or another fraction anthem with verses to be sung by a cantor or the choir during the breaking of the bread. See *WLP* 869 for a litany form, and *H82* S151, S167–S172 and *WLP* 875–877 for refrains with verses.

Following these portions of liturgical music in which a cantor may serve in an official role, a solo voice is required in some song repertoire that is now more commonly found in use:

- Recent repertoire, particularly that in a more contemporary folk style. In much of this music the cantor primarily sings the verses, and the people sing the refrains. There are several examples of popular Roman Catholic songs by St. Louis Jesuits in *WLP* and *ELW*: "Be Not Afraid" (811), "Here I Am, Lord" (812/574), and "On Eagle's Wings" (810/787). Even though many congregations have grown to know the verses of these songs, their range, rhythmic complexity, text, and soloistic style lend them best to the responsorial performance by the cantor and people in which they were originally intended.[10] Another popular piece, "One Bread, One Body" (*ELW* 496) works fine with everyone singing refrain and verse.

- Call-response music. This pattern is common in folk music from South Africa (see *Thuma mina* in *WLP* 808 and *ELW* 809), and South America (see *ELW* 164), and also in African-American spirituals such as "Swing Low, Sweet Chariot" and "Somebody's Knockin' at Your Door" (*Worship*, 3rd edition, 415).

- Some of the music produced for the Taizé community in France also requires the use of a solo singer who may begin the songs and also sing verses between the congregational refrains, or over ostinato refrains, when provided. For example, *WLP* 832 and 834 contain some of the cantor verses available, and there are verses for *WLP* 826, 829, and 831 and *ELW* 175, 348, 406, 472, and 642 in the Taizé accompaniment and cantor books published by GIA Publications.[11]

Where?

The design of any given worship space will determine the possibilities for the placement of a cantor. The location of the accompanying instrument(s)—organ (and piano)—and choir may also influence the decision. (If one is fortunate to have instruments at the front and back of a church, there is more flexibility on the location.) Perhaps the most important reason for the location of a cantor might be how much and when a cantor is utilized during a liturgy. In a church where the organ and choir are located in a rear gallery and the cantor only intones a plainsong psalm and sings a gospel acclamation verse, it makes sense to have the cantor be with the other musical forces, provided they can be heard and understood. (Printing the cantor's texts in a service leaflet helps.) The rear gallery, however, is not an appropriate place from which to conduct a preliturgy rehearsal of the congregation, and the inability of the congregation to see the cantor rules out any gesturing of the congregation on entrances of liturgical music, when necessary. If a choir is always present, and the congregation generally participates well and takes initiative for itself, the latter concern is not so important. Cueing in the congregation may also be aided by the ministers in the sanctuary leading the congregation by example.

The active role of the cantor in present-day Roman Catholic practice generally requires that the cantor be visible and in the front of the church. In many older structures with organs in rear galleries, this presents both the cantor and accompanist a challenge, particularly in psalm settings and other music with a freer rhythmic structure. For congregations just beginning to participate, assemblies of school children, and congregations without much musical background, however, it is helpful to have a cantor communicate and engage the people through facial expressions, hand gestures, and other motions (e.g., holding up a service leaflet or hymnal open to the music for a particular acclamation or hymn). The late Joseph Gelineau, French Jesuit, who developed a method of singing the psalms that is still widely used today, spoke of the cantor as the *animateur* (animator) of the assembly.

If the cantor is to be located in the front of the church, space will need to be provided for a location for some sort of podium or classy-looking music stand that is in proportion to the other furniture in the chancel or sanctuary area. Depending upon the acoustical capacity for speech and music to carry and be understood in the worship space, a microphone at this location will be needed, as well. If the lector and presider use a microphone from the altar, the cantor should, as well. At Transfiguration we are fortunate to have sound technicians who carefully control volume for the intercessor when he or she sings at the ambo microphone.

In many churches, the psalm is sung from the ambo (pulpit or reading desk), as it, like the scripture readings or lessons, comes from the Bible and deserves a parallel place. The Intercessions should also be sung from the ambo or from the same location where they would normally be spoken. It is very important in churches with modern architecture, particularly those with a wide front, that the cantor be visible to all and near the rest of the ministers—presider and lector. It is common in churches such as this to place the organ, other instruments, and choir off to the side and at the level of the congregation. The cantor should not be located far away, or on the floor, if they are to lead!

An example of poor placement comes from a recent experience at a large national denominational gathering. As common with convention center and hotel ballroom liturgies, a raised altar area was created in the center of one side of the wide and deep hall. This dais held an altar, the presider, deacon, and lectors as well as *an interpreter who signed for the hard of hearing*, but no room for a cantor. The musicians leading the assembly in song each day were positioned in an area far to the right of the altar and at floor level. The musical leadership varied greatly—from electronic organ, brass, and choir; to jazz ensemble; to gospel choir and piano; to a single voice accompanied by guitar. The only way that any musician was visible to the majority of the congregation was if they were several levels up on the choral risers, and this placement was still way out of the central activity of the liturgy. The music chosen for the services was as eclectic as the musicians who led the singing, and much of it was new to the gathered worshipers. We very much needed a trained cantor (or a large choir) to lead us. I was particularly disappointed to find out that a conscious decision has been made by the nonmusician planners of the gathering to deny a visible placement for a cantor, one which would have offered the leader of the assembly's song a proper place of respect on par with the ministers of worship and helped us all to better celebrate.

How?

- Finding and Training

    - Establish a procedure for interested singers to contact you.
    - Schedule an audition in which the candidate prepares a hymn or song.
    - Interview the candidate regarding vocal background and experience.
    - Instruct successful candidates in how they are to teach and/or lead the congregation.
    - Schedule the newly trained cantors for a service where you can observe them.
    - Initially give them frequent canting opportunities to reinforce their learning.

- Rehearsing

    - Schedule periodic gatherings of your cantors to fine tune procedures, learn new music, and clean up any sloppy habits. The frequency of these meetings will vary from place to place, depending upon the skill of the cantors and the scope of their responsibilities. Even a brief meeting after choir rehearsals will be useful.

- If possible have cantors sing for each other occasionally and treat it as a workshop for skill building.

- Be Consistent

  - Establish a routine and procedure for cantors, and require consistency from liturgy to liturgy and Sunday to Sunday.
  - Consistency is even more necessary in a congregation where there are many visitors who will look to the cantor for leadership.
  - Give clear instructions for the congregation in the printed service leaflet and in the presider's booklet about singing, especially if the cantor must be in the rear gallery.

- Let the Congregation Sing

  - A good cantor will inspire a congregation to sing by a confident intonation and a simple gesture to begin, and will withdraw—especially from the microphone—to let the congregation carry their part. For example, if the cantor gestures the entrance and post-communion hymns with a choir present, he or she will signal the beginning and then move away from the podium while holding the hymnal and singing.
  - Tailor this general rule when a particular liturgical situation such as a funeral requires more assistance initially for the congregation.

- Don't Show Off!

  - Cantors must always sing the printed rhythm when the congregation is singing. Doing otherwise is confusing.
  - Refrain from singing harmony or descants over the congregation unless it is over a Taizé-style ostinato refrain.

- Clearly Delineate Roles

  - If the cantor also serves as a musical soloist during a liturgy (e.g., a wedding or a funeral), do not sing the solo material from the cantor stand.
  - Move closer to the organ or piano when singing as a soloist and do not use a microphone, if possible.

Conclusion

At the end of this discussion, I find myself back at the beginning with my Lutheran experience in the 1960s and 1970s of the congregation singing *everything* in the holy communion service. (I refer to this as the "tyranny of the assembly"—if I'm not singing, it doesn't count!) What was missing?—psalm singing, and a role for the choir in the service beyond an anthem stuck somewhere near the scripture lessons, for a start. Move now with me to Saint Rita Catholic Community in the 1980s and 1990s, and a relatively good practice of Vatican II liturgy. What was missing?—the ability to tailor the liturgical music to diverse assemblies at different mass times, and the unspoken restriction against the choir enriching the liturgy much beyond anthems at the offertory and communion and occasional choral verses of a psalm. In other words: the freedom to explore more treasures from polyphonic choral traditions by singing a setting or portion of the ordinary in its proper place from time to time. In my current position at the Church of the Transfiguration, we are able to celebrate the established, traditional roles of presider, deacon, congregation, choir, and organ, and to increase the role of cantor by singing the gradual psalm in a responsorial manner from time to time, prayers of the people, and some of the newer repertoire employing solo voice. I believe that the ultimate goal of good, modern, restored liturgical practice is to end up in this place—where everyone has his or her role to play in liturgical celebrations, which are heightened by diversity and music from past and present, presented in the best of the liturgical tradition. By the presence of clergy and other ministers who enrich the rite with love and care, of a director of music who understands his or her role as leader of the congregation's song, and of well-trained cantors and choirs who fulfill their respective duties, one can have liturgical celebrations in which fully conscious and active participation involves great art and music, ceremony and procession, movement and posture, listening and reading, singing and reciting, sound and silence, and the best of all possible worlds.

Notes

1. The Lutheran practice for the *Kyrie* has long been to use a litany form, rather than a six-fold or nine-fold version.

2. Paul Westermeyer, *The Church Musician* (rev. ed.) (Minneapolis: Augsburg Fortress, 1997). ISBN: 0-8066-3399-9.

3. Todd Nichol, *Liturgical Civility, Upward Mobility, and American Modernity* (St. Paul, MN: Luther Seminary). www.luthersem.edu/word&world/Archives/3-2_Piety/3-2_Nichol.pdf

4. This document and the others to follow are easily obtained on the Web. See http://www.fdlc.org/Liturgy_Resources/DOCUMENTSVatican.htm. They are also published together with U.S. Bishops Committee on the Liturgy documents by Liturgy Training Publications. See "resources" below for the reference.

5. Roman Catholic documents from Vatican II and beyond have used the word "assembly" for the people gathered for worship in the body of the church. *The Book of Common Prayer (BCP)*, 1979, refers to this group as "The People." *The Lutheran Book of Worship (LBW)*, 1978, used a boxed and bolded "C" for "congregation," and *Evangelical Lutheran Worship (ELW)*, 2006, has now adopted the use of "assembly." In this article, I use the various terms interchangeably, though I personally prefer the traditional word "congregation," as "assembly" is most often used in the English language to refer to political bodies—e.g., the General Assembly of the United Nations—or secular gatherings—all-school "assembly."

6. The two quotations here are from *Musicam Sacram* (*Instruction on Music in the Sacred Liturgy*), 1967, article 21; and an article in the Bishops Committee on the Liturgy Newsletter, April 18, 1966, respectively.

7. "Cantor" is a noun, not a verb! One hears all too often, "I'm scheduled to *cantor* for the 9:00 A.M. service this Sunday." The proper verb to use is "cant," so one should say "I'm scheduled to cant at the 9:00 A.M. service this Sunday," or to "serve as cantor for. . . ." One also hears misuse of "lector" in this way. Substitute the words "presider" and "preside," and you'll break yourself of this habit in no time.

8. The Greek word *leitourgia* translated as "liturgy" means "work of the people."

9. See *Worship*, 3rd edition, 284 for an example by Richard Proulx. In this case, the introduction is used and the cantor or choir sings the entire refrain immediately. I also shorten the organ conclusion for the cantor's sing-through.

10. Thomas Day writes extensively about the theological reasoning for singing "Here I am, Lord" in call-response form in *Why Catholics Can't Sing: The Culture of Catholicism and the Triumph of Bad Taste* (New York: Crossroad Publishing, 1990).

11. Jacques Berthier. *Music from Taizé*, vol. 1: G-2433, vol. 2: G-2778 (Chicago: GIA Publications). These have the complete parts for cantor, instrumentalists, and keyboard. Several are published in separate octavo form.

Resources

Cantor Training

Associated Parishes for Liturgy and Music. *The Cantor: Leader of Song, Minister of Prayer.* 2002. www.associatedparishes.org

Hansen, James. *The Ministry of the Cantor.* Collegeville, MN: The Liturgical Press, 1985. www.litpress.org

———. *Training the Parish Cantor.* Collegeville, MN: The Liturgical Press. ISBN: 978-0-8146-7841-1. A 54-minute VHS video cassette. www.litpress.org

Hansen, Jim, Melanie Coddington, and Joe Simmons. *Cantor Basics*, rev. ed. Portland, OR: Pastoral Press (OCP Publications). Item 11837. www.ocp.org

Harmon, Kathleen. *The Ministry of Cantors (Collegeville Ministry Series).* Collegeville, MN: The Liturgical Press. ISBN: 978-0-8146-2877-5. www.litpress.org

Johnson, Lawrence J. *The Mystery of Faith: The Ministers of Music.* Washington, DC: National Association of Pastoral Musicians, 1983. This contains references from the Vatican II and US BCL documents on the various ministerial roles in the liturgy. OUT OF PRINT (used copies available at www.amazon.com).

Kodner, Diana. *Handbook for Cantors,* rev. ed. Chicago: Liturgy Training Publications, 1997. ISBN: 1-56854-097-3, www.ltp.org

National Pastoral Musicians Publications. *Psalmist and Cantor—A Pastoral Music Resource.* www.npm.org/assets/Publications.pdf

Vatican II and Bishops Committee on the Liturgy Documents

Lysik, David, ed. *The Liturgy Documents.* 4th, ed. Vol. 1. Chicago: Liturgy Training Publications. ISBN: 1-56854-468-5, www.ltp.org

The Music Documents—Music in Catholic Worship and Liturgical Music Today. Available through OCP Publications. ISBN: 0-01531-41-0, www.ocp.org

Church Music History

Westermeyer, Paul. *Te Deum—The Church and Music.* Minneapolis, MN: Fortress Press, 1998. ISBN: 0-8006-3146-3, www.augsburgfortress.org

Hymnals

(Episcopal) *H82 The Hymnal 1982,* www.churchpublishing.org
(Episcopal) *Lift Every Voice and Sing,* www.churchpublishing.org
(Episcopal) *WLP Wonder, Love, and Praise,* www.churchpublishing.org
ELW (ELCA) *Evangelical Lutheran Worship,* www.augsburgfortress.com
LBW (ELCA) *Lutheran Book of Worship,* www.augsburgfortress.com
(Roman Catholic) *Gather* (several editions), www.giamusic.com
(Roman Catholic) *Ritual Song,* www.giamusic.com
(Roman Catholic) *Worship* (3rd ed.), www.giamusic.com

Liturgical Music with Cantor Role

Ford, Paul F., editor. *By Flowing Waters—Chant for the Liturgy (A Collection of Unaccompanied Song for Assemblies, Cantors, and Choirs).* Collegeville, MN: The Liturgical Press. ISBN: 978-0-8146-2595-8, www.litpress.org

Jones, Peter, editor. *Glory to God.* OCP. 7148, www.ocp.org
   Congregation, SATB Choir/Cantor, Organ, Brass
   Nice refrain *Gloria*; best with full choir, but works with high voice cantor

Martinson, Joel. *Missa Guadalupe.* Selah Publishing. 410-910 (Full Score)
   Congregation, SATB Choir, Brass, Oboe, Organ

The *Alleluia* and *Agnus Dei/Cordero de Dios* use cantor
Blends chant with new melodies, modern rhythms, and harmonies
The *Agnus Dei/Cordero de Dios* also published separately (410-916) and
available also in *Wonder, Love, and Praise* (see above)

Plainsong Psalmody

Litton, James, editor. *The Plainsong Psalter*. New York: Church Publishing Inc.,
1988. Though originally intended for the Daily Office, I have been using
the tone and pointing printed in this book for our gradual psalm singing at
Transfiguration, as well as for our psalmody during compline.

Responsorial Psalm and Canticle Collections

Publisher Web sites:

Augsburg Fortress	www.augsburgfortress.org
Church Publishing	www.churchpublishing.org
Concordia	www.cph.org
e-Libris	www.e-librispublishers.com
GIA	www.giamusic.com
OCP	www.ocp.org
Selah	www.selahpub.com
Westminster	www.ppc.com

Gradual Psalms, BCP Lectionary and RCL Lectionary editions. Church
Publishing: 1988 and 2007
Evangelical Lutheran Worship—Psalms for Worship. Augsburg Fortress: 2006.
ISBN 978-0-8066-5305-1
Celebration Series, Psalms for the Church Year. GIA
Volume 1: Marty Haugen and David Haas (G-2664)
Volume 2: Marty Haugen (G-3261)
Congregation, Cantor, Choir, Guitar, Piano
I *do not* recommend volumes 3 (Haas/Cotter) and 4 (Rory Cooney/Gary
Daigle)
Volume 5 (Roy James Stewart) is African-American gospel style
Many of these are now included in GIA's *Gather* hymnals
Grail/Gelineau Lectionary Psalms. GIA. G-5040
Congregation, Cantor, Organ
Includes complete psalms for three-year cycle, with the revised Roman
lectionary
Refrain with both psalm and Gelineau tones
The Grail Psalms. GIA: 1993. G-4044
Congregation, Cantor, Organ

Inclusive language texts based on the Grail translation from the original Hebrew. Unfortunately, due to the current Vatican proscriptions on language, GIA is not able to republish the complete lectionary Psalter with these inclusive texts.

Forty-one Grail /Gelineau Psalms. GIA. G-4402

This volume uses the refrains from *Worship,* 3rd edition, with inclusive text for the verses from *The Grail Psalms,* 1993. The entire psalm is printed, not just the lectionary portion, for use in Daily Offices.

Guimont, Michel. *Lectionary Psalms.* Chicago: GIA Publications, 1988. G-4986

For the revised Roman lectionary; also available: CD recording, choral descants.

———. *Psalms for the Revised Common Lectionary.* Chicago: GIA Publications, 2002. G-5616

Hopson, Hal H., editor. *The Psalter: Psalms and Canticles for Singing.* Westminster/John Knox Press: 1993. 664254454

Hunstiger, Jay. *The Basilica Psalter.* 2 vols. (Cycle B & Cycle C). Collegeville, MN: The Liturgical Press. OUT OF PRINT. (Used copies of this Canadian resource are available from www.amazon.ca.)

Congregation, Cantor, Organ

Refrain with tone (his own, double tone); some given simpler settings as well

Cycle B is in hand manuscript; Cycle C is engraved

Psalm and Canticle Octavos

My Soul Rejoices. Owen Alstott, editor. OCP. 8727

Refrain and versification of the *Magnificat*

Congregation, Melody/Descant, Trumpet, Organ

Nice refrain, simple verses

Psalm 15. Joel Martinson. Selah Publishing. 421-015

Conregation, Cantor, Choir (canon), Oboe, Organ

Psalm 23, Joel Martinson. Concordia. 97-6491

Congregation, Cantor, Choir (canon), Flute, Organ

With two refrains

Psalm 34. Joel Martinson. Concordia. 97-6492

Congregation, Cantor, Choir (canon), Organ

Psalm 85. Joel Martinson. Concordia. 97-6587

Congregation, Cantor, Flute, Organ

Psalm 98. Joel Martinson. Concordia. 98-3225

Congregation, SATB Choir, Trumpet, Organ

With two refrains

Psalm 128. James Chepponis. GIA. G-2858

Congregation, Male and Female Cantors, Flute/Oboe, Guitar, Organ/Piano

Nice setting in middle-ground style; good for weddings

Shepherd Me, O God. Marty Haugen. GIA. G-2950
  Congregation, Choir, Cantor, Guitar, Piano, Optional C Instruments
  From *Celebration Series,* volume 2. (See above.)
Your Love Is Finer Than Life. Marty Haugen. GIA. G-2658
  Congregation, Choir, Two Treble Instruments, Guitar, Piano
  From *Celebration Series,* volume 2. (See above.)

Gospel Acclamation Collections

Batastini, Robert, ed. *The Cantor's Book of Gospel Acclamations.* GIA. G-4987
  Congregation, Cantor, Organ
  Includes *Alleluias* and Lenten acclamations from *Worship,* 3rd edition, and
  other sources with their appointed verses.

Gospel Acclamation Octavo

Alleluia in C, Howard Hughes, S.M. GIA
  Congregation, SATB Choir, Cantor, Organ
  Nice responsorial Alleluia setting with an extremely simple tone for the verse
Celtic Alleluia, Fintan O'Carroll and Christopher Walker editors. OCP. 7106
  Congregation, SATB Choir, Guitar, Solo Instrument, Trumpet or Clarinet,
    Organ
  One of the most popular *Alleluias* in RC circles (about worn-out in some
    parishishes), but really very nice if used sparingly
Missa Guadalupe. Joel Martinson. Selah Publishing. 410-910 (Full Score)
  Includes an *Alleluia*
Praise to You, O Christ, Our Savior. Bernadette Farrell, editor. OCP. 7126
  Congregation, Unison Choir, Guitar, Trumpet, Solo Instrument, Organ
  Can be used for Lenten acclamation

Joel Martinson is director of music ministries and organist at the Episcopal
Church of the Transfiguration in Dallas, Texas, where he coordinates the vibrant
musical life of the parish, including choral and instrumental ensembles for all
ages, a music series, and an exciting new organ project by the firm of Richards,
Fowkes, & Co. A product of two generations of clergy/musician families, Joel
has worked as a musician in Episcopal, Roman Catholic, Lutheran, Presbyterian,
and Reformed Jewish houses of worship.

  An award-winning and active composer, he has been commissioned by a
wide array of churches, musical organizations, and individual performers across
the United States. Joel is represented by a complete setting of the liturgy in the
newly released hymnal of the Evangelical Lutheran Church in America, as well
as compositions in the official hymnal supplements and new music resource

materials of both the ELCA and the Episcopal church. From 2000–2004, he was adjunct faculty in church music at the University of North Texas in Denton, where he taught a series of courses in the historical and modern practice of liturgy and church music.

Joel has been dean of the Dallas Chapter of the American Guild of Organists, as well as director of the Recital Series and a member of the Steering Committee for the 1994 National Convention. He has served two terms on the national Committee for New Music Competitions and Commissions of the AGO and is currently performance chair for the Region VII 2007 convention.

What About Choirs and Organs?

ROBERT P. RIDGELL

A church choir: antiquated . . . humdrum . . . stuffy . . . affected . . .
VIP club.
A pipe organ: tubby . . . traditional . . . cacophonous . . . unsocial . . .
moribund art.

Discovering the beauty that church music brings to our world is a difficult task
at times—especially when those who are involved in the life of church music
often critique the offerings of the very same art to which they are called through
their vocation of church musician, choir director, or organist. Or perhaps, it is
even more difficult to discover the art when support for church music and her
servants is taken away for the reasons that there are more important ministries
like, for example—a soup kitchen, a parish bus, or a small stipend for the volunteer steward (custodian) of the parish. Alas, it is even harder to comprehend why
there is often no sense of fostering the art by clergy or musician for the reasons
that sometimes there is no want of cordial relationship, creative energy, or a
fresh look at the beauty of liturgy.

It is true that the beauty the "king of instruments" (the organ) brings to a
church or the musical world as a whole has long been considered a dying art.
And with that the art of singing is currently seeing a lack of education, learning, and competence. Our culture and some of her artists have pushed the art
of church music to new lows that have sadly brought the cultural interest to just
about zero. One need not look at the average attendance at an organ recital or
the lack of lusty congregational singing of hymns and ritual songs. How and why
this has happened is a topic longer and larger than this article could ever debate.
In fact, there is no need to really debate and criticize any longer. This article will
focus on the ways that organs and choirs find tones given to a world that seems
to need beauty, redemption, and authentic forms of prayer.

The day will come when after we have mastered the winds, the waves, the tides and gravity, we shall harness for God the energies of love. Then, for the second time in the history of the world, mankind will have discovered fire.

Pierre Teilhard De Chardin
Quantum Theology

Perhaps the most visible choir in the world is the Mormon Tabernacle Choir. The choir is heard weekly through radio and TV broadcasts and many recordings. The Mormon Tabernacle Choir's mission allows a rapidly growing faith community to evangelize and in many cases convert others through the medium of music, both organ and choral. This is true for the many cathedral choirs in the United Kingdom like Westminster Abbey, Westminster Cathedral, and St. Paul's Cathedral whose choirs and organs are the examples of nobility and transcendence. The cathedral music example is one that effects the driving ambitions and dreams of many American parish musicians as well. One would never underestimate the power of such cathedral music to convert and change the lives of others. In many cases—both in parish and cathedral life, there are probably hundreds of thousands who are transformed through church music.

Though we travel the whole world over to find beauty
we must carry it with us or we find it not.

Ralph Waldo Emerson

A reality question should be asked: Are these transformations valid? In most cases, regrettably, they probably are not. The so-called transformation is just as good as any YouTube™ performance or razzle-dazzle of a Super-Bowl halftime event. The reality is that the majority of so-called transformations will come with a fleeting taste of heaven followed by a tourist camera flash followed by an exit into a world in which *Entertainment Tonight* is held at highest standard. The only way to help our world is to continue what we are called to do without holding grudges for what is "good" music or "bad" music.

Since the 1960s various attempts have been made to refine the criteria of the appropriateness of church music. We have all seen, however, the inadequate development of criteria for musical judgment. Given the lack of consensus in the church on what constitutes "good" music and the lack of serious discussion on the issue, it is imperative that an open heart and mind be applied to what music choirs and organs provide now as well as in the future. There is a fine line within our own conscience at times. There are often moments in which we cringe and become upset with the fact that change happens. Yet, how can we move with the times and adjust our temperament while producing music and producing it well? Certainly musical standards are not absolute or unchanging, and church history attests to this. One thing that lovers of church music could most certainly agree on is the fact that there exists a characteristic ethos. To identify this ethos with any specific period or genre in liturgical/musical history would certainly be a mistake. The church is never limited to any particular style of music for the liturgy. An ethos is discernable, however. In order for the music of choir and organ to move forward from a cultural downfall music of a cosmic, transcendent character that elaborates the sacramental mysteries is crying to be heard. Music, traditions, and techniques used by countless generations is the starting point for discernment. As this occurs, the ethos in church music will find new expressions. New forms and styles naturally grow from extant forms of church music. That growth will empower the musician with song.

> Come, labor on.
> Who dares stand idle on the harvest plain,
> while all around us waves the golden grain.
> And to each servant does the Master say, "Go work today."
>
> Jane Laurie Borthwick

I shall never forget that moment as a boy chorister when I sang that hymn in St. Thomas Church, New York City, with Stephen Cleobury conducting and Bruce Neswick playing the organ. I was in the 1988 Royal School of Church Music New York City Summer Course for Advanced Choristers. It was perhaps the moment that changed my life. I felt empowered to stay the course and to work harder than ever to be a church musician. To this day, I feel called to the vocation of church musician.

How and why do choirs and organs empower us? We might ask: Is it appropriate for a congregation member to actually stand and never sing the *Sanctus* (Holy, holy) during an Easter Day Eucharist? Is it appropriate for an organist to improvise a Messiaen-esque fanfare after the reading of the gospel on Christmas Eve, when in fact it's really a "silent night?" After all, the deacon might feel as if the improvisation is drawing attention to the liturgical ritual of her or his carrying of the gospel in the procession—never mind the fact that some in the congregation might think that the organist has gone mad. Why play a *fanfare* on the theme "*Dieu parmi nous* (God among us)" anyway?! We must remain confident of the moments when we as congregation, choir, clergy, and musician are empowered and inspired to create, for it is in those moments that the Holy Spirit enters our souls and fills us with the energy and passion to create over and over again. There are majestic moments when composers empower choirs and organs as in Dyson's *Magnificat in D*. There are also moments of reflective weeping and inspiration as captured so poignantly in Carissimi's final chorus of *Jeptha*. It is in these moments that we are taken to a place of beauty. Beauty is essential and we feel empowered because of it. Beauty is a sacramental sign of God's presence and action in the world and prefigures the glory of the liturgy of the heavenly

Jerusalem. Choirs and organs are instruments of those moments. They change lives—like they did mine. Even so, choirs and organs are not the sole proprietor of music-making in the church. Clergy and the congregation are the principal and fundamental bodies.

The leadership of parish clergy is the single most influential factor in the musical and liturgical life of a church. Yet, how many seminarians graduate without knowing how to sing, or for that matter without understanding the history and importance of the organ as a tool for accompaniment?

The church's legacy of music education and formation extends back to early medieval times. Our seminaries and private/state-run schools in much of the English-speaking world have significantly reduced artistic formation. The church is now in an excellent position to establish music education programs for the neighborhood and community. This is the mission of the church, especially in a day and age when Sunday is no longer considered the social or spiritual nucleus of the week or when congregational attendance is at an all-time low. The focus of music education and formation bridges the church's relationship with the secular world and their spiritual quest.

Equal to that responsibility is the need for the training of current parish musicians—particularly in teaching: voice, organ, and conducting; a broad knowledge of liturgical rites; and the ability to organize, lead, and communicate in an effective and compelling manner. Moreover, there is a considerable need for full-time musicians to support and assist other lesser-trained or part-time musicians in parishes and smaller communities. This common call to service is part of a church musician's vocation.

Some of the most wonderful organizations to help clergy and musicians unite and to help with educational opportunities are:

American Guild of Organists (AGO), www.agohq.org
American Choral Directors Association (ACDA), www.acdaonline.org
Association of Anglican Musicians (AAM), www.anglicanmusicians.org
Chorus America, www.chorusamerica.org
Conference of Roman Catholic Cathedral Musicians (CRCCM),
    www.crccm.net
Leadership Program for Musicians (LPM), www.lpm-online.org
National Association of Negro Musicians (NANM), www.nanm.org
National Association of Pastoral Musicians (NPM), www.npm.org
Organ Historical Society (OHS), www.organsociety.org
Royal School of Church Music in America (RSCMA), www.rscmamerica.org

> For I will consider my Cat Jeoffrey
> For he is the servant of the Living God duly and daily serving him.
> For at the first glance of the glory of God in the East he worships in his
>   way.

For this is done by wreathing his body seven times round with elegant
quickness.

Christopher Smart
Jubilate Agno

One of the most challenging agendas for any organist and/or choir director is to
plan new and existing repertoire for liturgy and other parish events. Since the
Second Vatican Council a prodigious amount of church music has been produced and published. So much church music is available now, and the turnover
is so great that a stable repertoire of music familiar to singers, organists, and congregations is difficult to maintain. This pastoral problem creates further disunity.
Clearly, parishes and cathedrals and those responsible for music-making must
seek to maintain music that is "custom" within their denomination, region, state,
and liturgical framework. With organs and choirs, this might be quite a challenge
given the wide range of abilities among personnel and diversity in resources to
choose from. Yet, when it comes down to congregational music—both the new
and old need to be gently and frequently used.

Hymnody that uses choirs and organ to the fullest advantage represents a
poetically generative form of time-tested value for stimulating congregational
participation. Yet, at times there is no creative element in the musical production of hymns. Why would a congregation sing all eight verses of a proces-
sional hymn if the aisle in the church is only ten feet long? Often, hymns are
like bricks thrown into the liturgy. When I say this, I am referring specifically
to metered hymnody and hymn tunes with at least more than three verses. As
wonderful as hymns are, they can often obstruct the flow of liturgical ritual and
action. For example, there is often a liturgical misunderstanding when parishes
use a "sequence hymn" or "gradual hymn" after the second reading or before
the Gospel. In this scenario, the hymn detains the progression of the Liturgy
of the Word. When we look at the history of liturgy there is no such thing as
a "sequence" unless sung before the Gospel acclamation "*Alleluia*" on Easter,
Pentecost, Corpus Christi, Our Lady of Sorrows, and if lucky—a requiem mass!
Moreover, in other sections of the eucharistic liturgy one would find that most
do not employ the use of hymns for moments such as the breaking of the bread
(fraction anthem), or memorial acclamation ("Christ has died"). A gradual is by
all means—a psalm. Whether it is called a gradual hymn or a sequence hymn,
it is my hope that not only publishers of "ready-made" liturgy preparation, but
parishes, clergy, and musicians use appropriate language when describing ritual
music whether it be hymn of praise, "Glory to God in the Highest," hymn at the
retiring procession, closing hymn, or gospel acclamation. Using similar if not
the same language only unifies our denominations in singing the same song!
Often publishers suggest hymns for musicians and parishes through yearly planning books. Many neglect through lack of detail which hymns one should use
in liturgy, often suggesting that a hymn (and the genre of hymnody) be used for

anything and everything. This is not helping choirs and organs use the fullest advantage of congregational participation (both as listening and actual physical singing). In closing, the use of such preparation books promotes little, if any, creativity. Let's all try to swim against the current, allowing our minds to venture into new, unchartered song!

The role of the choir urgently needs to be renewed. There is nothing in the life of the church that justifies elimination of the choir—developments that have unfortunately taken place in some corners. The voice of the choir and that of the congregation exist in dynamic relationship. As part of the congregation, the choir leads congregational singing and at times sings with the congregation in unison responses and at times sings alone for the congregation's edification. It should not be forgotten that active participation on the part of the people is ensured both through actual singing and engaged listening. In no case should the choir offend against the proper norms for congregational singing. In all situations, a careful balance between the choir and congregation needs to be fostered. Deeper theological reflection on the nature of the liturgical choir is necessary in the Western church. Some, unfortunately, would reduce the choir's role exclusively to supporting and leading the assembly's song; many seem insufficiently aware of the ability of fine choral music to enhance worship. The resources for a more intensive exploration of the choir's role in worship may be found in a closer examination of the structures of the liturgical rites, in the resources of Eastern liturgiology and aesthetics, and in modern theories of symbol and art. Such theoretical exploration of the role of the choir might well consider the following:

- The choir serves in a particular way to give voice to the glory and beauty of the liturgy.
- The choir bears witness to the eschatological fulfillment of the church, the song of which prefigures that of the saints and angelic choirs in the New Jerusalem.
- The choir is a joyful attendant of the pilgrim people of God and a festive sign of their heavenly home.
- The participation of the choir is crucial to the realization of solemnity and majesty in liturgical events.
- The choir manifests the variety of gifts described in 1 Corinthians 12:4 (New American Bible): "There are different kinds of spiritual gifts but the same Spirit; there are different forms of service but the same Lord; there are different workings but the same God who produces all of them in everyone."
- The choir ministers pastorally in humanly personal and social ways, but spiritually through one voice, and it is the choir director's responsibility (with the help of clergy) to encourage and nurture the positive, proactive aspects of this communal ministry.

It is madness to wear ladies' straw hats and velvet hats to church; we should all be wearing crash helmets. Ushers should issue life preservers and signal flares; they should lash us to our pews. For the sleeping god may wake someday and take offense, or the waking god may draw us out to where we can never return.

Annie Dillard

One of the most memorably awestruck moments I've experienced in liturgy was watching the funeral of Princess Diana on TV. I will never forget the song "Make Me a Channel of Your Peace" by Sebastian Temple (1928–1997). This song, which is still very much what one might call "hum and strum" Roman Catholic music for the reasons that it has been used mainly in the '70s and '80s as a guitar/keyboard standard, was probably composed with that intent. The song was chosen by the sons of Princess Diana and was claimed to be her favorite song. The song is currently owned by the nonprofit publisher Oregon Catholic Press. What made that song so moving for me was the manner and form that the choir and congregation sang, not to mention the fact that Martin Neary gussied up the song with a descant on my favorite word "ah" and the organ roared slightly with a medium-to-full swell. This was noble simplicity and it was done well.

> Do all the good you can,
> By all the means you can,
> In all the ways you can,
> In all the places you can,
> At all the times you can,
> As long as you ever can.

Peter Gomes
Sermons: Biblical Wisdom for Daily Living

Quite often church musicians are faced with that challenge of making something musical that we generally wouldn't like to play or hear but having to do it anyway. Perhaps it's the rector or pastor who wants it, or perhaps it's the congregation that has been clamoring to hear it. In either event we are put into a quandary. To make or not to make the music? That is the question! If we as church musicians were hired to pick and choose our own music at our own personal church service, I would pick my favorites—Maurice Duruflé's *Requiem* (for my funeral, maybe); the Gregorian chant mass, *Missa di Angelis*; the hymn tune "Helmsley"; and the organ choral prelude, "Schmücke dich" by Johann Sebastian Bach. Well, we can't have it all! And, no matter how we look at it—the vocation of the church musician is sensitive because like other vocations we often put our life at risk. Is there really any need for such sensitivity? No. On the other hand—the artist is always willing to put his/her life at risk for the purity of art itself. Yet, if we were artists in one sense of the word, most of us would not be employed by the church, rather we would freelance our gift to the world. The church is our employer, and no matter what trends, fads, and changes come our way—it is our vocation to find the charity and help build up the body of Christ. After all the church is the home of holiness. Perhaps it is like Sebastian Temple's song "Make Me a Channel of Your Peace"—let's find unique ways of gussying up hymnody, songs, and anthems that have hardened our hearts and those of others.

> Forth to high heaven let your praises ring
> But with caution—listen while you sing,
> Let there be in you unity and peace,
> Begin together, and together cease.
> No word or note should ever be begun
> Before the former one if fitly done.
> Be careful not to cut or syncopate,
> Each syllable music have its proper weight.
> For if you keep enunciation good
> The words are rightly heard and understood.
> When to the Lord you will your voices raise
> These simple maxims shall perfect your praise:
> Lift up your hearts to God in love and fear,
> Lift up your voices resonant and clear
> Lift up your minds by thinking what you say,
> Not noise, but prayerful music be your way.
> The cry that to the ear of God doth dart
> Is cry, not of the throat, but of the heart.
>
> Anonymous, fifteenth century

It is the duty, it seems, of every choirmaster to recruit for an array of voices. Very few churches are ever privileged enough to always have enough singers—never mind, the right singers! As we know the ministry of a "paid singer" continues in many churches this day. Yet, there are many smaller parishes that simply cannot afford the competitive prices of singers, especially those in large urban settings. As a community church, we often forget to work closely with our local schools and colleges and universities. One recommendation would be for the parish to consider instituting a new ministry—that of the "choral scholar". Often, one will find students both in high school or college who for a "scholarship" would be most interested in singing for smaller stipends—or, if their parents wanted—a bank deposit into their student account to help pay for education, books, etc. This ministry not only offers the student an opportunity for music education, but also a mentorship that congregations and choirs and church musicians can provide. One of the most successful programs I have seen comes from St. Paul's Methodist Church in Houston, Texas. Visit www. choralscholars.org for more information.

Whence hath the church so many organs and musicall instruments? To what purpose, I pray you, is that terrible blowing of belloes, expressing rather the crakes of thunder than the sweetnesse of a voice?

Abbot Ethelred (twelfth century)

The pipe organ is the most effective leader of congregational singing especially in large congregations. With its wide dynamic range and variety of tonal color and especially its air-supported, sustained sound, the pipe organ offers effective support for communal song. Recently upon blessing the new organ in the Regensburg Cathedral's "Old Chapel," the Holy Father, Pope Benedict XVI wrote:

In the Constitution on Sacred Liturgy of the Second Vatican Council (*Sacrosanctum Concilium*), it is emphasized that the "combination of sacred music and words . . . forms a necessary or integral part of the solemn liturgy" (No. 112). This means that music and song are more than an embellishment (perhaps even unnecessary) of worship; they are themselves part of the liturgical action. Solemn sacred music, with choir, organ, orchestra and the singing of the people, is not therefore a kind of addition that frames the liturgy and makes it more pleasing, but an important means of active participation in worship. The organ has always been considered, and rightly so, the king of musical instruments, because it takes up all the sounds of creation—as was just said—and gives resonance to the fullness of human sentiments, from joy to sadness, from praise to lamentation. By transcending the merely human sphere, as all music of quality does, it evokes the divine. The organ's great range of timbre, from *piano* through to a thundering *fortissimo*, makes it an instrument superior to all others. It is capable of echoing and expressing all the experiences of human life. The manifold possibilities of the organ in some way remind us of the immensity and the magnificence of God.

Psalm 150, which we have just heard and interiorly followed, speaks of trumpets and flutes, of harps and zithers, cymbals and drums; all these musical instruments are called to contribute to the praise of the triune God. In an organ, the many pipes and voices must form a unity. If here or there something becomes blocked, if one pipe is out of tune, this may at first be perceptible only to a trained ear. But if more pipes are out of tune, dissonance ensues and the result is unbearable. Also, the pipes of this organ are exposed to variations of temperature and subject to wear. Now, this is an image of our community in the Church. Just as in an organ an expert hand must constantly bring disharmony back to consonance, so we in the Church, in the variety of our gifts and charisms, always need to find anew, through our communion in faith, harmony in the praise of God and in fraternal love. The more we allow ourselves, through the liturgy, to be transformed in Christ, the more we will be capable of transforming the world, radiating Christ's goodness, his mercy and his love for others. The great composers, each in his own way, ultimately sought to glorify God by their music. Johann Sebastian Bach wrote above the title of many of his musical compositions the letters S.D.G., *Soli Deo Gloria*—to God alone be glory. Anton Bruckner also prefaced his compositions with the words: *Dem lieben Gott gewidmet*—dedicated to the good God. May all those who enter this splendid Basilica, experiencing the magnificence of its architecture and its liturgy, enriched by solemn song and the harmony of this new organ, be brought to the joy of faith. This is my good wish and hope on the day when this new organ is inaugurated.

Pope Benedict XVI[1]

Good pipe organs help attract competent musicians to leadership roles. Allowing a church or cathedral to become vibrant through the opportunity for concerts and school visits strengthens congregational development by allowing youth, as does the idea of "choral scholars," to see and learn about a pipe organ, thus becoming interested enough in the organ to perhaps study and play the instrument. This provides a feeder to the parish for future musicians. The pipe organ truly represents a commitment to future quality in sung worship.

One aspect of the quality of sung worship relates to that of acoustics. If anything can be done to improve the quality of acoustics—it must be done first, more than anything. Acoustics should not be regarded as a peripheral aesthetic consideration. Indeed, the principal beneficiary of an ample acoustic is the singing assembly; the church building itself is the primary resonating instrument of those gathered for worship. Lively interaction between building and assembly is essential both to the spoken and sung participation of the people and the dialogic character of the liturgy. A resonant acoustic is also crucial if choral music is to achieve its particular effect. All voices present in communal worship are well served by good acoustics: congregation, presiders, lectors, cantors, choirs, and instrumentalists.

Ah Music, a magic above all that we do here!

Albus Dumbledore
Headmaster of Hogwarts School
of Witchcraft and Wizardry

Every musician deals with reality by means of her or his fantasy. Our imagination is our basic musical tool for life. As we cope with reality, let us keep in mind that we have the absence of external restraint; we have the freedom to play and explore. We must look at the work of organs and choir as flexibly and imaginatively as possible. We must be able to have fun and enjoy that freedom. This will always be on a paradoxical level—disciplines that bring in us a capacity of seeking our freedom. It is through the care of our soul and connecting through others that we find our place as pastoral musicians.

I suggest the following freedoms and creative elements to you as you discern ways to continually use tradition and creativity as a mantra:

1. On an appointed Sunday, put your singers (choir) into the congregation and have them sing the hymns, descants, harmonies—anything and everything. If the room size permits, have the anthem sung from the midst of the congregation. This will not only help the choir to understand their role as congregational leaders, but will allow those in the congregation who might not have heard part-singing up close and personal to experience an "aural revelation"!

2. When the choir sings their anthem of the day, consider using other parts of your church building (a side chapel, the back, the front, the middle of the nave).

3. Use percussion (and organ, if appropriate) on greatly rhythmic hymns.

4. Specify a "choir-only" verse on a particular hymn, thus allowing the congregation to meditate upon the text.

5. Learn organ improvisation (HUGE IMPORTANCE). Consider the use of chant with the organ used as a drone (for example, *Veni, Emmanuel, Adoro Te Devote*). Use organ repertoire to "self-design" your improvisation for hymns, etc. Don't feel the need to "reinvent the wheel" every time improvisation is called for. An example on *Adoro Te Devote* would be to hold an organ pedal (flute) 16' "D" and with the left hand hold an 8' string or flute tenor "D" and "A" throughout the entire verse. There are numerous basic instructive books to help with organ improvisation. The best tool for improvisation usage, however, is actual organ repertoire. Use a few motives from Bach to Vierne, and use them when you can. The basic tool for organ improvisation (like in any improvisatory art form, such as jazz) is to constantly add to the "bag of tricks." If you start with a pedal drone on *Adoro Te Devote*, add on the next verse a slowly moving *obbligato* flute part, without drone.

6. Let the organ play a larger role in the entrance procession and/or retiring procession. A hymn is not always needed or appropriate. Consider the use of a choral postlude or prelude.

7. Offer a series of music theory classes to your congregation (with additional compensation, of course—unless used as a Lenten penance!).

8. Use "homemade" descants (take the alto line up an octave) on hymns; or in a contemporary hymn, rewrite the harmonic accompaniment part for voices on "ah" and keep it simple. Descants are the most effective tool and don't always need to be used on the last verse!

9. Consider the various uses of singing psalmody such as responsorial psalms using a choir member as a cantor with an antiphon for the

congregation, simplified Anglican chant, or a spoken psalm with an improvised organ accompaniment reflecting text painting.

10. Consider the use of ritual music—ostinato chants, refrain/antiphon repetitions, and solo instruments (flute, piano, etc.) as opportunities for ritual. This is particularly opportune during communion (when the choir receives communion) or when music is needed for a specific liturgical activity, such as a procession (baptism, for example) or the *mandatum* (footwashing). There are several composers who have shown great strength at writing chants of this sort, beginning with the Taizé community, Jacques Berthier, John Bell, Colin Mawby, Margaret Rizza, and Andre Gouze. The use of canons like *"Dona Nobis Pacem"* are also effective.

11. Not to forget: never be afraid to use the "silent" stop on the organ for at least forty-five seconds per liturgy. This might occur before, after, or during the liturgy (which is the most important opportunity to use this stop). I urge everyone who might not have this necessary stop to install one immediately upon his or her church/cathedral organ. Of course, John Cage said, "There is no such thing as silence."

Music is a divine art, not to be used solely for pleasure but as a path for God-realization. Music that is saturated with soul force is the real universal music, understandable by all hearts. Music is not only an art, but also a science. It has the potential for harmonizing mind and body and for developing the deep spiritual aspects of our being.

Paramahansa Yogananda

The kingdom of heaven is made of "every nation, tribe, tongue and people." The gospel unites all cultures together by its message of inclusion, not exclusion. All church music should reflect that. The key word here is "tongue." It's talking about communication. Music is a major form of communication.

Let us all remember that music is the language of the heart. The language itself is neither holy nor unholy. If the heart is profane then what comes out of the heart is profane. If the heart is pure, then what comes out of the heart is pure (Matthew 15:18, 19). It's not the sound of words that make them holy. It's the intention and motive behind the communication. We now have historical evidence that the Hebrew language grew out of the Canaanite dialects. So did their music. They borrowed from their contemporary culture and made it their own.

All music is sacred. It's all about the intent behind the communication—the spirit of music. All music is sacred if it glorifies God and celebrates God's creation. The mission of sacred music should always be concerned with addressing the human condition with hope. The ministry of grace. The ministry of reconciliation. The ministry of healing and mutual respect. Lyrically, we can accomplish that with theology. Sonically we can accomplish that with instrumental beauty. Music is God's gift to reconstruct the human spirit, not tear it apart.

God is the Creator of variety and diversity. There's nothing boring or mono-lithic about creation. It's full of surprises. God brings order out of chaos. That is what the artistic impulse is. And sacred music is full of surprises. Like good humor it employs that "ah-ha" moment when the light bulb goes on and you "get it." A great musical artist knows how to achieve that goal. Yes, there are a lot of predictable moments in sacred music, but let us keep in mind that God is not predictable. Sacred music should expand the soul and fill it with grace and insight into the delight of discovery. Nothing crosses boundaries and melts walls quite as powerfully as music. It's our most powerful tool of communication, as long as we use it wisely.

Note

1. Taken from the following Web site: http://www.vatican.va/holy_father/bene-dict_xvi/speeches/2006/september/documents/hf_ben-xvi_spe_20060913_alte-kapelle-regensburg_en.html

Robert P. Ridgell is the twenty-first assistant organist of historic Trinity Church, Wall Street in New York City, where he directs the Trinity Choristers, a commu-nity-based youth choir program. His prior appointment was director of music of the Philadelphia Cathedral in the Episcopal Diocese of Pennsylvania where he established neighborhood-outreach concerts, an after-school program, and the Cathedral Choir School for Girls, and guided one of the newest Episcopal cathe-dral foundations in the areas of modern liturgical renewal. He has also served as associate director of music at the Cathedral of the Madeleine, Salt Lake City, where he also directed the Eccles Organ Festival and was the choral/music the-ory professor of the Madeleine Choir School, the only coeducational full-time Roman Catholic choir school in the United States.

Robert has performed throughout the United States, Europe, and South Korea and remains an active clinician, teacher, and *improvisateur*. In 2004, he was a finalist of the American Guild of Organists National Competition in Organ Improvisation. In great demand as a conductor of children's choirs, Robert has prepared choristers for performances with the San Francisco Opera, the Mormon Tabernacle Choir, the Utah Symphony as well as several celebrity events including Robert Redford's Holiday Party in Sundance, Utah; the 2002 Winter Olympics; and a performance with EMI recording artist Ricky Fante. He has been founding director of the Trinity Choristers in New York, the Archdiocesan Youth Choir in Philadelphia, the *Alumnae Cantores* of the Princeton Girlchoir, and the Philadelphia Cathedral Choir School for Girls.

What About Unaccompanied Congregational Song?

DONALD SCHELL

A cappella—Accompanying One Another

Much of what I know of people singing together comes from thirty-five years of *a cappella* congregational singing, just people—and Spirit—risking singing together Sunday by Sunday and day by day. From that experience I've learned that people sing naturally, and singing takes us to a place of communion with God and with each other. Singing *a cappella* was a nearly accidental discovery. To begin with it was just wanting to sing even when we didn't have an organist.

Yale undergraduates who wandered through Dwight Chapel's big open doorway to the 5 P.M. weekday liturgy at the Episcopal church at Yale stayed and came back to build that gathering into two dozen or more regulars. It was a big, resonant space—mostly empty except for forty or so chairs. We filled it with our chanted psalms and sung hymns and the eucharistic music. We had some solid singers among us, but it wasn't a singing group, it was a congregation discovering a voice together. For Sundays, we hired an organist to assist our congregation, believing that forty to fifty voices would want and need the support.

I left that college chaplaincy in order to try what I'd learned about community in an ordinary parish setting. I became rector of a small-town congregation in Idaho. People were reluctant to sing, so I found us a good organist who stretched the limitations of our electronic organ to make surprisingly good music. With his help we sang not just the Sunday hymns but also the service music—*Trisagion*, *Gloria*, Creed, *Sanctus*, *Agnus Dei*, and the Lord's Prayer. The accidental learnings about *a cappella* continued there in our midweek liturgy, which grew to include almost a quarter of the congregation's average Sunday attendance (twenty or so people out of eighty). I put the liturgy in the parish hall because the space was flexible and allowed us to face one another for prayer, gather around the table for communion, and adjourn to the other end of the room for a potluck afterward. There was no instrument in the parish hall, and even if there had been, I didn't have budget to hire a midweek keyboard player, but my Sunday organist came to sing with us because he liked the singing.

Twenty-eight years ago, Rick Fabian (who worked with me in the Yale chaplaincy) and I led the first liturgy of St. Gregory of Nyssa, San Francisco. From our work at Yale and my midweek in Idaho, we trusted a small congregation to sing without organ, but in the beginning we imagined a bigger St. Gregory's would eventually require an organ to support and lead the congregation's singing. As the congregation grew, so did our satisfaction and skill at accompanying our own singing together, voices supporting voices. By the time St. Gregory's could expect 150 to 200 people for an ordinary Sunday liturgy or 300 or 400 for Easter Vigil or Christmas Eve, members were delighted that our singing welcomed strangers in to sing with us. It had become evident how the congregation claimed this *a cappella* tradition as their own when we moved into our new, acoustically live church building. We, the clergy leaders, thought an organ would become necessary, but the people filling the church and catching the joy of a bigger group singing *a cappella* said "no" to an organ. And that ownership doesn't just extend to bigger services. Because we're not dependent on an instrument, it seems natural to the lay leaders to sing even our smallest daily morning prayer. Even St. Gregory's staff meetings begin with improvised chanting of a psalm, a silence, and singing the Lord's Prayer together; vestry meetings too begin with a canticle or other sung prayer.

Our singing takes many forms, each one a somewhat different way that we find Spirit in singing together. The 10:30 liturgy grew from the root experience of the Yale student congregation. The music we'd adapted to the Trial Use ICEL texts of the 1970s created a framework of what we call "choral folk traditions," Russian chant, plainsong, simple polyphony, South African freedom songs, American shape note hymnody, and new music that fits that context.

The liturgy begins with a choir anthem (the choir is clustered as part of the informal gathering in the large open space around our altar table). Then the whole congregation sings a *Trisagion*. The singing gathers the people who were chatting and greeting one another and makes them a congregation. The choir (who are not vested) scatter themselves throughout the still-standing congregation, and our music director leads us through enough of the music we'll sing in that Sunday's liturgy that people including visitors learn to trust their own voices. We give everyone all the congregational music, *Music for Liturgy*, our collection of canticles and service music, and a hymn sheet. After the music practice, the whole congregation processes into our seating area for the ministry of the word, and the choir remains scattered among other people to support robust congregational singing. *Music For Liturgy* and a hymn sheet are ALL we put into people's hands, though our inspiration was Thomas Cranmer's example of giving everyone the entire liturgy in 1549. Renewing vernacular liturgy so shortly after Johannes Gutenberg's invention of the printing press, Cranmer's act boldly acknowledged peoples' literacy and honored the authority it gave them to see and understand what had so recently been priestly secrets. It would seem that reading music is today's equivalent of "secrets" in the liturgy.

Like Cranmer, we're concerned for Christian formation and the dignity of every person in the worshiping congregation, but for twenty-first-century people living 450 years after books became common, telling them to read along with printed scriptural and liturgical texts feels like a first grade teacher's ploy to keep order. Instead we offer people listening, singing, and a place for their voice. The message of the media we put into their hands gives music and singing together a place of privilege. Visitors say, "I could tell you really wanted me to sing." We never simply read text together, a practice that today seems numbing to mind and Spirit. After the sermon and in the prayers, our people speak up in their ordinary, individual speaking voices. But the voice of our whole congregation is a singing voice.

After the ministry of the word, when all gather around the altar table for the Eucharist, the choir regroups in the circle to sing their two *a cappella* anthems for that Sunday during the people's communion and during the money offering. With the help of music from both choir and congregation, energy continues to build right through the Eucharist to our final, danced carol (a danced hymn for any season). As we all encircle the table to dance, the choir has slipped back among us offering their solid support to our singing and dancing.

The other two liturgies at St. Gregory's grew up after the initial one at 10:30 and they approach the learning of music and practice of singing together differently.

For 8:30 we improvise some (literally making up chant together) and use the same music for several weeks to encourage people to sing from memory. We launched the 8:30 liturgy when St. Gregory's was about ten years old. It began in a converted space in the small office building on the property where we would eventually build our new church. Its inspiration was a visit my wife and I made to a 7:30 A.M. Rite I Holy Communion in a thriving congregation in a resort and retirement community down the coast from us. My wife and I were enjoying a quiet weekend and slipped into this church looking forward to the rare opportunity of being together in church, as we can't be when I'm working. We were surprised and pleased to find the church quite full and the people singing without organ accompaniment. I don't know how many times I've heard that the early liturgy group in Episcopal parishes are the people who don't like organ music. I'd never before seen a congregation explore that old maxim to find what music works with early risers who want a more contemplative, predictable liturgy. We didn't sing any hymns, it was just Merbecke's setting of the *Kyrie, Gloria, Sanctus,* and *Benedictus,* and *Agnus Dei,* and Old Hundredth as the bread, wine, and money offerings were carried up to the altar rail.

We concluded that people who would like an early Sunday liturgy would sing happily if the music was familiar and relatively unchanging. For our first years of the early liturgy at St. Gregory's the music never changed. Eventually we decided to make an annual cycle of seasonally appropriate music that changes every six to eight weeks (we divide the long post-Pentecost commons in half). We use an 8:30 music book, which contains service music, canticle, hymn in procession to the altar table, and a carol, for eight Sundays in a row. We do give people printed music for this, but over time they learn the music by heart.

This early liturgy at St. Gregory's grew slowly. By now it's twenty-five to thirty-five people on a Sunday including some children. The size of the group and their ease with the music reinforces a very strong sense of singing together. Regulars describe that liturgy as strong, tender, sweet, peaceful, refreshing, and comforting. Repetition of the same music week by week gives the small group (with no choir) the confidence to try harmonies. Singing the seasonal music becomes better each week as people learn it by heart. The group is welcoming to strangers and has a strong, natural pastoral care network, both signs that the musical formation is building a healthy congregation.

This liturgy also includes about fifty verses of psalmody (the lectionary-appointed psalm with a cluster of other psalms around it that are thematically in dialogue). We sing antiphonally, side to side, in the congregation, dividing ourselves into two groups of around fifteen people. Free chant gets people past the memory of whoever it was who told them they couldn't sing. Dissonance is a natural part of music; and in this singing, people become less frightened of dissonance and also find and enjoy consonances without the paralyzing fear of "wrong notes." They learn the feel of consonance in body resonance and because every note they offer fits, they don't hold back.

As the presider chants the words of collects and the eucharistic prayer, the people drone on a single note like the *eison* of Byzantine chant. Visitors are moved and astonished at this experience of everyone participating in offering the prayer, and regulars tell us that their listening has been transformed by the practice of this simple monotone and the resonance it sets up in their bodies as they're praying. Like visitors, they also say that they've never experienced such evident sharing in corporate prayer.

Our 7:30 Sunday evening liturgy is the newest and smallest Sunday liturgy. We've shaped it for younger adults at the end of their weekend and have set it in candlelight. We have welcomed the musical challenge that pools of light in darkness brought to our usual ways of singing. People's faces in candlelight are radiant. But we discovered that printed music in their hands was too hard to read in the soft light, so we began to re-create ancient practices of bookless singing to allow people to sing well without music they must read.

This liturgy began by borrowing music from many sources (including Taizé, Iona, and world music), but as we've developed it, we've begun creating new music that our volunteer cantors teach and model by ear. This is a way of beginning to renew an aural, preliterate musical tradition. How did people in other times learn to sing from the cues of a leader? We're gathering hints and recollections from camp songs and traditional choral song from Africa. We want to find ways to achieve harmony and satisfying complexity by layering music using multiple melodies, rounds, ostinato, and other such techniques. All this expands our understanding of learning by heart. Rediscovery of call and repeat and call and response forms of singing, as well the singing that comes from repetition in a round or canon takes us to new collaborative territory in communication, relationship, and exchange.

It seemed natural to St. Gregory's to explore new ways for a cantor to invite and embellish congregational singing, because we had already discovered such richness and variety of spiritual practice in *a cappella* congregational singing. Bookless liturgical music adds fresh hints that learning and shared learning of music are in themselves spiritual practice.

In all these different liturgies, we welcome all the voices present and nearly everyone does sing. Sometimes we falter. Some music may require choir support and more than one attempt to really own a new piece, but with week-by-week practice, people come to enjoy singing so much that they're willing to fail on the way to learning.

Singing together is a core practice of Christian (and human) formation. Where the church is facing life and death squarely, the place of singing is clear. St. Paul exhorts a struggling, persecuted church to sing frequently and not tire of singing God's praise. The Gospels remind us starkly that the last act Jesus and his disciples shared before he went out to face betrayal and death was singing a psalm. With these beginnings, what sort of church or community would decide singing was optional or decorative?

Or to turn it the other way, what could be more natural than our congregation, both choir and even a good number of "nonsingers" taking our singing to the bedside of parishioners in the hospital, at home, or in hospice care. Because our people are accustomed to singing without instruments, the congregation's familiar songs and canticles make their way to the bedsides of people who are sick, injured, or facing death. What we see there is exactly the same spiritual power of music.

I first experienced this power when a Roman Catholic friend asked me to come pray and sing at the bedside of a young Sudanese Catholic who had a severe concussion from hitting his head in a warehouse fall. I went to the intensive care unit dressed in white cassock and cross and was greeted by his Sudanese friends. We sang and prayed around his bedside for an hour with him showing no response at all. But the next day he awoke and thanked his friends for the music.

Suzanna's story makes the spiritual and community-gathering power of music even clearer:

A year ago as summer was ending, Zanna (as she is known to her friends), an alto in our congregation's choir, was hit by a truck downtown. Watching lights and traffic to make his turn, the driver gunned the truck too late to see Zanna in the crosswalk. The impact hurled her sickeningly through the air and she landed on her head. Physicians in the hospital trauma center warily evaluated her terrible headache and groggy state and saw things turn abruptly critical; Zanna lost consciousness and showed no response at all to stimuli.

Serious intracranial bleeding could do this, and it would kill her. Her doctors induced a coma to slow brain activity and in emergency surgery determined brain swelling rather than bleeding had provoked the crisis. They removed part of her skull to relieve the pressure and put it aside in the tissue bank, grimly hoping she'd recover and they'd eventually put it back.

Zanna's induced coma kept her on a respirator in intensive care. Over the next days, her doctors tried repeatedly to ease her out of the coma, but unsuppressed brain activity provoked dangerous seizures. The doctors doubted now that she could ever recover consciousness, and they began asking the family to consider removing life support.

Within a day of the accident the choir came to sing to Zanna. It was different from other times they'd sung at bedsides. Some felt so helpless; they assumed they were singing her a good-by that she'd never hear. Some came expecting to see a friend, and were dismayed to find a living body without evidences of Zanna's own spirit.

Still, because it was what they knew to do, they sang pieces and hymns they knew that she had loved, singing them in four parts. They took courage from the sound of their singing circle and sang some more. When they were done, the nurses thanked them, explaining that sometimes in a coma people can hear even when they show no response at all.

With the nurses' prompt we asked that anyone visiting Zanna sing to her. Even our shakiest, least confident singers heard the need and sang. Day by day she seemed unchanged, until one day when my wife and I, and a houseguest we'd taken along, were quietly singing to her, Zanna's eyes moved under her eyelids. We stopped. Her eyes stopped moving. We sang again. Her eyes moved again. I called the ICU nurse. She said it could be random nerve firings, but it also might be something hopeful. Hearing this flicker of response choir members and other friends came to sing more often.

A small group from the choir was singing to her when Zanna opened her eyes. But she seemed to see without consciousness. Her eyes darted frantically from face to object to face without any sign of recognition. If her ears connected us to her mind and soul, her eyes certainly didn't show it. Did she know the music? Did this disappointing presence recognize they'd sung one of her favorite pieces?

Her injured brain seemed to have lost everything. Weeks passed before she spoke her first words, which came muted and flat as she spoke them over and over as though she couldn't hear herself or recall what she'd just spoken. The words barely lived except for a disturbing edge of fear, confusion, and anger in their tone and on her face. We did what we could—we kept visiting and kept singing to her. Her listening was as intent and peaceful as we'd see her. Names appeared. A few sentences. Then she recognized people. Physical therapy taught her to stand and begin to walk. The doctors transferred her to an intensive rehab facility fifty miles south of us. Choir members drove down for visits, and so did my wife and I. A parish family that was nearby joined our effort.

As Zanna progressed, she seemed to grasp the magnitude of her challenge, and miraculously with it came the first signs of her own hope—initially in deadpan speech that hinted at humor. But one day she smiled.

Her treatment plan required moving her again. The next stage was the slow, slow work of long-term rehabilitation and the place for that was even farther south, a hillside ranch more than two hours from her congregation and friends. Choir and other friends were determined to keep visiting and singing, but the three-and-a-half-hour round-trip cut down on the number of visits. A little family of three became her lifeline.

A month or so after Zanna had been moved there, and ten months after the accident, my wife and I took three copies of our congregation's *Music for Liturgy*, book with us for our first visit to Zanna in the ranch rehab facility. We walked slowly outdoors to a picnic table in the shade of a fruit tree. Zanna could walk alone if someone walked close enough to help her if she needed help.

At the picnic table we three slowly leafed through the music book, singing piece after piece together, all hoping to find something she'd remember. Before the accident Zanna's clear, confident sight reading would have led us. Now we sang quietly to encourage her to keep trying, my wife and I negotiating as we sang to know which of us was holding pitches, rhythm, and pace, the throughline of the music.

Zanna sang like someone laboring to recall something, a person who knew for dreadful certain that she couldn't trust her memory. Sometimes she would chide herself with frustration and go silent. We kept singing and Zanna would once again take up the work and join in. No matter how frustrated she got, she kept saying, "Let's try that again." And so we did until she said, "Let's try another one."

Music held the three of us in a circle of learning and communication. Zanna watched herself on the verge of discovery as she worked to sing. I asked her how she experienced the effort. She said reading words and music together was difficult. I asked her whether it would help to read the words together aloud with each new piece. "Let's try that," she said. As hard as it was for her, Zanna showed no fear. The music beckoned. We felt the sheer physicality of the challenge and sensed how the brain stays alive, grows, and forges a self through the learning process.

Reading text together we all heard how fragmented Zanna's reading was. Like a bright first grader, she got most of the words on her first try, but she read sound by sound and word by word; hearing the words in sentences and complete ideas seemed beyond her reach and she knew it—except that after her reading, my wife or I would repeat what she had just read and Zanna would say, "Ah, yes."

With the words in mind, we'd try the notes, note by note on "la, la, la." As with the words, Zanna sang disjointed notes always hoping she might remember and recognize musical phrases or a whole melody. Sometimes she rushed ahead to venture a note. We felt her disappointment when it seemed the note had tumbled in from another melody. No one said it, but we all three knew she was looking and hoping to find a song that had somehow survived in her memory.

The slow work did turn notes into music, and as with the sentences, Zanna felt and recognized not the shape of a melody, but that piece by piece, the best she could say was, "I think I maybe sang that one before," a small victory after four or five repetitions of a piece she'd sung fifty or a hundred times in church.

After six or so pieces of music my wife suggested we try the old Shaker tune, "Simple Gifts," a congregational favorite. "'Tis the gift to be simple, 'tis the gift to be free . . . ,"

Zanna's relief and joy at simple recognition burst on us like a sunrise. We sang a little more together, "'Tis the gift to come down where we want to be," and then Zanna stopped us, wanting to test her memory of the way forward. "I know it. The next part goes, 'And when we find ourselves in the place just right . . .'"

And it was just right, tentative, but all there—words, tune, sentence, meaning, and memory in one conversation—musical declaration. Then briefly, "I don't think that part sounds quite right," and she tried words and notes as she thought she remembered them until she found her way to the tune our three memories shared. Then she sang the whole again from the first line and through to "We'll be in the valley of love and delight." Then once again, together, Zanna nodding her head as she sang with us. She greeted notes and words like old friends or even a friend where the relationship has begun to bud to romance. We sang again, and she kept in tune with us (as she had not done before) and her accurate pitches seemed to help join the words into sentences.

I asked her if she wanted to try singing it through by herself. She did, and as she sang through a piece that was finally her own, we felt her pleasure at singing something known by heart. "Simple Gifts" had remained mysteriously whole in her memory. Despite old neural paths that weren't working, "Simple Gifts" bridged the chasm of broken function connecting Zanna to her old self. We watched music guide her to a process of creation, remembering, and interpretation. Like a hidden spring deep in the forest, music bubbling up renewed Zanna's freedom, giving her back a self and a life.

Music we learn by heart rests whole within us and makes a vessel of our personhood, a refuge to meet and be held in God's Spirit. And the community of the three of us, welcoming, caring faces to Zanna, friends with context missing, was healed and restored as well. She remembered the music, knew us, remembered the congregation, pictured the church. The music led her from fragmented isolated self to speaking of "we" and "us."

Jesus knew that singing gives us life and makes us human. A poignant Gospel saying captures his frustration with the people to whom he preached in the marketplace, people not moved to mourning by John the Baptist's weeping and wailing, but also not moved to sing and dance by Jesus' piping a joyful tune—people lonely and alone in the jostling crowd of buyers and sellers.

Amy McCreath, Episcopal chaplain at M.I.T., once described her experience of leading ropes courses as part of leadership training and team building with her student group. Amy observed that the power of a ropes course is that success depends on the group. So too, a music leader who touches a group's hope and desire to accomplish something together quickly invites the group to discover the power in the learning itself. Human voices defining the melody and tonality unquestionably carry that power and authority.

Like a river, and not a museum or a variety show, a liturgy carries our thoughts, our prayers, our memories, and our feelings in the flow of breath and heartbeat, natural movement and grace. Even the plain speech of preaching or announcements finds cadences and resonance from the music that surrounds it. Liturgy and music are a single whole that unfolds over time.

Amy's ropes course leader is a person who takes the calculated risk (with real danger) of asking people to count on one another for the sake of community accomplishment and safety. Music leaders and clergy must develop a similar confidence, a calculated fearlessness that assumes people can find their way if they are allowed to plunge in and struggle a bit if need be. Yet vestries will scold a priest or church musician for asking the congregation to experience such struggle, as though "Sing to the Lord a new song!", the exclamation-command that begins both Psalm 96 and Psalm 98, is a curse or a punishment. Why? The obvious answer is fear, which is to say lack of trust and of love.

People fear making mistakes and fear their voice standing out on a wrong note. Leaders must face fearlessly into people's discomfort. The forgiving laughter of utter failure is too rare in church. Without mistakes there is no learning. Wrong notes and the creative forgiving response of "Good, now let's try that again" take us to a transcendent place where finding the notes we were looking for also gives us a glimpse of who and what walks beside us as we sing.

Just as untrained singers must let go of their fear of making mistakes, clergy and church musicians must let go of their fear of boring people. Repetition makes a musician of a "nonsinger." Trained musicians and musical sophisticates often project their own boredom onto the congregation. This is a place for a beginner's mind. With enough repetition of a hymn or other piece of music, untrained singers pass through their fear of mistakes to a blessed place of patient, childlike practice singing a piece until they finally learn it, and then singing it over and over again by heart. The most skilled of us relearning such openness can recover delight in the simplest music, the music that composers tell us is so difficult to write and that people recognize because it's so easy to love.

Music makes our bodies our teachers. Daily, after quiet morning prayer, I bicycle to Aikido practice, a reconciling martial arts practice where we take turns playing attacker and defender for the sake of learning to blend, join, and transform an attack into a flying, reconciling dance. "Mind follows body," my Aikido sensei, Jimmy Friedman says. "I don't care what you intend or mean. What I'm trying to give you is a way to let your mind find out what you intend. In this spiritual practice, you body is your teacher."

Our practice of singing makes our bodies our teachers. If our body and the making of our voices and our shared voice is the practice, we focus on how we make music rather than thinking of the music as a finished product. Voice training (depending on the teacher's approach) can take away trained musicians' ability to observe the embodied musical practice of nonsingers or nonmusicians. The physical resonance of our own voice and the voices of the people we're singing with make our bodies reverberate. The voices of friends and people we love touch us, literally making our bodies reverberate in comforting, recognizable ways. When we listen with our whole bodies, we find that music is much more than what appears on the page. There is music in our sharing it, our making it, and our hearing together what we've made. The music is in our bodies, and it's in our listening.

Music as we know it would not be possible except for the synthesis listeners and performers make. Our listening makes the music for each of us. Even in a concert, the music isn't up on the stage. What is on the stage is performers making a sequence of sounds one after the other. The music is in their hearts and memories, and we hear the music-makers' music by the music-recognizing within us.

All humans speak the language of music and even recognize some of its subtler grammar and vocabulary. In fact we learn language itself by our inherent musical gift of hearing sound patterns in modes, intervals, and rhythmic patterns; remembering them; and attaching them to meaning. Zanna's brain, her recovering self, just like a world-famous singer or instrumental performer, was working to create music by remembering an emerging sequence of sounds, holding it in memory, and joining the sounds together to find what sound, note, and chord say to the next and the next and so on.

Any child learning to speak inhabits the primordial world that renaissance opera composers imagined. They were convinced that the first humans sang everything. Some anthropologists suggest that those composers imagined something close to true. Voice and percussion music may be older in human history than speech itself. Pitch and rhythm are the fertile ground from which speech grew.

Music made us human, and singing builds and restores a human person and builds community. We find our way to communion by discovering our rhythm and voice, by shaping a tonality, by adjusting tuning together, and by our breathing (and perhaps dancing) that give us one breath and one movement.

Singing asks that we give generously while letting go of our competitive urge to control others. Singing disciplines a congregation or community to breathe together; it is literally a practice that brings us to common inspiration, one Spirit. As we learn that singing encourages us to add our sweetest and best voice to the community, we may finally notice that none of us sings as often as we're called to.

Certainly communities that depend completely on instruments don't sing as often as they're called to. The spiritual practice of singing is most immediately evident and accessible where the singing community collaborates exclusively in human voices. In other words, where the path of melody counts on human pathfinders to discover it together, the singers will discover God accounting within their acting together.

After enough "said, low mass" liturgies, people begin to imagine that music is an aesthetic nicety in worship—pleasing, decorative but unessential, like incense or flowers. The combination of convenience and a "merely aesthetic" rationale for music leads congregations to leave singing out whenever they fear they may not do it well enough.

All that I write about here is available to any congregation that sings. As I said, *a cappella* congregational singing was something I stumbled into. I have enjoyed congregational singing with instruments. But I've also seen how people who depend on instrumentalists and won't sing without them don't make the great communal discoveries of singing together. Strong instrumental leadership gives many people the impression that the organ or other instrument is making music while they're just singing along (or in many cases not singing along).

We begin and end at a place where words fail us. God waits for us in our singing. In the end there's no good name or adequate description for the practice of people singing together without instrumental leadership or support. "Unaccompanied" sounds lonely, but when we sing together, we're in the best company we can have. "Without instruments" says nothing about what's happening, only about what's not there. Even "*a cappella*" that I've been using hints at monastic chapel and general churchiness and makes music sound "special" in a way that silences many people's singing. We begin and end at a place where words fail us, which isn't at all bad when we remember that

Everything is music

We've come to the place where everything is music
Everything is music, let it play.

Why do you stay in jail when the door is wide open?
Let the beauty that you love be what you do.

Stop talking now, open up the window,
The one right here in the middle of your heart.
Let go your hands, sit down in this circle,
You know you got no need to keep yourself apart.

The day you wake up sad and empty, don't go back to sleep.
There's a million ways to kneel and kiss the ground.

Don't worry now, about saving all these songs,
There's so many more just waiting to be found.
And if all these instruments should disappear
We would still hear something coming up from way down in the ground

Because, we've come to the place where everything is music
Everything is music, let it play.[1]

Some Practical Suggestions

- Offer explicit blessing and encouragement whenever people stumble; forgive (even laugh at) mistakes and try again.
- Encourage people to sing naturally and to listen to one another.
- Notice which piece sings well quietly. Sing it enough to find confidence and then ask people to sing it more quietly. Quiet singing, particularly when people are beginning to sing in parts, is a huge help in listening.
- Risk singing at unexpected times and places.
- Trust enough in people's pleasure in learning to sing something new to allow them to sing the same thing many times. For example, using a new hymn or canticle for two or three weeks in a row.
- Develop a few special congregational songs to honor people's birthdays, anniversaries, and special accomplishments—try "God, Grant Them Many Years" (*Wonder, Love, and Praise*, no. 824, from Church Publishing) or find an *Alleluia* that people love and use it on many occasions—make a suitable piece a congregational theme song.
- Pace and phrase music to the breath (a little longer phrases at a somewhat brisker pace than typical hymn-singing or chant).
- Develop a clear distinction between rhythmic singing and chant; a drum helps sustain a steady beat in rhythmic singing; a drone, speech rhythm, and natural breathing between phrases helps find the natural ebb and flow or softer pulse of chant.

Note

1. Kris Delmhorst, track 12 on her CD, *Strange Conversation*, lyrics adapted from Jalaluddin Rumi as translated by Coleman Barks reprinted by permission of the author.

The Reverend Donald Schell is the retired rector of St. Gregory of Nyssa Episcopal Church in San Francisco, California, where he has developed a unique liturgy that is grounded in ancient orthodoxy while providing a "progressive" worship opportunity for Episcopalians. Music, dance, and dialogue are hallmarks of St. Gregory's unique worship service. The Reverend Schell, a dynamic speaker and a celebrated author, is on the front edge of leaders in Episcopal liturgy.

He is a founding board member of Spiritual Directors International, an Aikido black belt and certified teacher, and author (with Maria Schell) of *My Father, My Daughter* and *Pilgrims on the Road to Santiago*.

What About Additional Services?

First Friday at Christ Church Cathedral, Nashville, Tennessee

SHELDON CURRY

Silence—the air thick with anticipation. It is 6 o'clock on a Friday evening. People gather quietly, find a place and sit. Some kneel. Some pray.

Then . . . *THOOMB! THOOM-BA-DA! THOOMB! THOOM-BA-DA!*

Taiko drums—large, resonate low-pitched drums from ancient Japan—begin relentless pounding. Sound bounces from stone wall to stone wall. Not so much loud, as insistent. Then, out of nowhere—wind chimes and Tibetan prayer bells. Next, a solo bamboo flute followed by African oud (a relative of the European lute). Both slip almost unnoticed into the air. A whiff of incense sneaks into the candlelit cavernous room, inching toward the stained glass windows. Singers hum a long single pitch, weaving an aural velvet thread into the tapestry.

This is preservice music for an Episcopal worship service. Not in Macao or Bali, but Christ Church Cathedral, Nashville, Tennessee, a few blocks south of the Ryman Auditorium, mother church of country music—the original home of the Grand Ole Opry.

And I am conducting a group of six instrumentalists and thirteen singers. We are performing music that none of them saw until the preservice rehearsal ninety minutes ago. Thus begins "First Friday," an experimental liturgy started in 2000.

As do many others of the series, this service includes a professional dance company. Occasionally short theater pieces shed light on liturgical readings. Tonight throughout the service, in front of God and everyone, a professional artist creates, on canvas, images reflective of the liturgy. Roughly 250 people join in worship, singing a hymn they have neither seen nor heard before tonight.

How did this happen? And why?

A Call from the Dean

During the summer of 1999 I received a call from my friend and colleague, the Reverend Canon Anne Stevenson. For several years before and after Dean Kenneth Swanson became dean at Christ Church Cathedral, I served as cantor and sang in the choir there. I had moved on to direct music at other parishes within the diocese, but the cathedral staff, Dean Swanson, and I kept in touch often.

The cathedral's Sunday morning liturgies, long-standing, well attended, traditional, worked beautifully, but Dean Swanson wanted an added service—one that would explore the edges of what people expect in Episcopal worship. He charged the Reverend Canon Anne Stevenson with gathering a small group who would serve as guides on this liturgical journey. She asked me to direct the musical portion of those once-a-month services.

Collaboratively, this small group created the "First Friday" liturgies. Anne served as the group's leader. Alice Nichols, a wonderfully creative lay liturgist, helped craft each Eucharist. Grete Gryzwana, a choreographer originally from Los Angeles, new to Nashville and founder of Epiphany Dance Company, directed the professional dancers. Roberta LaBour, a lay member of the cathedral, added expertise in theater, costume, and set design. I was in charge of music.

Dean Swanson's idea was to provide a shortened, but complete Eucharist (no longer than an hour or so) for people who were finishing their downtown workweek. Those attending the service might or might not be Christ Church parishioners. He hoped "First Friday" might attract people who were not necessarily "church folk," but who were open and searching for a spiritual punctuation mark to end the week.

My job was to create music for this unusual Episcopal Eucharist; music designed specifically for a worship service whose attendees were decidedly NOT familiar with church history and liturgy. Worship would be at 6:00 P.M. on the first Friday evening of each month. There was to be a theme for each service and that theme would change month to month. One month might feature Celtic music, the next medieval chant, the next Hispanic or African or New Age or Big Band Jazz.

"First Friday" music was to be separate from the Christ Church music program. Instrumentalists and vocalists came from outside. I was to fashion music unlike that heard in a Sunday morning cathedral service. We never used their majestic new pipe organ.

Challenges flourished. Our budget was small. We could not afford to pay musicians for rehearsals. On the "First Friday" of each month, musicians arrived at 4:00 P.M. to rehearse. By 5:30 we had to be ready to go. Circumstances demanded excellent sight readers—people who could embrace a ninety-minute, pressure-packed, no-nonsense rehearsal, then turn around, take a deep breath, and calmly present top-notch musical offerings as if the notes were old hat.

From September through June, each service included dance—usually four to six minutes in length. Sometimes as long as twenty minutes. These dance pieces—music and choreography—were usually original creations. Each month I wrote original hymns, service music, incidental meditations, and music for before and after the service.

My task was daunting. I ate it up!

"Well, *That* Certainly Didn't Work!"

When I first discussed these services with Ken and Anne, they told me to take *real* chances. Taking *real* chances presumes foul-ups and failure. We had a few—many of which were mine—especially early on.

As I said, one of my goals was to use new hymns in each service. If you have been around church much, you know what an outrageous proposal that is! People did not know what to do. It took me a while to figure out (mostly by trial and error) how far I could go. Go, that is, and reasonably expect to keep eager explorers with me, willing to step off the ledge into musical unknown territory. Patience met experience and eventually we discovered a middle ground where all could comfortably meet—a place where the music might be new, but the text at least somewhat familiar, or vice versa. In some services, the hymns were entirely new to everyone. Worshipers began to expect the unexpected. So much so that one night after a service, a disgruntled regular attendee complained to me that she actually *knew* one of the hymns. You must understand; that doesn't happen in Episcopal churches! "Surprise" became an integral part of worship.

Anglicans are renowned for corporate psalm chant style that bears the denomination's name. When done well, it is stunningly beautiful, a gorgeous Victorian tradition. One evening I tried using this chant form with an unusual, unfamiliar poetic verse. The music was slow but used atypical chord progressions, and percussion interspersed itself randomly throughout.

It was a disaster. Worshipers limped through, sheepishly whimpering the words, heads cowed, embarrassed, desperate eyes searching, hoping for rescue that never came. We stuck our tails between our corporate legs and carried on.

Dean Swanson met me after the service, grinned, shook my hand and said, "Well, *that* certainly didn't work! Congratulations on finding the edge of the envelope."

The important fact in this incident is that, no matter what unorthodox idea I tried, the support I felt from clergy was unwavering. I never once heard the words, "Don't you EVER do that again!"

It was no secret; we were creating this liturgy as we went along. We couldn't look at an "owner's manual" to find out how to proceed, what to do next; no such manual existed. To my knowledge, it still doesn't. We followed the Rite II Eucharistic outlined in the Book of Common Prayer (This *was* a cathedral after all!), but many times we switched sections around to suit the flow of the service.

At some point during the second year, after much hard work, careful thought, and a lot of prayer, the service began to gel. We began to sense what unheard-of way of proceeding best met our corporate purpose—worship of an astonishing, graceful, loving God.

This blossoming happened because those creating the liturgy believed the task we were taking on was not only possible, but also necessary. Without total commitment from each member of the team, we would have stopped (or been stopped) before we found our stride. We had to trust one another and trust that God would lead us where God wanted. We believed in each other's gifts and skills and in God's ability to shape our loaves and fishes into a eucharistic feast. We had to listen carefully to one another and be honest in our communication. There were times we disagreed, our patience stretched taut in our time-crunched dealings with one another. Those occasions were few because we realized, I think, that we were striving together toward the same end. There were times in a liturgy meeting someone would ask me, "Are you sure this is going to work?" I would respond, "No. I am not sure. But this is where I feel led. If it *does* work, we'll open an area we haven't explored yet." And so we felt our way along.

Thanks be to God, we reached many redemptive, miraculous places together. We learned a lot about God and ourselves. We discovered how much we do not understand about the mysterious workings of worship. Looking back, I realize something. When unforeseen circumstances took events out of our control (i.e., the power went out, a reader didn't show up, an unplanned fire began smoldering on the reredos, as it once did *during* a service!); it was in those times, God blessed us with some of our rarest, richest worship experiences. LOVE grinned, took our well-intentioned offerings, mixed them with our weakness and openness and fashioned them into an awe-full adventure we never had in mind. One we relished.

So . . . Do I Dare Try This at My Church?

I don't know. I don't know that everyone should. I think there are churches where worship like this might seem inappropriate or forced. One cannot lead people where they do not, at some level, want to go. If my negative comments stop you from trying, yours might be one of those churches. And that is not bad!

If you want to go ahead, however, I offer these observations.

Music is a powerful, powerful tool. It ignites passions and incites riots. It can be a "Balm in Gilead" or a weapon of "mass" disruption. It can also split a parish into factions. The negative effect of music used unwisely and without regard to its influence has destroyed churches and ministries. The First Friday crew at Christ Church Cathedral was purposeful in keeping a wall between First Friday liturgies and Sunday morning worship. The respective purposes of Friday and Sunday, while in some ways similar, were not the same. We used worship tools for First Friday that would have been out of place in a traditional Sunday morning Rite I or Rite II Eucharist. I don't recall who said, "I like broccoli *and* vanilla ice cream, but both suffer irreparably when served together." The same is true in worship styles. Keeping these services intentionally separate kept the integrity of both intact.

> I cannot imagine a worship series like First Friday being successful without the full support of the clergy. The impetus must, I think, come from the rector, or at least be agreeable to her or him and have the consent of all concerned including the Vestry and other church leaders.

Be wary. Guard against "alternative" worship as concert event. We were careful not to use the chancel, altar, or reredos areas as "stages" in a strictly theatrical sense. Instrumentalists and singers were seated in the balcony; they were unseen leaders, not "entertainers." Usually, they appeared in the bulletin as "Gallery Musicians," not as individuals. Today's consumer-driven world gets us into the habit of attending "events." People expect entertainment, sometimes even in church. Worship is not that, or at least ought not be. Worship is exploring and celebrating and communicating with God. There is a time for concerts or fundraisers in churches, but that time is not worship time. "First Friday" could easily become a promotional gimmick; that is simply wrong.

We did not publicize the "theme" of an approaching service. We might hint in a poster or the church newsletter, but those attending the services soon learned to abandon preconceptions. If they went to a First Friday service, they were as likely to hear medieval hurdy-gurdy as they were to hear jazz or Middle Eastern whirling dervishes or a woman's choir chanting Hildegard *a cappella*. The diversity was intentional. We wanted to insure that First Friday could not become the "folk" service, or the "Celtic" service, or the "hip-hop" or "chant" or "fill-in-the-blank" service. The small liturgy group, working together, set the theme for each month's service. The lectionary always controlled our direction and decisions. For instance, one service in November came close to All Saints' Day. Nashville has an expanding Hispanic community, so we decided to offer a "*Dia de Los Muertos*" (Day of the Dead) service using mostly Hispanic music and musicians. The colorfully decorated sanctuary alluded to centuries old traditions. Paper cut-outs (*papel picado*) lined the chancel ceiling. The nave featured several homemade altars piled high with vivid, fanciful offerings or remembrances (*ofrendas*) honoring the departed. The service was bilingual. It was deeply moving and enlightening.

I wrote music for First Friday services—lots of music. I am a composer and writing was a part of my job description. But even if it had not been, I discovered that suitable music was simply not available. First Friday was not a praise and worship service in the typical evangelistic sense. Not "Blended" worship. There was no praise team. We did not project song sheets of contemporary Christian music (CCM) on jumbotron screens in the front of the sanctuary.

This is an important point. There exists today, not only in the Episcopal church, but also in many other Christian denominations deep divisions. Fights erupt and churches split. Emotional, spiritual, and even political factions take aim at choice of worship music and styles. Friends become enemies. Ministries are damaged; jobs lost. It is neither my intent nor place to use this forum to advocate for one side or the other in this debate, but the fact was and is, CCM was not what Christ Church Cathedral was about. In addition, the First Friday directive was to provide a worship experience that was distinctly "other" than the norm . . . whether that norm be traditional Anglican classic music or Willow Creek Community Church rock music. So we steered clear of both CCM *and* traditional Episcopal music. Even Taizé was off-limits.

Because Christ Church is a diocesan cathedral and sponsored First Friday services as a gift to the diocese and the city of Nashville, I was able to use singers and musicians from various places. If I wanted to use a musician from another church, I contacted that person with the full prior knowledge and consent of the music director of the church concerned. In keeping with the purpose of the service, many participants were not "church people" at all. Nashville is home to some of the most creative musicians in the world. Some work in the recording industry. Some tour with various artists. Some play or sing in bars or nightclubs. In my work as a professional musician and composer, it was my privilege to work with many of them. Usually if I asked, they would play for First Friday. In one service we used a percussion troupe from Ghana; only one of its members spoke any English. They came to my attention through a local international education center. In more than one case, Nashville instrumentalists and singers were as surprised as were the worshipers. They experienced unqualified acceptance. No-strings-attached grace. They encountered ultimate creativity far exceeding their own. For several of them "First Friday" became church.

"Well," some say to me, "that could only work in a large cathedral in a major city. And . . . I am not a composer!"

I won't say it was easy. It was not. And it won't be for you. But I firmly believe similar programs are possible anywhere—with little or no extra budget. Where 2 or 3 or 217 are gathered together there will be *someone* who plays *something*: someone who sings but not in "the choir." Talented composers and songwriters live everywhere. These people are often willing to join in, but no one asks. Look for a flute player or bassoonist from the local community college. Go to a song-writer night at a local club or coffeehouse. If there is a need, it is possible to search out singers and a small group of people who have the talent and creative energy to put toward fashioning liturgy. Again, I caution against using this model as a replacement for traditional worship in a traditional Christian community—a way of "upgrading" or "modernizing" the gospel. (First Friday was many things but never was it "dumbed-down" McWorship!) But as an adjunct to regular Episcopal worship, I think it served well. I know there are people attending Christ Church now because they once attended a First Friday service.

As I write this, I use the past tense on occasion because I am no longer at Christ Church Cathedral. In the summer of 2007, I moved to Houston, Texas, to work in a smaller church, St. Stephen's Episcopal. It is not an expansive Gothic cathedral, but it is a beautiful sacred place. These people share a history of exploring boundaries; they know about adventure and risk. Together we will see what the holy journey holds for us.

"First Friday" continues, however. If you happen to be in Nashville on the First Friday of the month, stop by the cathedral at 6 P.M. You can find more information at: http://www.christcathedral.org/firstfriday1.html.

Sheldon Curry is now the director of music at St. Stephen's Episcopal Church in Houston and the composer of hundreds of titles, both choral and instrumental, published in various national catalogs. He is a graduate of Baylor University where he studied choral music under Robert Young and Euell Porter, and composition privately with *Prix de Rome* winner Richard Willis.

He has written music for recording artists, recorded original music for film and television, and is a two-time Grammy-nominated record producer. In addition, he has directed church music for over twenty years.

What About Additional Services?

Taizé at All Saints' Episcopal Church, Beverly Hills, California

THOMAS FOSTER

> God of all eternity, Savior of every life, in the footsteps of the holy witnesses to Christ down through the ages, from the apostles and the Virgin Mary to those of today, enable us to dispose ourselves inwardly day by day to place our trust in the Mystery of the Faith.

Thus reads a prayer from the late Brother Roger of the community of Taizé. It speaks of the ethos of the miraculous French village that has drawn thousands in pilgrimage from all over the world for sixty-five years. While it may be true that the very word Taizé elicits a variety of responses, one can only be moved by the very ministry of prayer and reconciliation nurtured by this community. Worship in the style of Taizé, and its music, has spread worldwide as a result of this ministry.

I was blessed by many experiences leading worship in this style on a monthly basis during my tenure at All Saints' Church, Beverly Hills, for several years, as well as in other locations throughout the country. I can attest to the viability of such a worship form; it has found a home in many houses of worship.

In August of 2005 the world mourned the tragic death of Brother Roger, the founding prior of Taizé. The succeeding prior, Brother Alois Löser, had been previously chosen by Brother Roger, and the work of the community thankfully continues.

The following is a slightly edited excerpt from an article published in the *Journal of the Association of Anglican Musicians* in December of 1996 and again in 2001. In addition, I would commend the wealth of material on the subject of Taizé currently available on the Internet.

The title of this article should at once seem anachronistic. Those who know the simple setting in which the Taizé community flourishes might well wonder how worship born of that setting could possibly work in the cultural and social milieu of a community such as Beverly Hills. It does, in fact, work very well.

How did it begin at All Saints'? When we decided to explore the possibility of this style of worship as an added and alternative form, I, never having been to Taizé, set about learning the roots of the movement. Subsequently I was a member of a pilgrimage made to Taizé, which was a rewarding and enlightening experience. Taizé is a small ecumenical monastic community named for its town in the Burgundy region of France, just north of Cluny. The movement began in 1940 when Brother Roger arrived to find a small village with no proper road, no telephone, and no running water. The warm welcome of a few elderly people ultimately persuaded him to remain there. After an early interruption of his work due to the occupation of France, he returned in the fall of 1944 with other brothers whom he had met and resumed work toward his vision. From the outset, sharing the life of the world's underprivileged was essential for the community. Since the 1950s, hundreds of thousands of young adults from around the world have made pilgrimages to Taizé. In Brother Roger's words, "The pilgrimage does not seek to organize the young into a movement centered on Taizé, but encourages them to be peacemakers and to bring about reconciliation in their own neighborhoods, in their cities or villages, in their parish communities, together with people of all generations, from children to old people."

What is the attraction? Another quote from Brother Roger: "Many young people today are experiencing discouragement. In the times of prayer together here, in the times of reflection and in the silence, in seeking after the sources of faith, our great wish is for them to discover a meaning for their life. We would like to search together with them as to how they can discover a new dynamism and how they can prepare themselves to undertake responsibilities." Specifically, the daily life of the community is based on a simply structured routine of prayer at morning, midday, and evening. This prayer includes simple song, a psalm, a Bible reading, silence, and intercession.

The simple chants were composed largely by Jacques Berthier, then organist at St. Ignatius Church in Paris. This is functional music, sung as ostinato song, simple enough to be readily committed to memory by the thousands worshiping in their own language.

After worship in the evening, the prayer is sometimes continued by singing late into the night. Their worship space, called the Church of the Reconciliation, was built in 1962 and was enlarged during the early 1990s. Throughout this vast space symbolic candlelight is used; seating is oriented toward an obvious visual symbol. The room is filled with icons illuminated by the candles. In addition to worship, classes and counseling are offered. During their stay at the village, many visitors spend extended time in silence.

How can all this translate to our local worship spaces? It is important to remember that we cannot always copy exactly from another setting; what works in one place will not necessarily work in another. Details don't always transfer, but concepts do. I believe the phrase "bloom where you're planted" pertains to this point. In general, the ambience desired is a combination of intimacy and transcendence. As is suggested for any Taizé-style worship, there should be a central and obvious visual focus as described above. The space should be lighted only enough to follow the simple printed service, candlelight (candelabras as well as plentiful votive candles) being the predominant source of light, if possible. Seating should face the visual focus; symbolizing our quest for Christ; our prayer is not centered on ourselves. Seating in the round is therefore not necessarily desired, although some informal seating space on the floor might be provided.

A few years ago, my rector, Carol Anderson, challenged me afresh to investigate the worship in the style of Taizé for our setting at All Saints', Beverly Hills. Early in this process, I became convinced that the secret is in the *approach*, and that any sense of the trivial or casual is to be avoided. Knowing that the simplest music is often the most difficult to interpret, I set out to nurture singers to provide a *carefully planned* and even *elegant* musical ambience for worshipers. I soon became aware that the most attractive musical result hinged on choir singers providing quality leadership so that the congregation could join in as they would, or simply bask in the music floating through the nave from the gallery. I discovered also that these simple, repetitive tunes are prayers in themselves. I began writing obbligato lines for either high or low voices to sing over the repeating mantras. I began varying the choir's singing—sometimes parts, sometimes unison with the accompaniment occasionally improvising around the simple tune with mild harmonic departures. From the beginning, we often used a synthesizer and digital keyboard, since the sounds they produce are less familiar than those of the organ, adding to the sense of mystery that we attempted to sustain. Unobtrusive organ accompaniment sufficed on the Sunday mornings when we occasionally sang music of Taizé during communion time. The flexibility of the piano proved to be an advantage in accompanying this service. Other forms of music, not of the Taizé tradition, can also be effective as long as they fit the general mood. Plainsong psalms sung by assisting singers are also appropriate, perhaps with the use of congregational refrains or antiphons. Original composition is also encouraged.

Critically important to this worship is the synthesis of all aspects of the service. The leaders of the service (musician included) must be thoroughly open to the possibilities of what lie before them. The congregation will quickly sense from the service leader the degree of earnestness and intentionality in the approach to the service. At All Saints', the practice is for the worship leader and two torchbearers to enter quietly and ceremonially. The leader sits as candles surrounding an icon are lighted in silence, many other candles having already been lighted. Gentle opening music suggests origins from another space at another time, helping to set the stage with a sense of mystery. Periods of silence are essential in discovering the heart of prayer. Although congregations may be initially uncomfortable with these extended silences, they will soon grow to cherish the opportunity to express communion with God without words or music. (For those parishes that desire to begin the use of silence during Sunday morning liturgy, the Taizé experience can be for them an effective introduction.) Lastly, a leaflet is provided with the full service printed out, including rubrics noting the times of silence so they are not unexpected. The resulting philosophy of Taizé worship is that it is as carefully prepared and executed as any liturgy offered to the parish and community.

The approach described here has developed into a kind of art form, and as such is probably not necessary in all settings. It is important to note that it seems to provide for the people of our parish and community a service of serenity, strength, and comfort. On Friday nights at All Saints' during this service, one could almost feel the draining of tension from those coming from busy Santa Monica Boulevard after a work day. It was not unusual to find a group of people who wanted to remain in the stillness of the church for up to a half hour after the service.

Reflect on this quote from Brother Roger's words about Taizé: "From the depths of the human condition a secret aspiration rises up. Caught up in the anonymous rhythms of schedules and timetables, men and women of today are implicitly thirsting for the one essential reality: an inner life, signs of the invisible. Nothing is more conducive to a communion with the living God than a meditative common prayer with, as its high point, singing that never ends and that continues in the silence of one's heart when one is alone again. When the mystery of God becomes tangible through the simple beauty of symbols, when it is not smothered by too many words, the common prayer, far from exuding monotony and boredom, awakens us to heaven's joy on earth."

Hugh Dickinson, a former dean of Salisbury Cathedral, echoes this sensibility in a quote from a 1990 Taizé leaflet at that cathedral: "Surrounded by the quiet beauty of this chapel, BE STILL AND KNOW GOD, experience His peace enfolding you, relax in His love, and know Him with you now."

On the cover of each Taizé leaflet at All Saints', Beverly Hills, are the words of Carol Anderson, rector of the parish: "The worship tradition represented this evening began many years ago in the ecumenical French monastic community called Taizé. It is a quiet service of mediation, reflection, readings, and music. The experience finds its true meaning in the active participation of all the assembled and is meant to focus and deepen our faith through the power of prayer. Much of our modern personal need is for entertainment. We have 'busy' souls. The liturgy that has developed around the Taizé community is primarily for the worship of God but it is also meant to quiet the soul. This quietness does not happen at once, but gradually during the worship. There is repetition in the words of the music, there are many periods of silence, and the readings are read slowly—all so that we may have a deep sense of quiet grow in our hearts. Then we may be still and be at peace in the Presence of God." In my own experience, I have come to believe in the viability of "passive" participation; some desire to remain more quiet and let ourselves "marinate" (to use an expression of Carol Anderson's) in the experience.

I encourage you to consider worship in the style of Taizé as an added alternative form to a regular worship schedule. It can be an experience that sensitizes one to "worship the Lord in the beauty of holiness" in a simple but profound and powerful way.[1]

Note

1. *The Sources of Taizé* available from GIA Publications. www.giamusic.com. Used by permission. http://www.allsaintsbh.org/music/taize.htm

Thomas Foster was director of Music at All Saints' Episcopal Church, Beverly Hills, California, from 1976–2003 when the choir came to prominence through its four recordings for Gothic Records, its concert tours, and commissioned works. He has taught organ performance at Jacksonville University and California State University, Northridge, and conducting at the University of North Florida.

Tom has served on the faculties of summer church music conferences at Sewanee, Mississippi; Evergreen; and the University of Wisconsin and has been a lecturer/conductor in numerous dioceses of the Episcopal church as well as at Virginia Theological Seminary and the Institute of Sacred Music at Yale University. He is a contributor to The Hymnal 1982 and is a past president of the Association of Anglican Musicians.

Since 2003 Tom has served as interim musician at numerous cathedrals and churches across the country and given many recitals, most notably at St. Thomas Church, New York City; Methuen Memorial Music Hall; and Grace Cathedral in San Francisco.

What About Additional Services?

Before the Ending of the Day:
Compline at Christ Church, New Haven, Connecticut

ROBERT W. LEHMAN

> For the first time in my life, I had found a church where the divine presence felt as strong to me inside as it did outside. When I entered that sacred cave, I not only lost track of time, I also lost track of my self. At Christ Church, I discovered worship that took place inside God's own heart.[1]

Darkness is settling in. The deep grays and purples in the sky reluctantly fade and give way to murky blues, then to blackness. A stiff sea breeze kicks up and blows in from Long Island Sound and the air temperature begins a precipitous dive. It is Sunday night in New Haven, Connecticut, and the town falls silent as it hunkers down for the rigors of the coming week. This is the campus of Yale University where many of the world's best and brightest converge for nine months each year to teach, learn, and share great ideas. It is an exciting place where theologians—Christian and non-Christian alike—are asking large questions and, a stone's throw away, physicists are examining our world at the molecular and atomic level. Perched on the northwest corner of Yale's campus is a church whose gothic architecture and tower, rising majestically into the night sky, sit harmoniously amid the collegiate gothic structures that surround it. It is in this building that something astonishing will happen tonight.

It may seem ridiculous to begin a chapter on the singing of the night Office of Compline as if it were a bad mystery novel—carefully setting the scene where the crime is about to be perpetrated, replete with rhetorical clichés. But the image is important. To understand the success of the compline services at Christ Church, New Haven, one must understand that milieu is everything. Without the proper ethos, there can be no transcendence of *chronos*—chronological time. To truly enter into a reverent worship of God, we must suspend chronological time to find and enter *kairos*—sanctified time. Our time is not God's time.

The tower bells of Christ Church begin to peal. It is a summons to an experience unlike any other, which will soon begin within the hallowed walls of this building. Then they come. There are throngs of young undergraduates who have been pulled away from their computer keyboards, graduate students loosed from library cubicle bonds, young tattooed and pierced townies who have been inhabiting the coffee shops, and an octogenarian couple who have made a pilgrimage to this place for this night. As they approach the church building, they are met by a yellow school bus that has transported high school students from other Connecticut towns—from Westport and New Canaan—for what is about to transpire. In this time of postmodernism and materialism, of depravity and spiritual drought, they come.

What awaits these seekers is a twenty-minute period of quiet solitude, of peace and tranquility, of beauty, of otherworldliness. But most importantly, what awaits them is an encounter with the divine. They will hear the eternal truths of the Christian message, yet there will be no talking and no proselytizing. Each person will be fully and actively participating in what is to come, yet they will do no more than sit motionless and anonymously in their seats. Each person sits awash in the ancient Christian rites of nighttime—of thanksgivings for the day past and prayers for safe passage through the night. The pealing tower bells give way to a mournful tolling—then silence.

The Lord Almighty grant us a peaceful night and a perfect end . . .

Compline begins.

The church teaches that the sacraments, most predominantly the Holy Eucharist, form the cornerstone of public worship—and indeed the Holy Eucharist is celebrated three times at Christ Church each Sunday. So it is most curious that it is the Office—the *non*sacramental—that is attracting young people to church. A large percentage of the compline congregation at Christ Church falls into that age group that has been labeled "Generation X" by sociologists. "Generation Y," that group born after 1983, is now populating the pews as well. Much study has been undertaken by Yale seminarians on the phenomenon of compline at Christ Church, and as a result of their work, we have a well-focused lens turned on what it is that draws these young people to the church late on Sunday nights.

The segment of the population that is now enrolled in college or graduate school has never been without a computer. Easy access to the Internet and instant connection to the World Wide Web has made a "virtual" existence very much a reality to these individuals. They are attuned to a virtual reality that works for them on their own terms and draws them deeper inside at their own pace. The otherworldliness of cyberspace and the computer age can teach us a great deal about ways to worship and ways that religion can play an important role in the formation of our young people. Ironically, it has taken the computer age to awaken the senses to the ancient rites of the Christian tradition.

Seekers that belong to the generations that we see at compline generally describe themselves as *spiritual* but not *religious*. We have interpreted this to mean that there is a yearning for the mystical and beautiful, yet a distrust for, and lack of interest in, the organized church with its proscribed orders of worship; the expectation that the person in the pew will make responses, say prayers, and sing hymns is suspect to these young thinkers. Worse, to their way of thinking, many church experiences involve congregational interaction with one another— the passing of the peace or the signing of a pew register informing others who you are and whence you come. Spirituality to those of generations X and Y seems to be a private, personal matter that is best experienced by the engagement of the senses rather than through social interaction, exhibition of personality, or conversation. The active participation of listening, smelling, and seeing is a full and rich spiritual exercise; it is one that seems to satisfy the souls of those who gather each Sunday night.

Biblical interpretation, exegetical orations, and proselytizing, traditional agents of the organized church, are not reaching these worshippers successfully. Moralizing from the pulpit can be off-putting and insulting. The best preachers are those that draw the listener into the message and allow the hearer to live the story during its telling. (What church has ever won souls by having a dry, person-alityless cleric preach *at* the assembly?) In a virtual world, conversion and accep-tance take place through a process of discovery and osmosis, the speed of which is dictated by the one having the experience. To translate an everyday experience into church parlance, a person seated before a computer monitor is a "seeker" and all of cyberspace is filled with answers waiting to be discovered. Such is one of the great attractions of the World Wide Web. Likewise, the eternal truths of the Christian gospel are awaiting discovery in the darkness of the night Office.

The idea to begin a service of compline at Christ Church was first discussed in earnest in 1998. A new rector had been called to serve the parish and one of the facts of history was that Christ Church, though situated on the campus of one of the world's great universities, was never able to attract young people to its weekly solemn high mass on Sunday mornings. There were a small number of be-tweeded, professorial types present, but the aged-eighteen-to-twenty-five segment of the academic community was not to be found. We set out to find a way to serve that younger community.

We were all aware of the compline services at Saint Mark's Cathedral, Seattle—some of us had even attended them. The great success of those services is attributable to the enormous number of university students who come out and scatter themselves on the floor throughout that great cathedral church. Further, other university campuses were offering compline including the University of Pittsburgh and Columbia University. We decided that compline could work very well here if we could offer it with all the integrity of our worship tradition and without compromising who we are as a parish—liberal, progressive, and steeped in the Anglo-Catholic tradition.

We chose the hour of ten on Sunday nights, because after discussion and recollection of our own college experiences, we agreed that ten o'clock at night is a great line of demarcation. At this hour, the student world seemed to put a stop to whatever it was doing to take a break before embarking on whatever came next on the agenda. (I recalled that my college fraternity house came alive at ten o'clock and the starting time of our weekend parties was never earlier than this.) Amid groans of consent, we all agreed that this was late night to us, but just the beginning of the evening to a college student. Thus the time for compline was cemented.

It was paramount that our advertising and campus posting embody the other-worldly nature of the service we were going to offer. Many ideas poured forth, but the final choice was a poster that displays a hawklike gargoyle looking out from his place on the bulletin board while sharing this information:

> The last of the Eight Canonical Hours sung in the monastic tradition of the Middle Ages, COMPLINE is sung at night prior to retiring. The listener is bathed in ancient chant as it resonates throughout the gothic arches of CHRIST CHURCH . . . natural time is suspended as plainsong and polyphony combine to capture the cosmic rhythms of the spheres. Beautifully crafted CHANT and polyphony intermingle with the sweet fragrance of INCENSE and CANDLELIGHT, and the listener is transported beyond chronological time to a place where CREATION and eternity coalesce into ONE.

On first reading, it seems silly of course—a ridiculous, contrived paragraph. Yet, it contains some factual ecclesiastical history while, at the same time, spelling out exactly what one will encounter if one attends. The message makes it clear that this is something very unusual and special that has been going on for a very long time. It does not invite anyone; it merely imparts the information that this is happening. No proselytizing is done even at the initial advertising level. There are no "Come and meet Jesus" messages; that smacks of organized church.

Once individuals make the decision to avail themselves of this curious event, the experience is just as it was advertised. One of my colleagues at Christ Church, while an undergraduate at Yale, produced the following as part of a writing assignment:

> How old is the urge to pray in the gathering darkness? How old is the fear of night, the fear that dark will not always be followed by day?
>
> The night prayer of Compline is practical again now in a way unforeseen during the Reformation. At Christ Church in New Haven, people use it not as part of a daily cycle of prayer, not as one of the monastic Hours, but as the sole point of calm in a hectic week. Compline at Christ Church serves a new kind of worshipper. Through music that is centuries old, it draws people of all beliefs, or of none, and it joins them to one another.

Darkness and incense—heavy silence greet those who enter Christ Church on Sunday nights. Candles offer the only light. Sheathed in colored glass, red, blue, green, they cluster at the foot of the shrine to the Virgin Mary; they drape the High Altar; seven lamps hang suspended in the sanctuary like the Pleiades. People in their street shoes walk slowly up the long center aisle; some genuflect, bending a knee and crossing themselves. Some simply stare. They slide into seats that seem to be the right distance from the light, from the altar, from the door, from whatever is about to happen. Shortly before ten o'clock, the church bells begin to clang, distant and discordant. And then an unseen choir begins to sing. . . .[2]

The only task that remained was to draw up the order of service. It was the collective thinking of the Christ Church staff that young, college-aged people are asking lots of questions, most are embarking on an independent lifestyle for the first time, they are highly intelligent, and possess an innate sense of quality; great music in a sacred space is intrinsically appealing to people of all ages and temperaments. Yet, in the twenty-first century there is an ever-increasing secular world where popular culture insinuates itself into and pervades every corner of our society. We hoped to nourish the fundamental desire for beauty and a connection to the divine in our Sunday night offering. We viewed this as a way of appealing to young people without "dumbing down," which is so often the method that is employed to reach undergraduates.

Christ Church, New Haven, a beautiful gem of Gothic architecture, was a center for liturgical and theological thought when the ideals of the English Tractarians crossed the ocean and planted roots in North America. The genius of Anglo-Catholic worship is its idiosyncratic centrality of aesthetics. The evocation of mystery and the beauty of high art serve to convey the Christian message in a way that transcends the spoken word. In the Psalms, that ancient collection of the Church's song, God admonishes us, in the midst of roaring seas, earthquakes, and tumults to "Be still, and know that I am God!" (Psalm 46:10). God is calling us to know him in the quietness and the beauty of holiness. It was with this understanding that we set out to fashion our service of compline.

We have succeeded in creating an ethos that is at once attractive to those of Generations X and Y while offering a spiritual allure to those of more advanced age. The quietness—the introduction of long periods of silence—was at first unsettling, even to those of us who sing and preside at the service. In time, however, we have been able to stretch the meditative silences into long periods where calm prevails; there is no longer angst surrounding these silences. A great deal happens in those stretches of stillness; there is peace, contemplation, and whether they realize it or not, many are engaged in the practice of centering prayer.

The primary source for our service is *The Order of Compline throughout the year with the Musical Notation from the Salisbury Antiphoner* adapted by The Reverend G. H. Palmer.[3] The rubrics found in the Book of Common Prayer 1979 allow for more flexibility than the Sarum Order, and so we judiciously exercise some of the options from the BCP to allow for a greater variation of hymnody and for an anthem or motet to be sung toward the close of the Office. We strictly adhere to the seasonal antiphons provided by the Sarum Order, a richness that has been omitted from the Prayer Book. We have even gone so far as to write our own Orders of Compline for the Dead (compiled and sung when a tragic auto accident claimed the lives of several Yale undergraduates) and Compline in a Time of War.

At compline we employ early music exclusively. The entire service is chanted using plainsong melodies, and two components of the service, varying weekly, are sung to polyphony; a psalm and the Lord's Prayer might be sung to polyphonic settings at one service while the *Nunc dimittis* and the final votive antiphon will be sung to polyphony at the next. At the moment when plainsong seamlessly gives way to polyphonic texture it is as if the gates of heaven are opened. No one except the choir knows when that will occur and it is a moment of rare beauty when it comes. Someone seated in the darkness will for the first time experience the holiness of beauty; her heart will be uplifted; he will be brought to tears.

Compline at Christ Church is a visceral experience, one that transports the hearer and grants us a glimpse through the heavenly veil of the face of God—the perfection of all that is good and beautiful. It is toward this truth and wisdom and love that our hearts long and our souls incline. Through the most primal elements of creation—breath and song—the eternal, saving message of Christ is repeated week after week in the darkness.

> We are called to reflect in the beauty of our worship the immutable link between earth and heaven. We are called to lift up our praise to God, to elevate the soul with music, with word and with image, to boldly, beautifully, not faint-heartedly, proclaim the eternal Supreme Beauty of the divine . . . the unity and harmony and radiant clarity of the one true Godhead. We each are called to awaken one another to the theophany of beauty . . . to the power of the divine presence emanating from and through all things beautiful . . . to those things which incline our ears, direct our gaze, and turn our hearts to God.[4]

If we are successful in answering our call, then compline *is* a theophany, a living, breathing extension of the incarnation made manifest in humanity. *Kairos* becomes *Chronos*. Many understand immediately. Some may never understand. But Sunday night at ten, for whatever reason, they come. Those who attend compline at Christ Church are indeed given a glimpse—however fleeting—of the divine presence in our midst.

The almighty and merciful Lord preserve us, and give us his blessing. Amen.

http://www.christchurchnh.org/Compline.htm

An Order for Compline

as sung at Christ Church, New Haven
The Officiant begins

V. The Lord Almighty grant us a peaceful night and a perfect end.
R. Amen.

V. Our help is in the Name of the Lord;
R. The maker of heaven and earth.

> *or in Lent*

V. Turn us, O God our Savior.
R. And let thine anger cease from us.

V. O God, make speed to save us.
R. O Lord, make haste to help us.

Officiant and Choir
Glory be to the Father, and to the Son, and to the Holy Ghost: as it was in the beginning, is now, and ever shall be, world without end. Amen.

Then may be added Alleluia *or* To thee, O Lord, be glory, King of endless majesty *according to season.*

Psalmody

One or more of the following Psalms are sung with the proper seasonal antiphon
Advent
    Psalm 50 *Deus deorum*
    Psalm 80 *Qui regis Israel*
    Psalm 85 *Ostende nobis, Domine*
Epiphany
    Psalm 96 *Cantate Domino*
    Psalm 134 *Ecce nunc*
    Psalm 141 *Domine, clamavi*
Lent
    Psalm 25 *Ad te, Domine, levavi*
    Psalm 43 *Judica me, Deus*
    Psalm 143 *Domine, exaudi*
Eastertide
    Psalm 113 *Laudate pueri*
    Psalm 118 *Confitemini Domino*
    Psalm 136 *Confitemini*

Post-Pentecost
  Psalm 4 *Cum invocarem*
  Psalm 31 *In te, Domine, speravi*
  Psalm 91 *Qui habitat*
  Psalm 134 *Ecce nunc*

Short Chapter

One of the following passages of Scripture, is sung
Post-Pentecost
  Jeremiah 14:9, 22
  Matthew 11:28–30
  Hebrews 13:20–21
  I Peter 5:8–9a
Advent
  Amos 5:8
  Baruch 5:5, 9
  Isaiah 40:4–5
Epiphany
  Amos 5:8
  Romans 12:1–2
  Malachi 1:11
Lent
  1 John 1:8–9
  Joel 2:13
  Daniel 9:9–10
Eastertide
  Hebrews 13:20–21
  Colossians 3:12
  Hebrews 9:24
Following the Chapter, the Choir sings
  Thanks be to God.

Hymnody

One of the following is sung
Christe, qui lux es et dies
Te lucis ante terminum
O lux beata Trinitas
Deus Creator omnium
Lucis Creator optime
Jesu, Salvator saeculi (Eastertide only)

or the hymn proper to the day

V. I will lay me down in peace;

R. And take my rest.

Responsory

Post-Pentecost, Advent

    V. Into thy hands, O Lord, I commend my spirit;

    R. Into thy hands, O Lord, I commend my spirit;

    V. For thou hast redeemed me, O Lord, O God of truth.

    R. Into thy hands, O Lord, I commend my spirit.

Lent

    V. In perfect peace and safety;

    R. I shall sleep and take my rest.

    V. If I give sleep to mine eyes, and slumber to mine eyelids,

    R. I shall sleep.

    V. Glory be to the Father, and to the Son, and to the Holy Ghost.

    R. In perfect peace and safety; I shall sleep and take my rest.

    V. Keep us, O Lord, as the apple of thine eye;

    R. Hide us under the shadow of thy wings.

Then the Song of Simeon is sung with proper seasonal antiphon

Lent 1–2

    When thou seest the naked, cover thou him, and hide not thyself from thine own flesh: then shall light break forth as the morning and the glory of the Lord shall be thy reward.

Lent 3–5

    In the midst of life we are in death: of whom may we seek for succour, but of thee, O Lord, who for our offenses art justly displeased. O God most holy, O holy and mighty, O holy and merciful Savior, give us not over unto bitter death.

Eastertide

    Alleluia. The Lord is risen: *Alleluia.*

    As he said unto you: *Alleluia. Alleluia.*

Post-Pentecost, Epiphany

    Preserve us, O Lord while waking and guard us while sleeping: that awake we may be with Christ, and asleep may rest in peace.

Advent

    Come, O Lord and visit us in peace, that we may joy before thee with a perfect heart.

Lord, now lettest thou thy servant depart in peace, according to thy word; For mine eyes have seen thy salvation, which thou hast prepared before the face of all people, To be a light to lighten the Gentiles, and to be the glory of thy people Israel.

Glory be to the Father, and to the Son, and to the Holy Ghost: as it was in the beginning, is now, and ever shall be, world without end. Amen.

V. The Lord be with you.
R. And with thy spirit.

Officiant
Lord, have mercy upon us.
Choir
Christ, have mercy upon us.
Officiant and Choir
Lord, have mercy upon us.
Officiant and Choir
Our Father, who art in heaven,
hallowed be thy Name,
thy kingdom come,
thy will be done,
on earth as it is in heaven.
Give us this day our daily bread.
And forgive us our trespasses,
as we forgive those
who trespass against us.
And lead us not into temptation,
but deliver us from evil.

V. O Lord, arise, help us;
R. And deliver us for thy Name's sake.

V. Turn us again, O Lord God of hosts;
R. Show the light of thy countenance, and we shall be whole.

V. Lord, hear our prayer;
R. And let our cry come unto thee.

The Officiant then sings one of the following Collects according to season
Lighten our darkness, we beseech thee, O Lord; and by thy great mercy defend us from all perils and dangers of this night; for the love of thy only Son, our Savior Jesus Christ. Amen.

Be present, O merciful God, and protect us through the hours of this night, so that we who are wearied by the changes and chances of this life may rest in thy eternal changelessness; through Jesus Christ our Lord. Amen.

Visit this place, O Lord, and drive far from it all snares of the enemy; let thy holy angels dwell with us to preserve us in peace; and let thy blessing be upon us always; through Jesus Christ our Lord. Amen.

Look down, O Lord, from thy heavenly throne and illumine this night with thy celestial brightness; that by night as by day thy people may glorify thy holy Name; through Jesus Christ our Lord. Amen.

Christ our true and only Light: receive our evening prayers and illumine the secrets of our hearts with thy healing goodness, that no evil desires may possess us who are made new in the light of thy heavenly grace. Amen.

God of unchangeable power, when thou didst fashion the world the morning stars sang together and the host of heaven shouted for joy; open our eyes to the wonders of creation and teach us to use all things for good, to the honor of thy glorious name; through Jesus Christ our Lord. Amen.

Pour forth upon us, O Lord, the Spirit of thy love: and as thou dost replenish us with Paschal Sacraments, so of thy loving-kindness make us to be of one heart and mind; through Jesus Christ our Lord, who with thee and the Holy Ghost, liveth and reigneth in glory everlasting. Amen.

Lord God, whose Son our Savior Jesus Christ triumphed over the powers of death and prepared for us our place in the new Jerusalem: Grant that we, who have this day given thanks for his resurrection, may praise thee in that City of which he is the light; and where he liveth and reigneth for ever and ever. Amen.

The following collect is always added

Keep watch, dear Lord, with those who work, or watch, or weep this night, and give thine angels charge over those who sleep. Tend the sick, Lord Christ; give rest to the weary, bless the dying, soothe the suffering, pity the afflicted, shield the joyous; and all for thy love's sake. Amen.

Silence is kept.
A motet may be sung
The service concludes with the following

V. The Lord be with you
R. And with thy spirit.

V. Let us bless the Father, the Son, and the Holy Spirit.
R. Let us praise him and magnify him for ever.

V. Blessed art thou, O Lord, in the firmament of heaven.
R. Above all to be praised and glorified for ever.

or in Lent and Eastertide

V. Let us bless the Lord. *(Alleluia.)*
R. Thanks be to God. *(Alleluia.)*

Officiant
The Almighty and merciful Lord, Father, Son, and Holy Spirit, preserve us, and give us his blessing.
Choir
Amen.
Then one of the following is sung

Salve Regina (after Pentecost until Advent)
Alma Redemptoris Mater (Saturday before Advent I through The Presentation [Feb. 2])
Ave Regina caelorum (after The Presentation through Wednesday of Holy Week)
Regina caeli (Easter Vigil through Pentecost)

The Choir departs in silence.

Notes

1. Barbara Brown Taylor, *Leaving Church: A Memoir of Faith* (San Francisco: Harper, 2006), 29.
2. Kendra Mack, "As It Was in the Beginning" (English class paper, Yale University, 2000), 1.
3. G. H. Palmer, *The Order of Compline throughout the Year with the Musical Notation from the Salisbury Antiphoner* (Wantage: St. Mary's Press, 1953).
4. The Reverend Susan McCone, "The Holiness of Beauty" (sermon preached June 27, 2001, at Christ Church, New Haven).

Robert Lehman serves as organist and choirmaster of Christ Church Episcopal in New Haven, Connecticut, where he was appointed in 1994. He is a fellow of Davenport College at Yale University and has served on the staff of the Washington National Cathedral, the Princeton University Chapel, and Saint Bartholomew's Church, New York City. Active as a performer, Rob is often featured as conductor and solo recitalist both in this country and abroad, having appeared with the National Symphony Orchestra, the Handel Festival Orchestra, the Washington Chamber Symphony, and the Carnegie Brass Quintet. He has made several solo organ recordings and his numerous choral compositions have been recorded by leading choirs and are regularly heard over NPR and the BBC.

What About Additional Services?

The HipHopEMass at Trinity Episcopal Church, Morrisania, Bronx, New York

LUCAS SMITH

It's structured like any other traditional Episcopal mass and begins in the same manner with the minor difference being that it has a beat you can (and are encouraged to) dance to. In place of a choir there's likely a small table with two turntables set up, side by side, and a DJ, head bobbing to the prelude, with a hand on each, either syncing up the next beat, or putting the current track together. In a larger service there may be a full rock band providing the music, while in a smaller service as little as a powerful portable boom box may be doing the job. Leading the music, coming in generally when a choir would (and otherwise shouting encouragement when a choir would, likely, not) are a coterie of rappers. All in all, just another service of the HipHopEMass.

The music is loud and exuberant. The rappers call out "God is in the House!" and lead the congregation in the chorus. From song to song the music and the rap overlaying it move from joyous to solemn to intimate and back to joyous. For those unfamiliar with hip-hop, the power of the music and the service can be a bit surprising. Horace Boyer, editor of *Lift Every Voice and Sing II*, on the experience of first seeing the HipHopEMass, said "The sonorous and rhythmic phrases of the rappers and the tunes and harmonies of the singers brought a meaning and passion to the scripture, prayers and responses that must have been what Christ had in mind when he taught his prayer that begins 'Our Father . . . .'" For those already familiar with hip-hop, the experience is also usually described as surprising. The melding of authentic Christian feeling with mainstream quality rap and beats brings a look of "This is church?" to the faces of many.

Started in 2004 at Trinity Episcopal Church of Morrisania in the South Bronx of New York City, the HipHopEMass sought to bring the altar to the street and the street to the altar in a manner that would provide ministry to

181

a community, its young people particularly, that was largely at a remove from the church. For that community, indeed for most communities of young people, hip-hop is not merely the dominant musical genre but also the most powerful cultural force. Recognizing that, The Reverend Timothy Holder, who would soon found HipHopEMass, gathered together people with experience in hip-hop music, and set about producing hip-hop orders of service and organizing the means to enact them in a variety of situations.

A wealth of material was produced during that process, and it resulted in a service that could be musically innovative and powerful regardless of the circumstances. Indeed, the HipHopEMass, embracing the hip-hop ethos, was performed in circumstances as diverse as the small gym of a youth detention center in Virginia with minimal backing and personnel to the Episcopal Youth Event in front of well over a thousand people using a full band and seven rappers. The material of the Mass was published as *The Hip Hop Prayer Book* (Church Publishing). I'd like to share a piece—meant to be included but that had to be cut for space reasons from *The HipHop Prayer Book*—on the underpinnings of the music of HipHopEMass from one of its first musical linchpins, and current member of the Standing Commission on Liturgy and Music, Jeannine Otis:

The Music of the HipHopEMass
JEANNINE OTIS

The Music and Rhythm of the spoken word included in the HipHopEMass proclaims hope for the future. The word's existential foundation is built on tradition, which is the existence of a solid connection between the generations. The bridge is tradition: spiritual and African.

Cornell West states in his article, "Democracy Matters: The Necessary Engagement of Youth Culture": "Although Hip Hop Culture has become tainted by the very excesses and amorality it was born in rage against, the best of rap music . . . 'prophetic rap' (as he has labeled it) . . . and Hip Hop Culture still [express themselves] stronger and more clearly than any cultural expression in the past generation. Prophetic Hip Hop has told painful truths about the internal struggles and how the decrepit schools, inadequate healthcare, unemployment, and drug markets of the urban centers of the American empire have wounded their souls."

In African-American tradition, "Congregational singing is the means by which diverse individuals and groups worship the Savior as one committed union, and can provide expression for the deepest yearnings. Much of the congregational singing is executed in the responsorial (call and response) manner between a soloist and the congregation" (as stated by Horace Boyer in the preface to *Lift Every Voice and Sing II*).

The HipHopEMass music and rhythmical spoken word is used creatively, at its best, to explore the human condition, to express and expunge the doubt and uncertainty of being, and finally, to uplift and strengthen the spiritual community. From the opening choral introit, "God Is in the House", which is repeated with a rhythmic response to indicate knocking, the beginning of the worship is reminiscent of the beginning of any number of ancient rituals from various cultures. Then, following the "knocking" is the prophetic answer found in the lyrics of "Jesus Walks," recorded by Kanye West, which sets the tone for hope: "Jesus walks . . . Jesus walks with me." This brings us back in its sentiment to: "I Want Jesus to Walk with Me. All along my pilgrim journey . . . I want Jesus to walk with me."

This worship experience enlists the three primary characteristics of African-American music—call and response, syncopation/rhythm, and improvisation—to bring new meaning to the traditional service order in The Book of Common Prayer. For example, in the Liturgy of the Word, the prophetic, lyrical member (Niles) of the hip-hop group The Remnant offers this thought as a refrain/mantra:

> If my people who were called by my name
> Would cut the conceit, bend their knees and just pray,
> And seek my face in this heavenly place
> I would listen, forgive them, and heal the land that they waste.

Hip-hop culture has most assuredly co-opted the more traditional music of rhythm and blues/soul by continually using the lyrical themes of that genre as refrains or hooks. The offertory and communion of EMass both incorporate already recorded R&B/Soul and original music. A profound example of original Soul/Gospel/R&B can be found in the original music of Julio Herrera:

> We are redeemed of the Lord, so stand up and praise and magnify his holy name. . . . Let all of the Saints who believe in Jesus' name lift up holy hands and show that he Reigns.

> We are redeemed, renewed, and charged to believe in our faith and our culture and to continue to engage ourselves to grow spiritually so that we can engage others.[1]

It is important to note that structurally the EMass follows exactly the design of a traditional Episcopal mass. That said, the experience of attending an EMass is anything but traditional. Seeing children (and many others) dancing in aisles as a rapper stalks through the space, interacting with the assembled as he spits (rhymes) verses on the themes of grace and forgiveness and the empowering spirit, it is difficult not to be moved. Far from treating hip-hop music as an add-on to an otherwise normal service, music in the EMass is integral to the experience on every level. The prayers, with some exception, are spoken in hip-hop slang and at many times, during the homily for instance, a backbeat of drum and bass fills the background and drives the proceedings forward.

Following this chapter is an example of what the order of service from a hip-hop mass might look like with its moves from backbeat to backbeat and into the various performance pieces. For more information on the HipHopEMass, I recommend *The Hip Hop Prayer Book* (about which I have no rooting interest) as a resource. To hear the music of HipHopEMass there is a CD, also from Church Publishing, titled *And the Word Was Hip Hop* that includes original contributions from many of the founding rappers and musicians.

WORD!

You can find more information at http://hiphopemass.dioceseny.org/index.php.

Note

1. Reprinted with permission of Jeannine Otis.

Lucas Smith is acquisitions editor for Church Publishing and Seabury Books and is the editor of *The Hip Hop Prayer Book* and the executive producer of *And the Word Was Hip Hop*.

HipHopEMass.org DJ MASS
"Dear Momma + One More Chance"
TupacBiggie 2004–05

THE HOLY EUCHARIST *Let's Show God Some Love!*
THE BOOK OF COMMON PRAYER (Episcopal)
An Order for Celebrating the Holy Eucharist (400)

DJ MASS + MASTER MIX

Written, Compiled, Adapted, and Arranged by
Kurtis Blow, DJ Cool Clyde, Derrell Edwards, Julio Herrera,
Timothy Holder, DJ Lightnin' Lance, Tom Mercer, DJ Ol' School Sam & Shake,
Jahneen Otis, Martha Overall, Catherine Roskam,
& All the People of HipHopEMass.org!

ORDER OF HIP RITE		*TupacBiggie*
Minutes 0–20	Prelude Hip	
	Backbeat	Tupac/Biggie
	Loops	Kurtis Blow
	Welcome by MC/Celebrant	
	"Amen! *WORD!*"	*Loop*
	Eminem	
	I Can't Believe	Mary, Mary
Minutes 1–5	Procession Hip	
	Jesus Walks	Kanye West
Minute 6	Opening Acclamation and Prayer	
	Backbeat	Tupac/Biggie
Minutes 7–10	A Def Reading	*Continues*
Minutes 10–15	The Psalm *Rap*	*Continues UPBEAT*
Minutes 15–20 THE WORD	Gospel Hip	
	The Time Has Come	Corey Red and Precise
Minutes 20–25	The Holy Gospel	
	Backbeat	Koltai
Minutes 25–35	The Sermon	
	Backbeat	Tupac/Biggie
Minutes 35–40 ALTAR	Altar Call with Prayers, Anointing,	
	& Confession	
CALL & HOLY ANOINTING	*Backbeat*	Tupac/Biggie
Minutes 40–45	Offertory Hip	
	One Way	BBJ

Minutes 45–55	The Holy Eucharist	
HOLY EUCHARIST	*Backbeat*	Tupac/Biggie
	The Lord's Prayer and Holy Communion	
	Alleluia, Unity Klan	
	Holy Culture, Crossroad	
Minutes 55–57	Post-Communion Prayer	
	Backbeat	Tupac/Biggie
Minutes 57–60	Dance Recessional	
	Jesus Walks	Kanye West
Minutes 60–80+	Postlude + *Dance* Hip	
	I Know I Can	Nas
	We've Got Love	Third World

January 10, 2005